Practical
Apartment
Management

Practical Apartment Management

Edward N. Kelley
CPM·CRE

Institute of Real Estate Management

of the NATIONAL ASSOCIATION OF REALTORS®

430 North Michigan Avenue • Chicago, Illinois 60611

Standard Book Number 0-912104-21-X
PRINTED IN THE UNITED STATES OF AMERICA

About the Author

The author of *Practical Apartment Management,* Edward N. Kelley, is a Certified Property Manager. He is a member of the Executive Committee of the Institute of Real Estate Management and an officer of the Chicago Chapter of IREM. He is a dean on the National Faculty of IREM and is a frequent contributor to the Institute's *Journal of Property Management.* He won that journal's coveted award for the best article published in 1970. The author has served three terms as IREM's Regional Vice-President and member of the Governing Council.

Mr. Kelley also has been awarded the designation "Counselor of Real Estate" by the American Society of Real Estate Counselors.

The author of this book has earned his experience over the past nineteen years. He began his career somewhat accidentally when he was turned down in his bid for a position as a real estate salesman because he was too young. The same company, however, offered him a position as a property management trainee which he accepted. Mr. Kelley began his professional climb working as a weekend rental agent, summer janitor, and maintenance supervisor. In a few months he was assigned to a resident manager position and, by the end of his first year in the property management business, was promoted to head one of the company's branch offices.

Mr. Kelley soon found that property management offered many opportunities for advancement and individual expression and made the commitment to make property management his career. In less than two years he was supervising the management of more than 100 properties. He played a pioneering role in developing computerized accounting for property management offices. He also set up management programs for the first condominiums in the United States and played a key role in the design, lease-up, and management of some of the largest urban renewal developments ever built. This phase included the largest FHA-insured rehabilitation job ever undertaken in the United States.

At the ten-year point in his career, Mr. Kelley was the chief officer in charge of more than 18,000 apartment units. Three years later that number had grown to over 40,000 rental units, 60 shopping centers, 16 motels, and a number of office buildings, mobile home parks, and golf courses. Annual collections amounted to almost 100 million dollars. These properties were located in more than 100 cities in 34 states.

In 1973, Edward Kelley started his own property management consulting firm based in a Chicago suburb. His client list reads like a who's who in the business world and includes some of the country's largest lending institutions, corporations, universities, and private investors.

In his current book, Mr. Kelley shares his extensive skills and experience in the business of property management.

We at the Institute of Real Estate Management are proud to be the publishers of this important book.

Institute of Real Estate Management

August 1976

Contents

Low-rise to high-rise. Suburban garden apartment complex. Townhouses. Garden apartments. Mid-rise. High-
rise. Planned unit development. Other types. Furnished
apartments. Unit size/room count. Unit mix. Housing
standards.

Tenant. Tenants by choice. Empty-nesters. Career people.
Senior citizens. Tenants by circumstance. Families with
children. Swinging singles/young couples. Students. Income class.

Profit-motivated ownership. Interim or caretaker ownership. Not-for-profit ownership. Individual investor. Partnerships. Joint partnership. Limited partnership. Major

corporations. Life insurance companies/lending institutions. REITs. Co-op/condominium. Government.

Executive property manager. Property manager. Site manager. "Ma-pa" managers.

Office location. One office or two? Office appearance. Office hours. Recreation facilities. Supporting amenities. Parking.

Limitations. Unfurnished vs. furnished. Children. Pets. Other problems. Sex and morality. Security. Security deposits. Screening process. Application form. Application deposit. Checking credit. Lease agreement. Lease terms.

Tenant guidebook. Move-in. Improvements. Service and tenant turnover. Illegal and immoral uses. Tenant abuses. Tenant damage. Handling complaints. Tenant organizations. Arbitration. Emergencies. Personal injury. Property damage. Keys and lock-outs. Politics and voting. Soliciting. Tipping. Apartment transfers. Move-out. Security deposit return.

Selecting people. Checking out personnel. Job description. Licensing. Compensation. Wage and Hour Law. Employee benefit insurance. Permanent, part-time, and seasonal employees. Living on or off premises. Training.

Supervision. Reporting to work. Breaks. Uniforms. Tools. Guns. Gifts, kickbacks, commissions. Socializing with tenants. Controlling employee purchases. Pilfering and petty theft. Employee evaluation. Salary and wage adjustments. Incentives and bonuses. Holidays. Vacations. Death of a relative. Sick days. Education and tuition. Labor unions.

Landscaping. Paved areas. Trash. Lighting. Animal litter. Patios and balconies. Fencing. Snow and ice.

Entrance door. Vestibule. Door glass and metal. Lights. Mailboxes. Directory. Furnishings, plans, artwork. Doormat. Corridors and stairs. Elevator cabs. Corridor lighting. Odor. Exit signs. Fire extinguishers and hoses. Numbering. Foul-weather gear.

Ready-ready checklist. Drapes. Floor covering.

Laundry room. Storage locker. Garbage chute room. Recreation features. Real vs. mental walk.

Inventory mechanical equipment. Guarantees. Inspect the structure. Apartment maintenance. Painting. Exterminating. Grounds maintenance. Seasonal maintenance. Standard vs. custom checklists. Deferred maintenance. Staff requirements. In-house or outside personnel? Service contracts. Supplies and parts. Maintenance equipment and major tools. Getting the right start.

Monthly rent. Weekly/semi-monthly rent. Payment in advance. Aggregate rent. Graduated rent. Head rent. Seasonal rent.

Rent and the economy. The manager's role. Market feel. Identify most desirable. Status and rent. Views and rent. Floor pricing. Best-of-type pricing. Adjusting rents. Upward adjustments. Downward adjustments. Valuation of investment. Concessions. Deficiency discount. Exchange for service.

Manager's resistance. Raising rents on vacant units. Raising at turnover. Ability to pay. A typical example. Tenant resistance. Ways to raise rents. Discriminatory pricing. Avoid divided raises. Once-a-year adjustments. Tax and utility pass-throughs. Escalator clause. Now is the time.

A matter of habit. Make your policy known. Rent bills. Site office. Computers and lock boxes. Forms of payment. Advance payments.

Enforce on the first. Spotting trouble. Penalty charges. Discounts. Excuses. Payment program. Damage deductions. Test your skills.

Powers. Obligations. Associated risks. Compensation. Termination or cancellation.

Unscheduled collections. Security deposit accounts. Owner's custodial account. Purchasing. Bill payments. Payroll periods and taxes. Reserves. Monthly statement.

Application form. Time record.

Tax file. Insurance.

Types of budgets. Budget tips. Analyzing budgets.

OSHA. Antidiscrimination laws. Building code violations. Posting of notices and licenses. Contract and guarantees. Correspondence.

Graphic Design—David Jungel

Pen and Ink Illustrations—Nicholas J. Nowicki Jr., A.I.A.

Introduction

You don't have to travel very far in this country to be confronted by owners and property managers desperately searching for answers to their day-to-day problems. The current popularity of apartment management seminars, conventions, and workshops, drawing as they do large numbers of property managers, developers, investors, and others associated with multi-family housing, further indicates the immediate need for more published information on the subject.

The housing industry since the late 1950s has demonstrated that it is capable of designing, financing, and building very large and complex housing developments. But we are still trying to develop the necessary skills to effectively manage such properties.

Until very recently, the question of who was going to run an apartment building rarely entered anyone's mind during the development stages of that project. Now, with billions of dollars in existing housing, containing millions of units, and with the addition of hundreds of thousands of units yearly, the urgency of treating the practice of property management in a serious way cannot be disputed.

In the pages that follow, the student and the practitioner of the subject will find a structured presentation of practical ideas that can help them succeed as property managers. The main emphasis will be on the management of multi-unit residential investment properties.

For our purposes our discussions will center on the management of multi-family housing containing 50 or more rental units which are owned and operated for their investment potential. With today's costs of both construction and operation, the economy of

1

scale is critical to a property's ability to generate a return. Properties smaller than 50 units can and do present attractive investment potential to some owners, but they cannot always justify the cost of skilled management administrators as part of their operating expense. This must be furnished by the owner and requires a substantial commitment of both time and involvement. The larger investment properties, on the other hand, generate enough revenue to cover the professional management as a normal—indeed necessary—operating cost.

Many of the topics discussed here are applicable in fact to the management of the smaller housing types such as duplexes and small apartment and isolated townhouse buildings. There the goal is the same, namely to produce the greatest possible net operating income (collections less expenses) over the economic life of the property. Even the management of housing which is operated without the profit motive—institutional, government, co-op, and condominium housing—can benefit from portions of this text. While in such cases there isn't a need to maximize income, there still is the need to minimize operating expenses, just as with investment housing. Many of the same maintenance procedures need to be established in all types and styles of housing. Handling of the various types of residents also has a common thread.

This book is written as though it will have only one kind of reader, namely those who wish to be informed about practical ways to manage rental housing on behalf of owners who expect a return on their investment. Property administration is a most difficult undertaking today and requires all the information and skills that can be brought to bear. The new breed of property managers who can accomplish this goal are finding and enjoying lucrative career opportunities.

Incidentally, throughout this book when we use terms that refer to gender, such as "he" and "she" or "his" and "her," we frequently use the masculine term when the intent is to refer to both sexes.

Some Historical Footnotes

Residential property management had its start in the United States around the turn of the century. For a number of reasons, it was babysitting or caretaker management more than the total administering of real estate. Owners of rental housing were too busy, too rich, traveled too much, or were too ill to assume the task themselves. Such owners would contract with local real estate agents to look after their investments. Accordingly, properties were managed in the early days for the same reasons that chauffeurs were hired to drive cars—more for convenience than necessity.

The original concept of property management was to collect rent and to report any unusual circumstances to the owner. The agent was expected to remit to the owner the monies collected less payments for any bills which the agent incurred at the property. And, typically, no other responsibilities were involved. The agent was regarded as the rent collector who also served as a buffer between the tenants and the owner.

This style of property management continued through the 1920s when the boom in multi-family housing started in the United States. Since the largest properties of this period rarely contained more than 100 units and usually less than 35, caretaker property management continued to be in vogue.

As real estate companies in the larger metropolitan areas began to acquire more multi-unit housing business, the need for specialized managers became apparent. It was natural for real estate companies to welcome this sideline activity. It provided a fixed monthly income to help cover overhead costs, leaving the brokerage commissions as profit. Keeping the units occupied was not a matter of great concern since housing then was in short supply and turnover rates were far lower than experienced in more normal times.

During the depression years property management got an extra boost when mass foreclosures brought control of many properties to life insurance companies, banks, and other lending institutions. These organizations had to set up special departments to operate the reclaimed properties.

Lending institutions, particularly the life insurance companies, were not happy in the position of day-to-day dealings with tenants, especially when those dealings often involved eviction proceedings. Since it was a time of national crisis, the image of seeming to profit from the misfortunes of victims of the depression simply was not good public relations.

In addition, the lending institutions soon became unable to handle the volume of properties that eventually were foreclosed, spread as they were throughout the country.

To meet this need, prestigious local real estate companies were retained to assist in the management of growing numbers of repossessed properties. Since the brokerage business at that time itself was all but dead, they had the incentive either to expand an existing property management department or to create one. The real estate companies had no staffing problem since there were plenty of brokers and other office personnel who were no longer being kept busy in real estate sales.

During the early and middle 1930s, property management began to bloom as an industry of its own. Standardized procedures and forms appeared. But by the late 1930s, the economy was recovering and investors and syndicates began to purchase foreclosed properties from the insurance companies and the lending institutions. These properties were small by today's standards, however, and were easily handled by the new investors who looked to save the added cost of a managing agent. Once again, therefore, management came to be thought of as a convenience rather than as a necessary service.

World War II brought both good and bad for the business of rental housing and property management. Occupancies were at an all-time high, but rents were frozen as part of a price control program to guard against runaway inflation. With government-imposed ceilings on rents, and with labor and materials in short supply, owners began to neglect maintenance of their real estate holdings. Tenants had little choice but to accept the deteriorating conditions and shoddy maintenance. Property management was an extra expense many owners could not afford. In some cases, if the owner was engaged in profiteering, the manager became an obstacle. Some owners charged as much as $5,000 for the "right to rent" a choice apartment in a prime location. With rents frozen and maintenance costs increasing, the manager couldn't produce a cash return on apartment buildings as great as what some owners could gain from bonus-payment profiteering. That's the way it was during the war years and for several years thereafter when housing continued to be in short supply.

Throughout this whole period, tenants were forced to take whatever housing was available. Since rents continued to be frozen up until the mid-1950s, and expenses continued to rise, the cost of property management was one which owners tried to avoid. The consequence was that the management business showed little growth from its original period of importance (in the mid-1930s) until the late 1950s. Many of those who had been managers returned to their original occupation as mortgage bankers and real estate brokers.

Management continued well into the 1950s mostly as a caretaker enterprise. The manager's prime duty was to collect rents. He had few leasing and virtually no maintenance duties to perform. Preventative maintenance and other long-range planning activities so common today were unheard of during the period under discussion.

It is true, of course, that some major real estate companies in large metropolitan areas had built up portfolios of several thousand units over the years, and accordingly were beginning to systematize reporting procedures for the properties in their charge. Even so, there was still little sophistication in the actual operation of properties, and great variation reflecting the differing policies, requirements, beliefs, and whims of the various owners.

Keep in mind that residential properties of twenty years ago were not as large as they are today. A building containing 25 to 80 units was considered to be a good account. These smaller properties were almost devoid of the kinds of amenities that are commonplace today. Perhaps there would be basement storage space and a coin-operated laundry room, but not much more.

Some time after rent controls were lifted in 1953, a building boom followed. The supply of new rental apartments began to catch up with the demand, and the balance point was finally reached in the early 1960s. But the new properties being built were still mostly small single-building developments. The merchandising and leasing of these new properties became important only when supply began to exceed demand. Still, the promotional techniques were primitive compared to those then employed in other industries.

Rent collection problems became more difficult as the supply of apartments increased. Property maintenance also began to take more and more of the manager's time, especially in cases where this had been neglected in the past. Those managers who developed the best systems for servicing existing tenants, and for marketing and merchandising vacant units, saw their portfolios of properties increased by the new business opportunities. After some 60 years, it could truly be said that property management was emerging from its earlier caretaker status to that of a highly respected profession.

This emergence was given a further boost by the continued boom in apartment building that continued up through the mid-1970s. Whereas apartment buildings constructed up to the 1960s were comparatively small, the new decade saw a transformation. Urban renewal provided an impetus for residential developments covering dozens of city blocks. Developers created huge complexes of garden apartment buildings on relatively cheap suburban tracts. Governments began building more and more public housing. Passage of condominium laws triggered a rush to put up all types of condominium structures. Liberal government programs and tax shelter provisions prompted individuals to come into the housing field, followed later by corporations who saw opportunities in residential real estate, thus prompting more building.

Since the 1960s, literally hundreds of very large, multi-unit developments have been built each year in communities throughout the country. Even the most modest apartment community today will cost $3 million or more, while some of the larger projects now run in excess of $50 million.

All of this resulted in hugeness and complexity. In consequence, the demand for good property managers has never been as high as it is today, and all present indicators point to a growth in future demand for such professional service. This is because small single-building developments are rarely built today, while large city-like communities with 1,000 or more units are becoming commonplace. Many of the newer complexes have schools, shopping centers, clubs, and recreational facilities, all contained within the grounds of the development. Rent collections within a single complex can exceed $1,000,000 yearly, and normal annual turnover for a single property may require as many as 300 rentals to replace moving tenants. Professional management of these properties is a necessity and no longer a matter of convenience to busy and absent owners.

Above we have traced the history of how traditional caretaker management is being replaced by professional management capable of administering large sums of money and of supervising large staffs. This means that problem solvers are needed now as the business of property management takes on a truly professional character. It presents an exciting challenge to persons willing and able to master the techniques of professional management. That is what this book is all about.

Chapter One

The World of Apartment Management

If you are already engaged in apartment management you may feel like skipping a further introduction or orientation and jump into discussions of apartment management techniques. This is faster, of course, but you won't receive a complete foundation for the subjects to follow. While your concerns today may deal with a particular property or tenant type while employed by a specific owner, the situation may change, so an overview of the total management picture will be helpful. Here in this chapter we identify the stage and cast of characters found in the business of managing multi-family housing.

Types of Properties

The stage or type of property is first. For the most part, the property manager is assigned to properties that already exist or are at least committed in terms of design, mix, layout, and equipment. The property manager may feel he should play an important role in helping plan the design, unit mix, unit layout, and equipment package of a new apartment development. Because of his daily exposure to both present and prospective tenants, he is clearly in the best position to know what the tenants want and what features draw the greatest response. Unfortunately, property managers seldom get such an opportunity. More often, they must deal with an accomplished fact—a completed property with many built-in management problems.

7

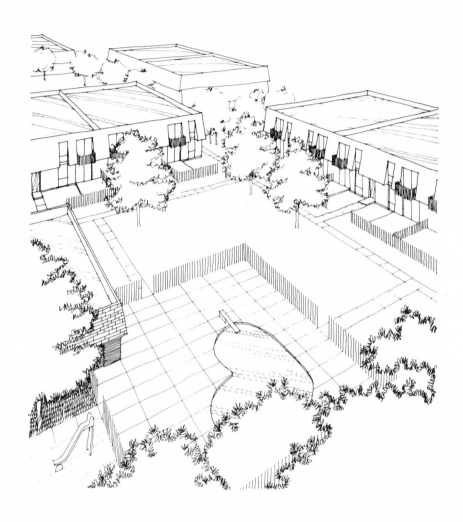

Suburban Garden Apartment Complex

This type of rental housing accounts for almost three times as many units as all other housing types built in recent times. Its popularity is credited to generous green space, ample parking, modern living units, recreational outlets, and competitive rent levels.

Regardless of how badly the property is located, designed, or equipped, there is nevertheless an optimum level at which it can be operated. There is a point at which income is at a maximum and expenditures at a minimum. The property manager must make the necessary adjustments to reach this point which produces the greatest possible net income.

All housing provides the basic need of shelter, just as all automobiles provide transportation. Both housing and automobiles can and do vary widely while performing their basic functions. Housing is available in all sizes, shapes, and prices. In the paragraphs that follow we will be describing the different styles of buildings which house multi-family units. You should note that the same classification of building designs can be used for public housing as well as the most expensive luxury housing. The difference, of course, is determined by location, size of units, and the equipment or amenity package. It is the tenant profile that adds the final character and identification to each building type.

There are many ways you can characterize the types of housing properties in the United States. Old and new, big and small, furnished and unfurnished, luxury and basic, permanent and temporary, desirable and undesirable, urban and suburban on one side, and inner-city on the other are a few possibilities. We shall be talking in the main about those property types that currently exist and/or are being built and developed, and particularly the large investment properties that have 50 or more separate units.

Low-Rise to High-Rise

Height is a good starting point to distinguish types of apartment buildings. Where land is relatively cheap and the developer is under little or no pressure to increase the number of housing units per acre, he can build lower buildings and spread them out. As land costs rise, the developer starts to think of getting more units onto a piece of ground, so he puts up higher buildings. In this book we have elected to distinguish buildings of varying height as follows:

Low-Rise: Buildings with one to five stories. If the building has an elevator, we call it an *elevator building*. If it has no elevator, we refer to it as a *walk-up*.

Mid-Rise: Buildings with six to nine stories. Elevator service is assumed unless otherwise stated.

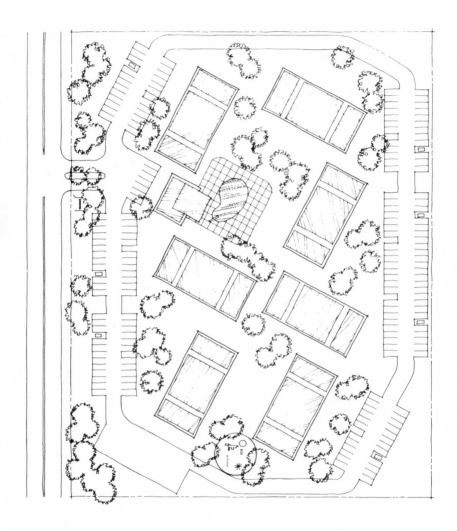

Site Plan

This is simply a plan, drawn to scale, showing the location and shape of buildings, roadways, parking areas, recreational amenities, and other important improvements. This can even detail building addresses and unit placement. Site plans are very helpful as part of the promotional material for a multi-building development.

High-Rise: Buildings with 10 or more stories.

Keep these distinctions in mind, because what may be a mid-rise building in one community may be considered a high-rise building in a smaller town.

Suburban Garden Apartment Complex

The first low-rise type of building we will consider is the *suburban garden apartment complex*. This is a property type that became popular in the 1960s, and that is destined to remain so for a variety of compelling economic and demographic reasons. This type is so prevalent that examples of it can be seen in almost every community across the land; it accounts for almost three times the number of residential units provided by all other types of new rental housing. This property type is easily recognized at a glance because of its many uniform features. For one thing, suburban garden apartment complexes are built on large tracts rather than city lots. This means that the identification and location of the development tends to be by name rather than by a city street address: e.g., The Terraces, Mission Valley, Farmingdale, Harbor Manor.

These complexes are generally located in growing suburbs and often completed in phases. The streets in the development typically are private. The land plan provides for a cluster of buildings usually two or three stories high, of more or less similar appearance, grouped around recreational features and parking lots that are shared by all of the tenants.

Many suburban garden apartment complexes are occupied by the younger set, including newly formed families with an average tenant age of less than 30. By offering modern, clean housing at rents which fit the pocketbook, such units gain quick acceptance from renters. They provide a welcome alternative to the older, more conventional housing stocks available in the city centers.

There are other factors that explain why the suburban garden apartment complexes are so popular. Ample parking—say, two spaces per unit, so scarce in urban locations—is included in the rent. More than that, the rents themselves tend to be substantially less than rents for comparable city housing.

These complexes frequently are built on raw, undeveloped land on the outskirts of a city, town, or village. The cost of a ten-acre tract might not be much more than a large city lot. At first, the building

Townhouse Development

Rental townhouse units have consistently enjoyed a strong market appeal. This is primarily because of their separate entryway, large living areas, and private patio or fenced yard. In many ways, townhouses provide the features of living in a single-family detached house at substantial dollar savings.

codes of these young growing communities generally are less restrictive than those of the municipalities they surround. This allows for lower construction costs. Finally, at the beginning, real estate taxes are lower than taxes on land closer in, providing for a major cost advantage. When added together these savings provide modern housing at affordable prices.

There is a life-style factor that has also attracted hordes of the younger set to the suburbs. The apartment complexes are built with generous use of green space and with lower density than city counterparts. These new properties lack the congestion of the crowded city. Many offer a wide range of recreational amenities. These almost always include a swimming pool and sometimes a clubhouse. Tennis courts, saunas, exercise rooms, playgrounds, sports fields, even putting greens and par-3 golf courses may be seen in the more luxurious settings.

From an operational standpoint suburban garden apartments don't pose the problems that their size and scope might suggest. The many buildings are usually cookie-cutter replicas of one another. The equipment is simple, usually a scaled-up version of single-family home equipment. Common areas are kept to a minimum. The tenants are responsible for carrying their garbage to central locations outside. Operating problems arise from the size, not from the complexities of this property type.

Townhouses

Another popular and easily recognized low-rise property type is the *townhouse*. Sometimes called row-houses, these have been built in the larger cities of America for many years in densely populated urban areas where land has been scarce and expensive. Centuries-old forerunners still can be seen in European cities. While the majority of these units were built for the owner-occupant, a great many of them are for rent.

Townhouses provide tenants with individual identity and living style usually reserved for occupants of single-family detached houses. They commonly are two stories high; some have basements, adding even more useful space.

New townhouses continue to be built in rows on adjacent city lots because of their high demand in the market place. To satisfy much the same demand, townhouses have been built in large

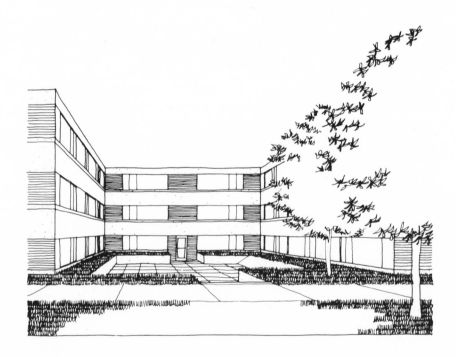

Garden Apartment Building

This building type is usually located in urban areas or established suburbs. Garden apartments are sometimes referred to as patio or terrace apartments because the first-floor level is a few steps below grade. Unlike their larger suburban counterparts, these buildings offer little in terms of recreational amenities.

numbers in recent years in suburban areas. Following the same principles as the suburban garden apartment complexes, they are set on large tracts, in clusters, surrounded by open space and with ample parking and shared recreational amenities. Many of these developments are commonly and originally intended as rental units.

Large numbers of young families are attracted to the suburban townhouse complexes. Some couples rent them as a stepping stone to eventual ownership of a single-family dwelling. The principal attractions of the townhouse are privacy and spaciousness, both in square feet and number of rooms. The separate entrance is a major feature. Once inside, tenants can enjoy the illusion of being in their own private detached house. There may be a private patio or small fenced yard, allowing for outdoor living enjoyment. While rents are higher than comparable apartment building space, it is considerably cheaper to rent a townhouse than to own a home. This makes the townhouse a good compromise for the needs and wants of so many people today.

Operationally, townhouses are easier to manage than rental apartment developments. Most of the upkeep burdens are left with the unit occupant the same as they would be in a single-family home. There are few common areas except lawns, grounds, and recreational amenities. Laundry facilities and tenant storage are almost always contained within the individual units. Equipment is also handled individually and is made up of simple widely used brands. Because townhouses are larger units they attract larger families which can cause headaches to the operator. But market demand for this type of housing is consistently high; therefore their merchandising is relatively easy.

Garden Apartments

As noted, townhouses can be found in suburban and urban settings alike. The modern city-located apartment buildings that are the counterpart of the suburban garden apartment complexes are called *garden apartments*. This important property type may be thought of as the present-day version of the old English basement walk-up apartment buildings that were so common in the 1920s.

Garden apartments are sometimes called *terrace* or *patio apartments*. Usually they are built on several city lots. These low-rise

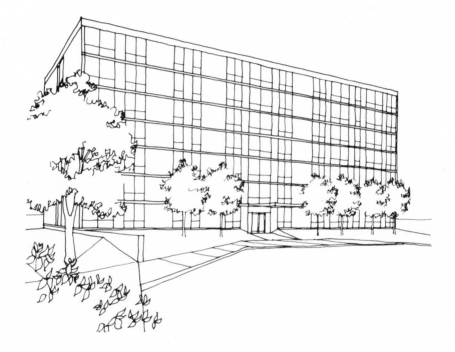

Mid-Rise Building

Ranging in height from six through nine stories, the mid-rise building can be found almost anywhere. Its features include a single front entryway, usually a lobby or waiting room, and a service core with elevators and stairwells. A common corridor provides access to apartment units on each floor. Parking and recreational amenities vary depending on age, location, and rent level.

structures may contain between 20 and 100 units. Their green area is usually limited to a front lawn and perhaps a small courtyard.

Typically, the lowest floor of the garden apartment building will be a few steps down from ground level. If there are more than two upper levels, elevator service is provided. The ground level is considered by most tenants to be as desirable for occupancy as the upper levels, unlike the old English basement apartments whose appearance was marred by small windows and overhead utility pipes hanging from the ceilings. Not infrequently, several garden apartment buildings will be put up in a neighborhood and then sold to individual investor-owners. While these buildings may have distinctive facades, they typically have identical interior layouts.

Garden apartments provide little in terms of additional amenities. A laundry room, storage locker room, and bicycle storage facilities usually are all that are offered. Occasionally a game room or tenant "club room" is provided. Because it has relatively few rental units, as compared to large suburban counterparts, this property type does not enjoy the same economy of size. Owners of small garden apartment complexes rarely maintain on-site management, but rather a live-in maintenance person who typically handles the re-renting of vacated units. Owner-management of this type of rental property is commonplace.

Mid-Rise

The *mid-rise* building, six to nine stories, can be old or new, located in either city or suburbs. A typical floor is located around a service core containing the elevators, staircases, meter room, and trash depository. A common hallway provides access to the individual apartment units. Apartment types are usually located in the same position on each floor, simplifying plumbing and mechanical installations. Either hydraulic or gear-type elevators are used. This building type usually contains between 40 and 140 rental units. One common lobby and mail room are typical. Amenities beyond laundry and storage facilities might include club and exercise rooms and perhaps a swimming pool or sundeck. The building is more complicated in construction and equipment than a low-rise structure, and therefore requires more technical knowledge in both its operation and management.

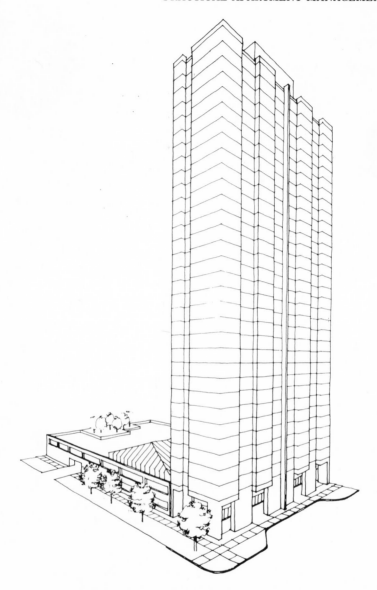

High-Rise Building

This type of building makes possible the greatest density of land use. This increased density helps to offset premium prices charged for scarce lots in choice locations. Or, because of the building's smaller land coverage, more area can be devoted to green space. Depending on size, location, and rent level, the extra services and amenities offered will vary widely.

High-Rise

There appears to be almost no limit to how high a *high-rise* building can be. High-rise structures containing residential apartment units now exceed 100 stories. The typical building, however, is more in the 20 to 30 story range. In addition to greater use of the land, the economics of height are needed to offset their much higher construction costs. One building might contain 900 units or more with the average of about 250. The same basic service core described for mid-rise buildings will be present although it may be expanded to accommodate a greater number of apartments per floor. Tier arrangement and typical floor layouts are also used. Because high-rises serve more people, they need more and faster elevators, usually gearless. Elevators with speeds of up to 1,800 feet per minute can be found in apartment buildings. The supporting amenities are larger in size and scope, and include receiving rooms, commissaries, valets, doormen, garage attendants, and a host of other services. While extra services do not necessarily come with high-rise buildings, greater complexity does. The equipment is often custom-made, one of a kind, requiring special training and attention to operate and maintain.

Planned Unit Development

A property type which has just recently come into its own is the *planned unit development, PUD.* Examples tend to be large in scale and often built in several phases over a number of years. They are found at in-city locations where large tracts of ground have been made available through urban renewal, or on large tracts of suburban or countryside land. Through a prearranged agreement with local planning or zoning boards the overall size and scope of a planned development is decided. The placement of the buildings, their height, size, unit mix, parking area, and green spaces are all considered and agreed upon before approval is granted. They often contain a mixture of all the property types we have just discussed; they may even include single-family detached homes and condominiums as well as rental properties. Some are so large and encompass housing for such a wide segment of the housing market that they become self-contained communities or small towns. Provisions for

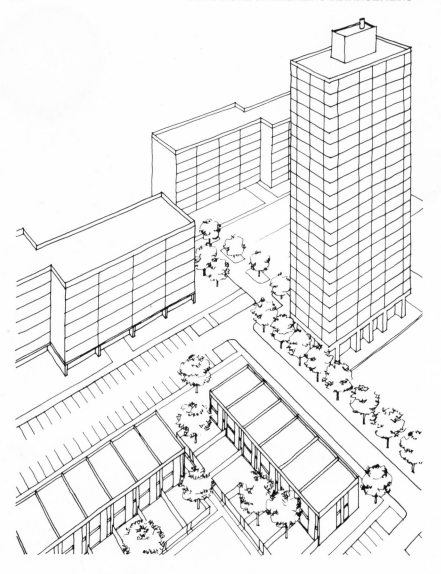

Planned Unit Development (PUD)

Because of their comprehensive planning in advance of any construction, planned unit developments often provide a better use of land and a variety of housing types. This illustration shows the high-rise, mid-rise, and townhouse types integrated into a single development. Some PUDs have been built using every housing type including single-family homes.

churchs, schools, shopping, and public transportation are often incorporated into the development scheme.

Other Types

Finally, there are still other types of rental housing available. Some of these are in the traditional mode while others are of a more modern character. Some of these are of lessening importance like the old *3-story walk-ups* and the corridor-type *apartment hotels.* In addition, there are *mobile home parks*, which afford more permanence than mobile housing. *Vacation* or *second-home cottages* or units also are presenting new challenges for property management. Buildings converted or built to provide rental units for the elderly offer specialized accommodations together with some unique management problems.

Above we have described the principal property types, and we have referred to them using the designations that are commonplace today. Property type is the basic feature that reflects a certain kind of land usage. And while the property *character* ultimately is derived from the property type, there are other factors involved, too. For completeness, we close this discussion by mentioning some of these factors.

Furnished Apartments

Any of the property types discussed above can be operated either furnished or unfurnished. The property type remains the same, but the character and operation change dramatically. With the exception of some of the specialized and miscellaneous property types, the addition of furnishings as part of the rental package increases the risk, work, and problems without any noticeable increase in net operating revenues. For example, a new 200-unit suburban apartment complex may have only enough serviceable furniture left to outfit 100 apartments after two years of operation. High tenant turnover is the reason. Furnished apartments for the most part attract mobile and transient tenant types. Such people occupy apartments as they would a motel room. They tend to have little or no commitment and rarely think of the furnished apartment as a "home." Instead they typically subject their rental space to hard abuse.

Owners who add furnishings usually do so to provide more

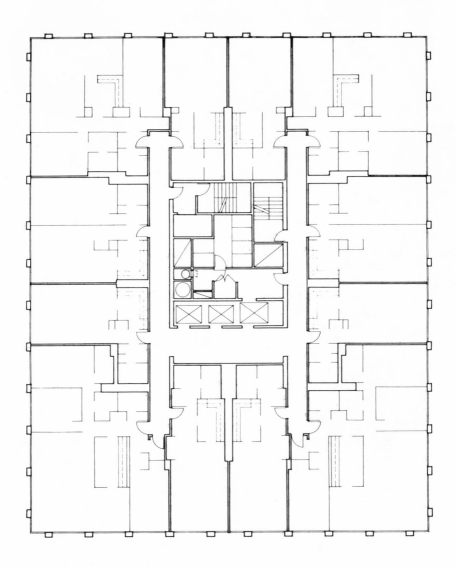

Floor Plan

Illustrated here is a typical floor plan of a large elevator building. The plan shows the unit mix configuration which is usually repeated on each floor level forming tiers of identical apartment types. This makes construction easier and less costly. Note the central service core which contains the elevators, rubbish chute, ventilation shafts, electrical service risers, and other necessary building components.

service and attract a larger market. There are ways to do this without offering apartment furnishings. We will refer to these later in this book.

Unit Size/Room Count

A second factor that fixes the character of the various property types is *unit size*. Apartment sizes are usually distinguished by the number of bedrooms and bathrooms they contain, or they can be referred to by their total number of rooms.

A small apartment without a bedroom is usually referred to as an *efficiency* or *studio* apartment. (In some parts of the country, a studio unit means a small apartment with two levels.) Usually they contain a small walk-in or pullman kitchen (a kitchen built along a wall), a dining and living area which is frequently the same room, and a bathroom.

When making a *room count*, the kitchen, no matter how small, is considered one room. The bathroom, which contains a toilet, lavatory, and tub (or shower stall), is called a "full bath" but is not included in the room count. Bathrooms with just a toilet and basin are classified as "half baths" and also are not included in the count. The living room is counted as a room, as is a separate formal dining room. A living-dining room combination is counted as 1¹/₂ rooms unless the combined space exceeds 300 square feet, in which case it would be counted as two rooms. A dining or dinette space of less than 100 square feet is regarded only as a half-room. Each bedroom with its own separate entry off a service hall is counted as a room. Dens and family rooms are also each counted as one room. Outside patios or balconies are not included in the count, nor are closets, no matter how large.

The following examples illustrate the room count method:

1. An apartment containing a combined living-dining room area, a kitchen, bedroom, and bath is referred to as a one bedroom apartment. (The presence of a complete bathroom is assumed and not mentioned, unless one is not included, or unless more than one is provided.) The room count then looks like this:

Living Room/Dining Area	1¹/₂ rooms
Kitchen	1 room
Bedroom	1 room
	3¹/₂ rooms

2. An apartment with a living room, dining room, kitchen, two bedrooms, and a full bathroom plus a partial bathroom is referred to as a two bedroom, $1^1/_2$ bath apartment. In this case, the room count would be:

Living Room	1 room
Dining Room	1 room
Kitchen	1 room
Two Bedrooms	2 rooms
	5 rooms

Unit Mix

Next we must consider that almost every apartment building or complex contains a number of different size units. This distribution, whatever it is, is referred to as the *unit mix*. The unit mix can greatly affect the character, ultimate use, direction, and success of a particular property type. Any of the property types described above would take on a different character if they contained only one size of dwelling unit. For example, a building with all efficiency units would have a distinctly different tenant profile than one with, say, all two bedroom units.

It follows that a building's location and intended market should influence the builder's decision when establishing the optimum mix. Differing economic conditions also will affect the desirability and demand of particular unit sizes.

An example of this can be seen during periods of a depressed economy, when efficiency apartments enjoy their greatest demand. Many people decide to scale down their living accommodations to a bedroomless apartment in a desirable building rather than move to a one bedroom apartment in an older (cheaper) building, or lose privacy by taking in a roommate to help share the costs. In these same hard times the two bedroom, two bath apartments correspondingly will be in minimal demand. Families requiring two bedrooms settle for apartments with only one bath. And two and three bedroom townhouses are in scarce supply during a poor economy as occupants wait for better times to purchase a single-family home.

At any point in time, economic conditions will affect the demand for the types of units, and therefore the mix, that a building has to offer. Obviously, no one unit mix will remain continuously at the same level of demand. The goal, therefore, is to provide a wide range of unit types, in varying percentages, to sustain a healthy occupancy and demand over the long haul of a building's life.

One example of a balanced unit mix intended to accommodate the widest range of market-place demand, and to provide stability throughout changing economic periods, might look like this:

Apartment Type	Distribution
Efficiency	15%
One Bedroom	40%
Two Bedroom, One Bath	25%
Two Bedroom, Two Bath	10%
Three Bedroom, Two Bath	10%
	100%

Such a mix, of course, will not be optimal for every location, nor as a hedge would it be advisable to provide such a mix for each building of a multi-building development. Tenants occupying the efficiency and one bedroom units are rarely compatible with families with children occupying the multi-bedroom units of the same building or vice versa.

Managers don't often get the chance to dictate the unit mix of a development. Still, they should be aware of the differences and the respective advantages and disadvantages of one against another.

Housing Standards

We have been discussing the major types of multi-family housing, their sizes and mixes that have been (and are being) built for investment potential. In each category we may further distinguish between properties built to *luxury* specifications, versus *middle-range* and *low-cost (subsidized) housing units*. The same property types take on a wide range of characteristics depending on the *tenant classes* they are intended to serve. Management concerns of leasing, services, maintenance levels, collections, tenant relations, and a host of other facets change dramatically between high-rise properties built for occupancy by the luxury class, the upper middle class, and the low-income classes of people. Some of these differences simply reflect the cultural background, history, desires, training, and demands of the various classes of tenants. These differences compound the difficulty of the job of management as will be seen in the next section.

Tenant Types

The easiest property to manage is an empty one. The life of a residential property is marked both at the beginning and at the end by the condition of no occupancy. As the presence of tenants adds a new dimension to the character of various property types, so can the application of management skills alter a property's character.

Tenant

In recent years there has been a movement to replace the word "tenant" with another designation, one thought to be less odious, such as occupant, resident, or lessee. This reflects the ingrained view held by many Americans that a tenant is a second-class citizen. Some operators and organizations believe that a softer word will change that feeling.

The fact remains that tenancy is really the only way in the English language to refer to people who gain the privilege of occupying land or buildings by paying rent. After all, every tenant is an occupant/resident, but not vice versa. The latter may be an owner-occupant, for example. More than that, some of the richest people and some the world's largest corporations are tenants in the premises they occupy. Why then should there be this stigma about the word "tenant"? In what follows, we shall use it without apology.

Tenants come in all sizes and shapes. Examples: singles and families, swingers and straights, students and the elderly, squatters and empty-nesters, quiet and loud, good and bad, and so forth. Managers of residential rental properties must be able to recognize these tenant types, to be aware of what is to be expected from them, and to know which ones are preferred occupants for given properties. The type of tenant that a building is designed for will affect many key aspects of management, including merchandising, marketing, maintenance, and tenant relations.

Some may object to thinking of tenant types, claiming that every tenant is an individual human being and must be treated as such. True, tenants are individuals. But insurance companies categorize people by height, weight, sex, medical history, occupation, etc., for insurance purposes, on the principle that groups demonstrate certain tendencies. Scientists do likewise in studying behavior. Property managers can do the same, because experience has demonstrated each of the groups mentioned above can be expected to behave in certain predictable ways and to make certain demands. Without such group standards, management would be hopelessly chaotic.

Tenants can be grouped in two broad categories, namely, *tenants by choice* and *tenants by circumstance*. Tenants by choice are likely to stay longer, cause fewer problems, and overall make better residents. They choose a place to be their home and back this up with commitments of money and energy.

On the other side, we find apartment dwellers who are *not* necessarily happy with the arrangement. They accept renting only as the best (immediate and temporary) way to compromise their inability to achieve other long-range ambitions. Frequently the real wish of these people is to eventually own their own private housing.

No doubt about it, the special attraction that real estate holds for the American public reflects the common way of thinking that one should buy before all of the land becomes "used up." It also reflects the viewpoint that property owners are the ones who have succeeded in life. This idea has had a very compelling influence on a certain class of rental tenants who see their present housing arrangements as a rude indication of their own shortcomings and disadvantages.

This attitude may be changing. Since the end of World War II, renting has spread beyond housing to other commodities—autos are a major example. Equipment leasing is a fact of life in the business world. The person who rents today is no longer as apt to be regarded as a second-class citizen the way he might have been in the 1900s.

Tenants by Choice

Career people, settled people without children, empty-nesters (couples whose children have grown and left), and retired senior citizens typically are tenants by choice. Maybe their situation is one in which the extra space available in purchased housing is not needed. Maybe they want the freedom that renting provides. Or maybe they choose to rent because it is the most economic way of living in the area of their choice.

Empty-Nesters

Given complete freedom to select tenants, an experienced property manager would try to fill all the units with *empty-nesters*. These typically are married couples who have raised their children—perhaps in a single-family home—and who now have chosen the carefree ways of apartment living. They invest in furniture and furnishings to provide comfort and convenience. They pay their rent promptly, live in peace and harmony with neighbors, and pose few management problems. They are the most selective of all tenants in their housing decisions. They insist on quality in housing, services, and management. Before they rent they shop around, since they are looking for accommodations that will remain satisfactory in the long run. Empty-nesters, however, make up only a small fraction of the prospective tenant market.

Career People

Next in terms of tenant desirability are the established *career people*. These can be bachelor men and women or childless couples. Their life-style is career-oriented. They have made the choice to rent rather than buy a home. The character of the place they live in is important to them and to their small circle of close friends. They tend to choose smaller apartments in established neighborhoods that are convenient to work and entertainment activities. Because of the career orientation, they may move from time to time, so their occupancy does not offer the same stability to management as provided by the empty-nester.

Senior Citizens

The *senior citizens*, married or not, who are secured by retirement benefits, are also a favorite tenant type. Characteristic of this group is that they tend to be quiet, prompt paying, and adept in good housekeeping. Such people also tend to choose small apartments especially when they are constrained by fixed, inflation-eroded incomes. Budgetary limitations may keep them from choosing locations in preferred neighborhoods; still they will be discriminating in finding a place where basic daily needs can be met. It is true that the medical problems associated with advanced age may pose some management problems. Beyond that, these people form a most desirable part of the market.

The tenant categories just mentioned—and indeed others—all have in common the fact that renting is done by choice. The priorities, life-styles, and conditions of age and health are such that the temptation to become homeowners is subdued, perhaps entirely absent. Maybe it's just that they don't like to cut the grass. Maybe they are convinced that in the long run there is greater economy in renting. In any case, such tenants are satisfied with their situation.

Tenants by Circumstance

On the other hand, there are those tenants who rent because of their current circumstances. A student attending college away from home, for example, needs temporary housing. Young families want a place to live until they have a down payment for a home. Swingers and live-together couples require a place to sow their wild oats before eventually settling down. In all of these cases rental housing is being occupied on an interim basis. Decisions about ultimate living arrangements are still to be made. Because of the temporary aspects, there is a reluctance to make commitments of their time, money, and energy to create a home-like environment. The rental unit is occupied without commitment. Naturally, management problems increase dramatically in such instances.

There are other renters, too—for example, those who are young and inexperienced—who sometimes may be classified as tenants by circumstance rather than by choice. We have already alluded to those engaged in trial marriages and whose tenancy in apartment buildings is nothing more than the modern-day version of a week-end in a motel.

From the management point of view the desirability of different classes of tenants by circumstance is measured by how long their occupancy will be prolonged and by the absence of costly problems their tenancy presents. After all, with good service, tenants by circumstance can be transformed into the more permanent tenants by choice. And every time the need to re-rent an apartment is avoided, net operating income will increase.

Families with Children

Families with children make up a significant part of the rental market. This will be true under economic conditions where the cost of buying and maintaining single-family housing is increasing faster than a family's ability to make these payments. Renting then becomes a compromise of the goal for home ownership.

Many managers prefer to avoid the special problems caused by children. The obvious reasons will be outlined in Chapter 2 under Rental Policies. But there is a positive side, too. Families with children are less mobile than other tenant classes, meaning that the need to deal with moves will be minimized. Also the skip-out rate tends to be low. The conclusion: with a creative management program which channels the energies of youngsters in non-destructive directions, you can take advantage of the large size and relative stability of this segment of the market. Families with children may be tenants by circumstance, but there are lots of them, and they are good tenants in the best cases.

Swinging Singles/Young Couples

We usually think of *swinging singles* and *young newly married couples* as tenants by circumstance. In any case they make up the largest segment of the rental market today. Because of factors such as inexperience, lack of maturity, shortage of possessions, job insecurity, and lack of long-range commitments and attachments, they form a very mobile group. Because of their large numbers they present a way for apartments to be filled quickly. By the same token, however, they bring with them the prospects of short tenancies and quick departures.

The apartment selectivity of young people is not keen. They tend to be attracted by superficial gimmicks. But they have high taste levels from having grown accustomed to the living styles that their parents took a lifetime to achieve. Not infrequently they earn good money, but because of poor budgeting they have meager savings and constantly fall short in financing all of their needs and desires. Rent collections thus become difficult. There are few markets in the country where full occupancy can be achieved without this tenant class. They are needed in spite of the management problems they cause.

Students

Finally, and lowest in terms of desirability, is the most temporary of all tenant types, the *student*. They come in large numbers to college towns, bringing with them few possessions and even less money. Their stay will be short. This and their lack of commitment to the place they are renting present management problems that only those who specialize in the student market will care to face. Occupancy terms are for ten months or less. Rent collections will be difficult. Wear and tear will present enormous maintenance problems. And then there is the competition to cope with, where the colleges themselves offer subsidized housing (e.g., dormitories, student-staff apartments, and the like). In periods of falling school enrollments, investment properties are left with more and more vacancies.

Income Class

Our discussion of tenant types so far has made no reference to *income class*. It is a touchy subject, but certain general conclusions can be drawn. By and large, white-collar and professional tenants present management with fewer problems than blue-collar workers. And the latter tend to be easier to deal with than low-income (unskilled and casual labor) workers. The fact is clear: the management of low-income housing complexes is far more taxing than that for tenants of greater affluence. It would be beyond the scope of this book to deal with the socio-economic reasons for this observation, but for completeness the matter simply has to be mentioned.

The major opportunities for property management involve dealing with people in middle- and upper-income brackets. These are the tenants of most of the newer and larger properties built in recent years. In this sense, the more difficult management of low-income housing must be regarded as a fairly specialized subject to which only limited portions of this book pertain.

In this connection, however, we should observe that not infrequently tenants moving out are of a higher economic status than the incoming tenant replacements. That is, people who move for the most part are moving up the ladder. The same situation is seen where a person sells a car to buy a new one, with the used car then being bought by someone less prosperous. It is also seen in the sale and purchase of single-family housing. Of course, housing requirements finally do diminish with time (as when grown children leave home), and economic disasters can occur (as when the breadwinner becomes unemployed). From time to time, some tenants have to step down the ladder.

Putting the people who comprise the rental market into classification groups, especially the small number we have used, is arbitrary and obviously very general. The exceptions to our descriptions are many and varied. In the final analysis, the individual quality and desirability of each tenant can only be gauged by his or her performance.

Ownership Types

Regardless of what the property types are and who the tenants are, all properties have owners. Like tenants, some owners own property by choice and some through circumstance. Some look for cash profits while some have other goals in mind. The manager of real estate must know of and understand these differences.

Profit-Motivated Ownership

Investment real estate has historically held a fascination and opportunity not present in other forms of investment. The vast majority of owners of investment rental housing are motivated by the profit potential of cash return. Other motivations include the potential of appreciation in value as a hedge against inflation. Some owners hope to sell at a later date for a price higher than what they bought for, thereby enjoying capital gains. Others want the tax benefits of owning real estate which may shelter income gained from other sources. Still others play a financing game of borrowing to buy a property, seeing it increase in value, refinancing it, and using the proceeds to buy still another property, and so on. In each case, the profit motive is the guiding principle.

A major advantage gained by real estate investment is that the investor maintains some degree of control over the outcome. By contrast, in the stock market, the investment follows the ups and downs of prevailing trends over which the small investor (at least) has absolutely no control.

There are disadvantages, too, in investing in real estate. A wrong decision in the original purchase and/or in the method of operation may be enough to wipe out the investment. Market conditions, fluctuating as they do, as well as local laws and ordinances, likewise can adversely affect the situation. More than that, real estate ownership means loss of liquidity of the investment capital. For example, while stocks, bonds, and savings account investments can be quickly cashed when funds are needed elsewhere, real estate may require up to 60 days to liquidate—and perhaps then at a loss because of the quick sale.

Investment in income-producing real estate involves a burden of business management that doesn't appear in most other forms of investment. In addition to professional management needed to operate the property, there must be supervision of the management itself. More than that, investors in properties face the fact that the brick and mortar do not last forever. It must be understood that eventually all that will be left is the land itself. But few investors expect to live long enough to face this eventuality. Even with these formidable pitfalls, private investment in multi-family housing properties still may be regarded as offering outstanding opportunities for profit. In fact, it can be said that investment in all forms of real estate enjoys an attraction as does no other form of investment. This is because land with or without improvements, is something real, something that is exhaustible, and something that historically has appreciated in value.

Interim or Caretaker Ownership

A great many multi-family residential complexes are not now being operated as a profit-making entity. The ownership can be by circumstance or by choice. Properties held by receivers, government agencies (FHA), or by lending institutions following foreclosure come about through circumstance, not choice. The goal in these cases is not cash profits but the final disposition of the property. Their ownership is that of caretaker rather than investor. The goals of these owners will have an effect on the caliber and direction of management.

Not-for-Profit Ownership

On the other hand, there are owners of multi-family housing who intend to operate as not-for-profit. Churches, unions, and social organizations often sponsor housing for members and others alike. Governments (local, state, and federal) all sponsor some housing which is operated without profit. Large companies, schools, hospitals, etc., often own not-for-profit rental housing. The various forms of cooperative housing operate to break even, not to profit. When the profit motive is missing, management is different, often more difficult.

To complete this discussion of ownership types, we should look at the common ownership entities to understand their basic differences. This can only be handled in the broadest manner as there are limitless ways to arrange real estate ownership. We will point out popular ownership types in their most conventional form without the many variations.

Individual Investor

The greatest number of owners of income-producing apartment houses most certainly fall into the classification of *individual investors*. They frequently use the capital earned from other business pursuits as the investment ante by which they enter the real estate world. They are attracted by the allure real estate holds and all the advantages we outlined earlier.

Partnerships

Small *partnerships and syndicates* are simply an extension of the individual investor. By having more people involved, the risks are spread, and larger purchases can be made that may be more profitable because of the economies that come with size. The advantages and disadvantages are about the same as those of individual ownership, except there is always the problem of how to control and deal with disenchanted partners. Partnership agreements help but are never enough when disagreement arises. Some partnerships are formed involuntarily through inheritance. These can be the most trying for a property manager.

Joint Partnership

In the *joint partnership or joint venture*, typically one partner furnishes the investment capital while the other furnishes services and know-how. Builder-developers frequently will be seen to supply their construction knowledge and capabilities, while their joint-venture colleagues come up with the cash. Many large lending institutions and other major corporations have funded such operations as an investment. There aren't any rules for how profits are split and each case is usually negotiated separately. The success or failure of this arrangement rests solely with the attitude and skills of the partners involved.

Limited Partnership

Another popular form of ownership is the *limited partnership.* Here there will be two classes of ownership, referred to as the general partner and the limited partner(s). Essentially the general partner is the quarterback who organizes and calls the plays. He controls the real estate and makes up operating losses that may occur. Meanwhile the limited partner invests capital in an agreed-upon amount which becomes the "limit" of his investment, responsibility, and control. This limit, however, only holds so long as the general partner is solvent and performs his functions. If he does not, the limited partners may have to perform on his failures to protect their investment, but they are under no legal obligation to do so. Property managers who deal with properties owned by limited partnerships are responsible to the general partners, not the limited ones.

Major Corporations

Many major corporations over the years have plunged into the business of owning multi-family rental housing. These attempts at diversification have not always been successful—notwithstanding the general tendency for real estate to appreciate in value with the passage of time. Real estate enterprises and developers, of course, succeed more often than not because they have the gambler's touch. They move quickly in ways that are dynamic, even flamboyant. But this is not the operational characteristic of major corporations, whose teams of business administration experts cannot compensate for lack of savvy and flexibility, no matter how big the computers are. It will be some time before the major corporations that have suffered substantial losses will forget their disillusionment.

Some large corporations have entered the multi-family housing business, not as an investment, but as a way to provide convenient, safe, and clean residential accommodations for their employees. In such cases special holding companies may be formed to hide the real ownership, and to avoid the adverse publicity of creating a "company town."

Life Insurance Companies/Lending Institutions

Some of the largest companies in America are to be found in the residential housing business as owners. These include life insurance companies, banks, and thrift institutions who are the prime lenders of the capital needed to finance apartment houses in the first place. Often, however, this kind of ownership is involuntary and comes as a consequence of the need to foreclose on delinquent accounts. When ownership develops in this manner it usually becomes the interim or caretaker brand. The goal is to wait out the bad times and resell the investment at the least possible loss. Certain properties are acquired, however, as investments and are added to the institution's portfolio to produce income and for their ultimate appreciation in value.

REITs

Real estate investment trusts, referred to as REITs, are a relatively new form of ownership. Their aim is to give small investors the profit opportunities and the tax shelter advantages that come from participation in real estate ownership. In their operation, the REITs get approval from the Securities and Exchange Commission to make a public offering of shares of beneficial interest. The funds so generated then are put into the purchase of investment real estate, or used as short-term mortgage money for real estate properties. This form of ownership succeeds only when prudent investments and strict supervision are made by the REIT management. The value of the investment is also subject to the whims of the stock market and not necessarily to the values of the properties; therefore, an important advantage of real estate ownership is missing.

Co-op/Condominium

Another form of mutual ownership is the cooperative or condominium housing development. This ownership type is interested in personal benefits, not profit, although many condominium buyers hope their investment will appreciate. The owners are primarily users, not investors. They are self-governing via committees and they present the most difficult challenge to professional management.

Government

Our final ownership type is also a form of mutual ownership in the strictest definition: government. Government ownership is not restricted to federal but also includes state and local governments as well. The involvement of government is becoming much broader than just ownership of public housing projects or through subsidies to various sectors of the housing market. The Federal Housing Administration (FHA) is an agency of the federal government set up to insure loans on a wide variety of housing types including very large and very expensive developments. If these developments falter, FHA pays off the private lender with cash or debentures and accepts the ownership of the collateral. Today FHA is one of the largest single owners of multi-family housing.

So we have it: a variety of property types with even greater variations of tenant types all owned in different ways for different goals.

Manager Types

Before we get down to the business of describing manager types, let's first understand what the property manager does. Primarily a manager is an agent, an extension of the owner he represents. The owner's interest should always be uppermost in the professional manager's mind. He should ask himself, when faced with decision making: "What would I do if I owned this property?" Because the manager has acquired experience and specialized skills, he is in a much better position than the owner to produce an answer. He is in effect a "professional substitute" for the owner. In this respect, the property manager is like the lawyer and accountant whose specialized skills are applied in the owner's best interest.

The basic goal of the property manager is to produce the highest possible *net operating income*. This is defined as collections less operating expenses. Some owners would like the property manager's role expanded to include the production of the highest possible *cash flow*, which is net operating income less debt service (payment on the mortgage). But the amount and payment of debt service has nothing to do with successful management. An analogy might help in understanding this. A commercial airline captain has as his first priority the safe flight of the airplane and its occupants. If the company he represents is in financial difficulties, he can try to save money but not when it begins to endanger his primary function. The same is true of property management. If the property manager has produced maximum rent collections and has kept operating expenses to an effective minimum, he has done his job, regardless of what debt service the owner must pay.

So with the goal and responsibility of management in mind, let us look at what is involved in property management. You must be first equipped with a lot of information about the property and its location, the market area, operating experience, maintenance techniques, reporting procedures, and a host of other items. You must have good common sense, be resourceful, and be willing to work hard, as these are the principal ingredients that make a good property manager. Unfortunately, not all managers have taken the time or have had the experience and training to really act as a "professional substitute." They are "problem finders," not "problem solvers." The sole purpose of this book is to offer the manager the knowledge which has been gained by others through years of experience, allowing him to grow faster in an industry begging for talent.

The real and most exciting part of the management business is the handling of investment properties for profit. Caretaker assignments and not-for-profit housing don't offer as many opportunities or challenges. In the main, this book is directed at managing income-producing investment housing, so let's start there. Investment housing is intended to generate profit. In fact, *the value of investment real estate is in direct proportion to the property's ability to generate net operating income (collections less operating expenses).* The manager's role is *to produce the highest possible net operating income over the economic life of the property.*

The skills in managing profit-producing housing are more demanding and more fulfilling than those needed for caretaker or not-for-profit management. In fact, the management of these latter two can be very frustrating because the presence of a material goal just isn't there. Without the need to produce a profit, the manager is often deprived of the purpose and spirit needed to succeed.

The differences between the manager types we are about to describe are really just varying degrees of knowledge possessed at the different levels. Granted, the amount of authority is also changing, but this is just a further reflection of the particular manager's skill and experience. Managers are employed in one of two ways: as direct employees of owners, who can be individuals, partnerships, corporations, or even the government, and as employees of real estate companies in the business of property management. The first class covers the greatest number of property managers. The manager types outlined below can fall into either class.

Executive Property Manager

An executive property manager is a supervisor who oversees and directs other property managers who are actually in the field handling the management affairs of various properties. His primary concern is often with running a business which manages properties rather than the actual management of those properties. His knowledge for this position usually stems from long and broad experience in actually managing investment real estate. He uses this knowledge to establish long-range policies and fiscal plans and to guide the property manager in his charge to solve difficult management situations. The executive property manager is frequently an officer of the company and in fact might very well be an owner of that company. Typically, he is compensated by a regular salary; additional incentive bonuses are common.

Property Manager

The individual actually responsible for the management of a particular property is called the property manager. The key to this title depends on several things. The title means in effect that the person holding it is the chief operating officer or administrator of a particular property or group of properties. He or she is responsible for fiscal planning, setting rent levels, establishing marketing and maintenance procedures, supervising on-site employees, and reporting and maintaining liaison with owners and superiors.

Site Manager

At the next level of management is the site manager. Responsibilities of this person include day-to-day dealings with tenants, renting units, making collections, and follow-through supervision of maintenance. The site manager is truly the person on the firing line.

Some people mistakenly refer to the site manager as the resident manager, implying that the person lives on the site. This is not always true. The place of residence has nothing to do with the responsibilities of this position. We shall use the term site manager in referring to this level of management.

"Ma-Pa" Managers

So called Ma-Pa management, also popular in small hotel units, is fast becoming a vanishing species and well on its way to extinction. The wife performs the renting and bookkeeping duties while the husband handles maintenance and maybe even problem collections or disturbances. While less expensive in the short haul than professional management methods, this arrangement is inadequate and ineffective in today's demanding times.

These are the people who play the game of property management. They enjoy career opportunities rarely found today. The success or failure of privately financed investment real estate falls on their shoulders. Those who learn their lessons well will be rewarded both financially and in the satisfaction of performing a vitally needed service.

Chapter Two

Policies

The development of proper policies is important in the smooth operation of multi-family housing. Policies also play a key role in the successful marketing of rental apartments along with four other major elements. The five elements are:

- **Policies**—establishing fair and reasonable guidelines, designed to attract and keep good tenants and discourage others.
- **Product Preparation**—making the property as attractive as possible, to attract the greatest number of qualified prospects.
- **Price**—regulating demand and desirability through rent changes.
- **Presentation**—blowing the horns and whistles of marketing, to catch attention and build desire.
- **Promises**—This is the common thread which ties all of the preceding principles together, and is implicit in setting your policies, preparing and presenting your product, and establishing prices. Because of this integration, we will not discuss promises separately, but you should be aware that promises are part of everything a property manager does every day.

In this chapter we will explore the first of these five P's, policies. These must be established before you begin your management operations.

Every business, large or small, is constantly confronted with situations and problems that call for decisions. Policies are pre-thought-out answers to anticipated problems. Some of these answers will help you avoid problems in the first place. Others will enable you to deal swiftly and thoroughly with problems when they do come up.

Even the one-man management operation needs to have policies, because it will face the same problems that the large management company faces. For the large company with hundreds or thousands of units to manage, the problems are much the same in kind, but they are more numerous and they occur faster. Without policies, management would have to make decisions on a one-by-one basis. This would not only lead to chaos, but also would produce inconsistent results.

Policies help to avoid all this. They clear the air. They let everyone involved know where he stands, what's expected of him, and what will be done if things go wrong.

The right policies enable you to put much of your management business on a routine basis and enable you to concentrate on the really demanding aspects. With policies, you don't have to spend time constantly re-inventing the wheel, your work becomes more efficient. Once a pattern has been set, you continue to follow it until something occurs that lets you know the policy is no longer useful.

Yes, policies need to be reviewed and changed when necessary. Policies are guidelines, not straitjackets. You can't anticipate every situation to which a given policy will apply. From time to time you'll encounter problems that can't be dealt with unless a policy is bent a little or changed entirely. But for the most part, policies will save you the trouble of making constant individual decisions.

Another important thing policies will do is compel you to study your business and know it thoroughly. You really can't make good policies until you know everything about your business. If you are taking over a property for the first time, you are going to have to do a lot of creative thinking—just like a chess player does—to plan your moves and consider the alternatives.

But you don't have to rely entirely on your own ability to anticipate problems. While in the beginning property managers had to innovate, because they had no professional expertise to fall back on, you're more fortunate. You can learn from the experiences of others; what follows is a sharing of those experiences.

Policies are important not only for you, the manager, but also for rental agents and maintenance people who work for you; the prospects and tenants in the building; and your owner. Each has a right to know what to expect. The time to fix those expectations is before a crisis erupts, when you have time to reach a cool, unimpassioned decision, rather than be forced to act hastily.

To be useful, policies should be written down and made available to everyone they apply to. When policies are changed, the change should also be communicated to all parties.

Policies should be reasonable and enforceable. You'll only weaken your position and appear dictatorial if you establish policies that you can't make stick.

In what follows we will discuss policies that:

1. Ensure high levels of office efficiency.
2. Attract the right kind of rental tenants and discourage undesirable ones.
3. Maintain good tenant relations, thus keeping management-tenant problems to a minimum.
4. Set standards for personnel staffing.

We'll point out areas that call for policies. We'll suggest what the alternatives are to various policies. In some cases we will recommend a policy. But in the end, it will be up to you to set the policy that best suits your objectives.

General Policies for Better Operations

Office Location

You probably will have several possible locations for your rental and management office. Since the office is in the business of serving prospects and tenants, it should be in a location where it will be easy to find, particularly for prospects. From this standpoint, the *closer to the road* or visitor parking lot your office is, the better.

One of the best places to locate your office is close to or in your *recreation facility.* This has several advantages:

- It ensures that prospects will see the recreation facilities. This often doesn't happen, particularly in the later stages of a rental program when the agent showing the prospect around will skip a tour of these facilities. When the prospect must come to the recreation facility to get to your office, he sees the facility which is an important plus in your marketing program. In some properties, the facility is kept closed or even locked during daylight hours, thereby losing its effect on prospects who visit at those times.

- You can supervise the recreation facility without adding the extra staff you would need if the office and facility were separate.

- Finally, because you're located in the recreation facility, you will have a better check on maintenance and can see that the facility is kept clean at all times.

Ideally, your office should have its own separate entrance from the outside. Prospects then don't have to enter the building lobby. This makes for better security.

Some managers like the idea of making the rental office part of the model apartments, or of taking over a regular apartment next to the models for the office. Both of these are poor choices. They breach security by bringing outside visitor traffic into the building and by having a commercial purpose intrude into a residential area. Tenants who live on the same floor will dislike this combination.

Putting the office in with the model apartment itself usually destroys the merchandising appeal of the model. You would then be better off in having only an office with no model. Taking over a next-door apartment for the office deprives you of the rental revenue of that unit. Circumstances may force you into this, but avoid it if you can.

One Office or Two?

Because the rental office or, as we will come to know it, the rental information center serves prospects while the management office serves tenants, you may consider the idea of having two separate offices. But it's generally best to combine the two functions in a single office. Such an arrangement uses manpower more effectively. At slack periods, when you may have only one person in the office and he or she has to leave for a few minutes, that office is without staff. By having the two functions combined, the rental and management people can fill in for each other; thus each gains a better understanding of the entire property's operations.

The exception to this suggestion occurs in extremely large complexes where, because of the large number of people involved in each function, it's best to have two separate offices.

Some managers think it best to separate the two functions regardless because they don't want the risk of having a complaining tenant come into the office and discourage a prospect who overhears the complaint. But this danger is highly unlikely, especially if you're managing the property in the right manner. If a tenant complains, it's likely to be when he pays the rent, which is apt to be early in the morning or late in the day; or he'll complain just before a major holiday like Thanksgiving or Christmas when he wants you to get things looking right for the friends he has invited over. In both cases, these are light rental periods when prospects aren't apt to be present.

But if you feel having tenants and prospects running into each other is undesirable, then you can still have a private area for tenants in the same office. The point is that a combined office gives you added efficiency.

Office Appearance

Despite the old saying, "You can't judge a book from its cover," people can and do judge by appearance. A management office that's messy-looking, with service requests stacked in the file tray, half-empty coffee cups lying around, wastebaskets overflowing, and ash trays filled with cigarette butts may make a rental prospect wonder just how well the rest of the building is maintained.

Maintaining a good appearance is essential. Desks should be clean and uncluttered. Ash trays should be emptied several times a day and wiped each time. Keep coffee pots and cups out of sight, except when coffee is being served. If there are magazines for prospects to read while they're waiting, make sure the copies are fresh. Windows should be sparkling and the floor cleaned or vacuumed daily. Good housekeeping in the rental office will pay off in increased prospect confidence.

Office Hours

Again, because the office exists to serve prospects and tenants, the hours you choose should conform to the habits of the people you serve.

Consider *prospects* first. Experience shows that Sunday is the day when you can expect the greatest activity. Some managers dispute this. They say they never see any prospects on Sunday. Why? Because their offices aren't open. Don't doubt the importance of Sunday: it is the busiest day.

Holidays are as important as Sundays. The only exceptions are Thanksgiving, Christmas, and New Year's Day, when most people stay home. But Easter Sunday, Memorial Day, Fourth of July, and Labor Day bring out the apartment-hunters.

Monday evening is another prime time for prospects. Saturday, contrary to what some may think, is a poor day, because people reserve that day for grocery shopping and other chores.

Knowing this, it's a good idea to keep your rental office open on Sundays and holidays in addition to weekdays. That means seven days a week. A further study of prospect traffic will reveal that few show up before 11 a.m. So generally if you establish rental hours from 11 a.m. to 6 p.m.—longer in the summer when daylight saving time is in effect—you'll catch most of the prospect traffic.

It's also a good idea to post your rental hours so prospects know when you're open. Your actual office hours can begin at 8:30 a.m. or 9, to allow your office staff to handle paperwork before the traffic starts coming in.

Now consider your existing *tenants*. Their habits usually conform to the normal workweek. They have little demand for routine office services (outside of emergencies and maintenance) on Saturday afternoons and Sunday. So for normal management hours, you can be open from 9 a.m. to 6 p.m. during the week and from 9 a.m. to noon on Saturdays.

Be aware that service is your goal. If you need to change hours to serve your prospects and tenants better, don't be afraid to do so.

Recreation Facilities

Whatever recreation facilities you have—and these can be anything from a single room with a Ping-Pong table to a lavish clubhouse—you need policies governing hours of use, guests, and fees. Otherwise these facilities will go uncontrolled, a situation which will irritate tenants and reflect poorly on your management abilities.

In setting hours, consider the preferences of tenants and also the effect on tenants who live near the facility.

Guests can be a problem. You want to tread a thin line between being so restrictive that tenants will be discouraged from having guests (and may move out for that reason) and being so relaxed that the entire neighborhood can use the facility.

A policy that many managers have found workable is to limit guests to *two at a time* in the company of the tenant. That means the tenant must be present. If he invites his sister, brother-in-law, and their 10-year-old-son, only two can use the facility at any one time.

As for guest *fees*, avoid them if you can. Tenants dislike them and they make your place seem unfriendly. They also create bookkeeping work.

Don't staff your facility with any more *personnel* than you absolutely need. Unless you are legally required to have a swimming pool lifeguard, for example, don't hire one. But once you do, understand that you've set a precedent which you may have to maintain.

Avoid regularly scheduled management-sponsored *events* such as parties, in recreation facilities. They run up costs, add to wear and tear on the facility, and they seldom engender the goodwill they're intended to produce. A limited number of such events, say three or four a year, will provide maximum impact and interest.

The manager is in the business to manage. That means he shouldn't be a *social director*. If tenants want to organize a bowling league, hobby show, knitting circle, or amateur theater, let them do it on their own. You'll only add to your costs without producing any marketing advantage if you get involved.

Finally, establish a policy governing use of the recreation facilities by special-interest groups such as political organizations, commercial enterprises, etc. Generally the policy should discourage such use.

Supporting Amenities

Your property will most likely have many supporting amenities designed to meet basic tenant needs and to make life more comfortable for them. Consider what your policies should be in each case.

- **Laundry room.** This is a basic facility that is important in satisfying prospects and tenants. Expect it to get heavy use. It should be well equipped; a ratio of one washer and one dryer for every 12 apartments is a good rule of thumb. There should also be a sorting table. The room should be properly ventilated, brightly decorated, well-lit, and cleaned daily. To aid in keeping it neat, provide a wide-mouth trash receptacle. As a tenant convenience, a bulletin board is a good idea.

The laundry room should be kept open the maximum number of hours each day, depending on its location. For security reasons and to minimize disturbing tenants who live nearby, 11 p.m. is a typical closing hour. But if conditions permit, consider keeping it open 24 hours a day; tenants who work odd hours will appreciate this.

Soap dispensers and change-making machines in the laundry room are subject to failure and pilferage, adding up to tenant irritation. Most tenants will bring their own soap and change. Avoid having the management office make change; you'll be forever making change for a parade of tenants if you do.

Should the property own the laundry room machines? From a financial standpoint, you're better off if you do. But the burden and expense of maintaining them, plus the risk of theft, are major negatives. If you deal with a concessionaire, be sure you reserve the right to approve prices charged to operate the machines. Otherwise you may discover that tenants will become irritated and blame you if concessionaires have the right to set and change prices on their own.

- **Vending machines.** Cigarette, candy, soft drink, and ice dispensers are appreciated by many tenants. These machines are best housed in their own facilities, preferably in or near the recreation room or clubhouse, in their own separate room, or in the laundry room.

  The disadvantage of these machines is that they are subject to vandalism and theft. In time they become unsightly, especially if they're exposed to the weather, and they create a maintenance problem.

- **Coin-operated amusements**. In a complex with families and young singles, coin-operated games such as pool tables, pinball machines, and air hockey can generate considerable revenue for the property. But these devices are subject to abuse, robbery, and frequent breakdown. You're better off having a concessionaire put in the equipment and take care of the maintenance. Concessionaires may in turn demand that you supervise the equipment to keep maintenance costs down.

- **Pay telephone**. This can be a big convenience to tenants during their move-ins and to site employees. But it should be located outside the building in an out-of-the-way spot. If you have it inside, the telephone will become a gathering place for young-sters and litter.

Pay telephones are subject to vandalism. They often don't generate enough revenue to pay for themselves. The telephone company may then demand that you pay a monthly fee to help sustain the service.

- **Storage**. A well-kept, organized, well-lit, and secure tenant storage facility is a building asset. Some complexes have a storage room that's just that—a room where tenants can put stored items at random, without benefit of lockers or other separation. This arrangement lacks any kind of tenant benefit. Even if outsiders can't get into the room, other tenants can. The possibility of tenants taking one another's goods is very real.

  It's far better to have separate tenant lockers identified by apartment number to avoid confusion and to help the manager identify the tenant's locker if the tenant can't be found. To prevent tenants from taking unauthorized lockers or more than one locker, keep all vacant lockers securely locked, and unlock each only when the tenant moves in.

Parking

Parking is one of the perennial problems of management. Uncontrolled parking of autos, motorcycles, boat trailers, bicycles, and baby carriages is a major detraction from the good appearance of your property and adversely affects your merchandising. It also causes tenant relations problems. The following are some sugges-tions.

- **Don't establish reserved parking**. This general recommenda-tion applies everywhere except where parking spaces are en-closed as in high-rise garages or individual private garages. The reason for this recommendation is simple. Reserved parking is extremely difficult to enforce. Tenants who have reserved park-ing expect their space will always be available to them. If they find another car in their space, they become very upset and create a scene, usually after midnight. Reserved parking that can't be enforced will only irritate your tenants.

  If you must assign reserved parking, your best bet is to use an arbitrary number for each space to thwart burglars. If you use the person's name or apartment number on the space, that makes it easy for a burglar to find out who is not at home simply by looking for the empty stalls and then matching the name or number with the mailbox identification.

- For **motorcyles,** provide a heavy steel rack embedded in concrete at various locations. For **boat trailers**, have a parking facility away from the buildings. This not only contributes to a more uniform appearance but even gives a recreation-oriented look to your property. As for **buggies and bicycles**, provide separate facilities for these in or near the buildings and insist that they be used.

In summary, these are major areas in which general policies are needed. When you have formulated the policies, they will set a useful framework within which you can approach the specialized areas of rental, tenant, and personnel policies.

Rental Policies that Attract the Right Tenants

If you rent to the right people at the start, half of your management problems are over. By doing a good job of screening applicants, encouraging the good ones, discouraging the bad ones, and educating people to what your property is all about, you will wind up with a much higher percentage of people who will pay their rent on time, observe your rules and regulations, and remain with you year after year. At the very start you have to anticipate all of the key questions that good rental policies should answer. Will you rent to families with children? What about pets? How many people can live in an apartment? What kind of security deposit will you ask for? Will you rent to unmarried couples? Homosexuals? These are among the policy considerations this section will discuss.

Rental policies are needed to minimize the subjective factor when deciding to whom we'll rent apartments. Most of us tend to prefer people who are like us. Property managers and rental agents are no exception. They will judge rental applicants by whether they fit the manager's or agent's preconceived notions of what a good tenant should be. They're apt to say:

- "We won't rent to any families with children because they'll just tear up the place," and there goes 54 percent of your market.

- "We won't rent to people with pets because they'll just soil the carpets and make a terrible mess," and there goes 60 percent of the market.
- "We won't rent to people over 65 because they'll just up and die on us," and there goes 10 percent of the market.
- "We won't rent to hippies, homosexuals, or lesbians because we don't like their morals," and another market segment is lost.

By the time this process is finished, there are precious few left to rent to. You may decide that you don't want certain people in your building; that's your decision. Just be aware of how you are trimming your market.

Once you determine who you'll rent to, establish a firm set of criteria in advance and make sure all your rental agents follow them. That way you'll avoid subjective judgments in accepting or rejecting applicants. You'll also minimize legal hassles which may come up because an applicant was turned down on subjective grounds.

Before you open the door to greet the first rental prospect, a number of very important policies must first be established. These are listed here under Rental Policies rather than under General Policies because of their enormous impact on the rentability of the apartment units in a particular complex. Your decisions with respect to these policies can spell your success or failure in the market place.

Limitations

While you have a lot of room to maneuver in setting rental policies, there are some restrictions you can't do anything about. These include:

- Antidiscrimination laws that prohibit rental discrimination on grounds of race, nationality, sex, religion, or creed. These are federal laws and they are rigidly enforced. Don't try to get around them.
- Type and mix of units in your property. If all you have are studio, one, and two bedroom units, you can't very well accommodate large families.
- Predetermined nature of your market. Your building may be located in a specialized market, such as a college town or a retirement area. Accepting tenants who don't "fit in" these

special categories may alter the character and marketability of the property.

Beyond these limitations there still is a lot of opportunity for you to establish good rental policies.

Unfurnished vs. Furnished

Whenever prolonged downturns in the economy develop and unusual vacancies appear, managers begin considering the advisability of furnishing their apartment units. They do this in an effort to maximize the market audience. They hope to attract couples and families who lack the money to buy furniture. There is no question that furnishing apartments adds an additional dimension to the market.

But experience has shown that renting furnished apartments is a burden and a drag on net operating income. A tenant who rents a furnished apartment has little commitment to his residence. Even with a damage or security deposit, he is less likely to take the same good care of somebody else's furnishings as he is of his own. Consequently the furnished apartment needs constant refurbishing. At the end of two years, a new complex with every unit furnished will be able to completely furnish only one half of the original units because of abuse and theft. Moreover, furnishings require substantial money; the cost of the furnishings is seldom repaid by the higher rent for the apartment.

There are special market conditions where renting furnished apartments makes some sense. Housing for students and for seasonal occupants in vacation areas represents two such situations. Otherwise, if tenants want furnished apartments, they can easily satisfy their needs by renting their own furniture. That way they can get furnishings which will suit their tastes, and the burden of paying for and taking care of furnishings is on them, not you.

If you're managing a building that already has furnished apartments, you may want to consider selling the furniture. The best potential buyers are usually the tenants currently renting the furniture.

Children

Children, pets, and trash, not necessarily in that order, are said to be the property manager's three biggest headaches. Trash is an unavoidable result of daily living; the best you can do is control it. But what about pets and children? Can't you deal with them by prohibiting them from your rental property?

Let's consider children first. Fifty-four percent of American families have one or more children under 18; that's better than half of the housing market! Be aware, too, that many communities have laws forbidding discrimination against families with children. You can quietly discourage these families, but you're still reducing your market.

Whether you accept children and how many you accept are directly related to your *unit mix* and your *occupancy standards*. For instance, if your property has mostly studios, efficiencies, and one bedroom apartments, families with children are not likely to be attracted. But if you have two and three bedroom units, children will be very much a consideration. In most communities, two bedroom units make up most of the vacancies, which is why property managers are brought face to face with the question of renting to families with children.

You may think you can avoid this problem by promoting your two bedroom apartments as "bedroom plus den" units, seeking to attract couples, not families. Or you may play up these larger units to singles, hoping they'll bring in a roommate. Or you may try limiting the apartments to families with high-school age children only (which is probably illegal). But in most cases you'll have to accept children as inevitable. Certainly you'll face the problem if a childless couple has a child. Even in singles-only complexes, some children may arrive on the scene.

Occupancy standards are a good way to determine how large a family can live in a given apartment, and to deal with cases where a childless couple living in a studio has a blessed event, or where a family with two children greets the arrival of twins. In such cases, your occupancy standards should require the family to find a larger apartment at the expiration of its current lease, even if that means moving out of the property.

There are other ways you can minimize the problems caused by families with children. In a multi-building garden complex, you can *designate certain buildings* for such families and see that these buildings are convenient to children's recreational amenities. In high-rise buildings, which are generally less attractive to families with children, you can *reserve certain floors* for family apartments. This way, you can maximize your marketing appeal by accommodating families and at the same time leaving other areas free from the noise and commotion of children.

One thing is certain: children are here to stay. They can be controlled with the right kind of recreational outlets. On the positive side, families with children tend to be less mobile than other tenant groups, lending desirable stability to any property development. Economic necessity is usually the determining reason why you must accept families with children.

Pets

Pets have long been a bone of contention between property managers and residents. With the pet population booming, the situation could become more troublesome.

Estimates place the pet population, including animals, fish, and reptiles, at 700 million, or more than three times the human population in the U.S. An estimated 60 percent of the nation's households, or 70 million households, have a pet of one kind or another.

While homeowners account for a greater number of pets than do renters it's estimated that from 45 to 50 percent of renters have pets. This means that if you have and enforce a "no pets" policy, you are effectively cutting yourself off from nearly half the rental market.

That's about the same as having the airlines and restaurants ban all customers who smoke. It might be the right thing to do from a health standpoint, but the loss of business would be disastrous.

The wrong answer to the pet question can slow up a rental program and affect tenant relations. So establishing a workable pet policy is important for the smooth management of a residential rental property.

Don't make the mistake of thinking you can avoid the issue by having no pet policy at all. That's worse than a policy forbidding pets. A nonpolicy is an invitation for pets to creep in. The damage is done when the first dog shows up. You should decide on a policy early, ideally before opening. If your building has been in existence for a while, there are still ways to implement a workable pet policy.

We can begin by sorting out the *dedicated* pet owner from the *casual* owner. The dedicated pet owner considers the pet a part of the household and will make sacrifices to see to the pet's needs. The casual owner does not look upon his pet with as much seriousness and usually is not willing to sacrifice his comfort and convenience for the pet. To him the pet is a whim.

One way to separate the dedicated from the casual pet owner is to charge the pet owner more. Some property managers, for example, charge a monthly pet rent of $5, $10, or $15, while others require a nonrefundable deposit of, say, $100 to $150. This is wrong, because once the owner pays, he thinks he has paid for all the damage the pet will cause. He is no longer concerned with what his pet does to doors, carpets, and plants. He feels he has paid for it.

A better way is to ask the pet owner for an additional amount to be added to the security deposit. That way the pet owner has some hope of getting the money back if his pet behaves. If the pet causes damage, or if the owner damages the apartment, you have the enlarged security deposit to cover it. Asking for the extra money is a good way of discouraging the casual pet owner who may decide the pet isn't worth the added cost. Or if he does decide to keep the pet, he'll be more careful with it.

Another way to tell the dedicated from the casual owner is to *ask who will take care* of the pet when the owner is out of the apartment. This is especially important if you're dealing with a working person or couple. The dedicated owner will provide for the animal; the casual owner may not have given thought to this problem and may not realize or care that a barking dog left alone can be a nuisance.

You can further sort out the dedicated from the casual pet owner by *designating certain areas of the property for pets only*. If you have several buildings on your property, for instance, take no more than 25 per cent of them—preferably those in the poorest, most remote locations, near a road or vacant lot, where a dog run can be located—and reserve them for pet-owning renters. All the rest of the buildings are then pet-free. In a high-rise building, reserve the lower floors or the least desirable wing for pet owners. The dedicated pet owner will accept the less desirable apartment for the sake of his pet.

This kind of physical separation is easiest to do in a *new property* before the rental program starts. In *existing buildings*, you may not want to take the risk of antagonizing long-standing pet-owning tenants. But over a period of time, you can restrict new tenants who are pet owners to certain parts of the property. Let the non-pet owners have the other apartments. You can also tell present residents who are pet owners that when their pet dies, they may not have another one in the same apartment, but they can move to an apartment designated for pets elsewhere on the property.

Whether or not you have this kind of separation, you should make your pet policy and rules known when the prospect applies for the apartment. This is important. Make your policy known early in the renting process so there can be no misunderstanding. Have it written out. Among the items that should be in the policy are these:

- Residents may have no more than one dog or cat, or two lovebirds, canaries, parakeets, or one mynah bird. No pet offspring are allowed.
- Dogs must be no higher than 14 inches or weigh more than 20 pounds full grown.
- Tropical fish limited to a 20-gallon tank are permitted.
- No other animals, fish, or reptiles are permitted, including monkeys, snakes, turtles, hamsters, or gerbils.
- Dogs and cats must be on a leash at all times when out of the apartment. They can't be staked out or allowed to run loose. Birds must be caged at all times.
- Animals must be walked in designated areas. If the pet leaves droppings in other areas, the owner must clean them up.

These rules should be spelled out in a pet agreement which the prospect signs along with the lease. The agreement amounts to a revokable license which applies to a specific pet. You should ask the owner to bring in the pet so *you can see it*, and so it can be weighed, if it's a dog. Have a scale in the office.

Besides giving the owner permission to keep the pet, the agreement also states (a) the tenant agrees to pay for all damage caused by the pet and (b) if the agreement is violated or if the animal becomes objectionable, the manager may demand the removal of the pet without affecting the validity of the lease or the tenant's responsibility under it.

The pet agreement is an important psychological tool in impressing the pet owner with management's seriousness. He knows what the rules are and he knows he'll pay a penalty if he breaks them. At the same time, you don't rule him out of the market.

Non-pet owners appreciate this kind of policy, too, because they know they won't be surprised one day by finding that someone with a Great Dane or a monkey has moved in next door. That kind of protection is an incentive for them to rent in your building.

In short, you have the best of both worlds: a maximum market for your apartments and preservation of peaceful relations between pet owners and non-pet owners who are your tenants.

Other Problems

Children and pets are not the only thing tenants bring with them which can pose problems in the peaceful and orderly operation of an apartment house. Without being negative, the rental agent must try to learn if the prospect possesses any problem articles and you should have policies to deal with them. They include:

- **Waterbeds** violate most floor loading regulations. They're messy to fill and empty. If they rupture, they can damage the apartment and the one below. And even if they remain intact, the bleach put in the water to keep it from souring will usually leach through in gaseous form and ruin the carpet.
- **Electronic equipment**, such as ham radios and CB radios that require special outdoor aerials are not good. For TV, a master antenna should be provided. If a tenant puts up his own antenna on the roof, he's apt to punch a hole in the flashing and break the water seal in the roof. Furthermore, the antenna could blow off, posing a danger to people below.
- **Noisy equipment** includes drums, stereo gear played too loud, hobby tools, and the like. Other tenants will object to these sounds being transmitted through walls and floors.
- **Flammable articles**, such as torches for glass blowing and welding equipment for metal sculpture, are obvious dangers.

Sex and Morality

Should you rent to unmarried couples? To homosexuals and lesbians? These questions may be more pressing in some communities than in others. Individual owners may also have keen feelings about them.

Unless there are local laws outlawing such arrangements, you are shutting off potential income if you decide against renting to such people in today's liberated society. Men and women living together without benefit of clergy are a fact of life. Even if you establish a policy forbidding unmarried couples, you will undoubtedly end up with them living in your complex. One party will apply and lease the apartment; in a short time the second party will move in and set up house. You will have a difficult time in court and may very well end up with two people in residence with only one person responsible under the lease. You would be better advised to have both parties responsible. Your policy should be not to judge their morality but to determine whether they will co-exist with the other tenants. The same goes for homosexuals.

Security

Prompted by reports in newspapers and over the radio and television of soaring crime rates, local assaults and rapes, and increasing numbers of burglaries, many managers have seized upon security as something to lure the rental prospect. A quick reading of apartment ads in most cities will prove the point. One building advertises 24-hour security. Another claims regular security patrols. A third touts armed uniformed guards. Still another boasts of electronic surveillance, with TV monitors and magnetic identification cards. And so it goes, with each manager attempting to rent his property with the promise of maximum protection to the life, limb, and property of the tenant. There's good reason for the public to be concerned. One in every five suburban residents has been the victim of burglary, vandalism, mugging, robbery, or car theft in a year's time. A recent poll concluded that one out of six Americans feels that security is a major problem in his own home.

No wonder that managers think they're on to something when they promise security. But making such a promise, either in the form of a direct claim or an implied commitment, should not be done lightly or without a clear knowledge of the consequences. Certainly your prospective tenants won't take the promise lightly, nor will the public or the judge and jury.

To begin with, by promoting security, you're raising fears in the minds of prospects, or aggravating fears already there. You are making the prospect think about security when he might not otherwise be unduly concerned about it. You may even cause the prospect to think that your security protection is not what it should be, and off he goes, looking for something better. The truth is that no apartment property can afford what it would take to make the premises 100 percent secure; it would take an entire army to do that.

Consider that security is a frame of mind. Hotels generally do a superb job of providing security, but they never promote it. Yet try something funny in a hotel lobby and watch how quickly the house detectives materialize. Hotels know that the mention of security is disturbing to guests, so they go at it quietly. Apartment managers would do well to do likewise.

What happens when you promote security? Not only do you raise people's fears, but you may very well undertake a liability that you normally would not be exposed to. That liability could come into play if a tenant is robbed, injured, or killed and you are blamed because you didn't provide the security that was promised. No matter how good your security system is, the injured party can always claim you could have done more. You could have doubled or tripled the guards, put in more surveillance, trained your guards better. There are court cases pending now, and cases already settled, in which just this principle decided the issue.

If you are thinking of stressing security to attract prospects, don't do it. If you have already made the promise, you may face risks, but we'll come to those later.

When we say don't promote security, we mean two things: don't put in any systems that promise security, and don't mention security at all in your advertising or literature.

The guiding principle to follow in avoiding systems that promise security is to stay away from anything that involves a person other than the tenant to control it.

For example, avoid guard service and security patrols. Stay away from electronic systems that require someone other than the tenant to monitor them. If you have a gatekeeper or doorman, make sure he's not dressed like a guard and don't give him a gun. Don't use canine patrols. Don't give an apartment rent-free to a policeman in exchange for having him act as a part-time guard in his off-duty hours. All of these imply that you are assuming responsibility for security.

What you *can* do is provide tenants with security devices that *they* can use. For instance, dead-bolt locks are satisfactory; they require the tenant to set them. Apartment-to-lobby intercommunication and TV systems, which allow the tenant to screen callers, are acceptable, because the tenant has to use them. In short, anything which can be controlled by the tenant is acceptable; anything which involves another party is not.

Doesn't the owner have an implied duty to provide security beyond putting locks on the doors? This question is being debated in the courts. As yet, there is no clear-cut answer. One decision that seems to have set a precedent requires the owner to provide a standard of protection commonly provided in the community. That would mean that if most of the buildings in the community have 24-hour doormen, your property must have the same; but it also suggests there is no need for you to provide anything more than what others are offering.

Most crimes in apartments occur because of tenant careless-ness, such as holding the lobby door open for a stranger, failing to screen callers before pushing the switch unlocking the door, or propping open an exit door for convenience. You can warn your tenants against such practices. The best way to do this is to ask your police department for literature on security, and pass this out periodically to your tenants. Don't reproduce security advice under your own name, because you may be implying liability. Use the police literature, because the police play the major role in any security situation.

Now that you have avoided any system that implies security, your next step is to make sure that security is never mentioned in your advertising, sales literature, or by your rental personnel. Not only should the word "security" never appear, but you should refrain from describing any feature that implies security. If you deal with an advertising agency, be sure that it adheres to this rule.

You're fortunate if you have avoided security promotion to date. If you are already in it, you have problems with which you'll have to live. There is a definite risk in pulling back, because if an incident occurs a week later, someone may claim you are reneging on your security promise. If you maintain the status quo, you still run the risk of not having provided "enough security." Your first recourse is to increase your liability insurance to cover this added exposure. Of course, if tenants start a rush of security suits, rates will skyrocket, just as they've done in malpractice insurance.

It's not a very secure situation to be in. Perhaps the whole situation might have been avoided if owners had refused to play on tenant fears and instead had focused on the positive aspects of their development.

Security Deposits

Security deposits grew out of the practice of owners asking prospects to pay two months' rent in advance. This was done to increase the prospect's commitment to the apartment, to weed out people with minimum cash, and to provide a cushion in the case of tenants who skip out or leave without paying the last month's rent.

But the Internal Revenue Service ruled that the last month's rent was prepaid rent and therefore taxable as income in the year collected. To avoid this, owners began calling this payment a security or escrow deposit, to be held as a guarantee of faithful performance of the lease. This means that if the tenant leaves the apartment in good condition after fulfilling his lease requirements, his security deposit is returned to him. If there is damage, the owner deducts an amount from the security deposit to cover repairs. Meanwhile, for the period of the tenants' stay, the owner has had the free use of those funds to use or invest as he pleased.

The subject of security deposits brings opposing reactions. Managers usually regard the full month's security deposit as a sacred right. Without it, they say, they have no protection against the tenant who damages the apartment or who violates a provision of the lease. The tenant on the other hand strongly objects to the security deposit on the grounds that he is giving the owner free use of a month's rent money for as long as he remains in the apartment.

When you request the payment of a security deposit from a prospective tenant, you also trigger fears in his mind about the fate of his security deposit in the hands of an unknown owner or agent. The tenant has doubts of ever seeing it again. Either from stories heard or through actual experience, the tenant expects a struggle. The defense used by most tenants is simply to vow not to pay the last month's rent. In doing this they avoid the risk of their money being withheld and at the same time, it helps to cover the advance payments required at the new apartment. Even while *provoking the tenant,* the manager does not provide himself with the protection he seeks with the full-month security deposit policy. The tenant who has breached the lease or caused damage to the property or suspects problems in getting the deposit back solves his problem by simply withholding his last month's rent and telling the manager to apply the security deposit.

If the manager agrees, he may come up short. This is especially so if the tenant rented the apartment when the monthly rent was $225, and the rent now has gone up to $250. The $225 security deposit originally required will leave the manager $25 short on the rent, in addition to having nothing to cover any damage to the apartment.

Of course, the manager may not agree to apply the security deposit to the last month's rent. He may put pressure on the tenant to pay up, or he may take court action. This is expensive and takes time. The tenant will probably have vacated the apartment before the case comes up. When it does, the manager will usually find that the court will order the security deposit applied as an offset to any rent owed, leaving the manager in the same spot as if he had originally applied the security deposit to the rent, again without any money to cover damages.

Security deposits are also coming into disfavor for another reason: many states now have laws that require owners to pay interest and give an accounting to the tenants whose security deposits they hold. The method of accounting and the amount and frequency of interest payments vary between states. Some states forbid the use of this money by the owner, requiring that it be held for eventual return to the tenant. Owners of property insured under the various FHA titles are required to invest security deposits in government bonds or with institutions which are insured by the federal government. The laws of some states exempt interest payments on security deposits if they are under a certain amount. These are usually nominal amounts and are generally under $100. Some exclude interest on security deposits collected on student-occupied housing and/or furnished apartment units. The laws change from city to city with regard to security deposits, but tenants' feelings on the subject don't. Payment of a security deposit remains a big, sharp thorn in landlord/tenant relationships.

But the biggest reason security deposits are not what they used to be is that they put the property at a marketing *disadvantage*, particularly when a competing property is being rented without a security deposit. Where all competing properties require a one-month security deposit, you can gain an advantage by reducing or eliminating yours. You might want to consider asking for a deposit of $100 or a figure substantially below one month's rent as an alternative.

Most prospects, when they sign a lease for a new apartment, are already paying rent on their present one. In addition, they are now required to pay a full month's rent in advance on the new apartment plus the security deposit, equal to another month's rent. While most tenants today are able to afford high monthly rents, not as many have the savings which will permit them to pay two months' rent in advance plus all the other costs of moving. So given a choice of two apartments with the same rent, features, and amenities, they will usually take the one with the lowest security deposit requirement.

For all of these reasons—tenant ill-will, administrative cost, and marketing disadvantages—the traditional security deposit is no longer a useful device. But the purpose of the deposit—the commitment of the tenant and the reserve to pay for damages—is still valid. So what you may find useful is a policy of asking for a *deposit of substantially less than one month's rent*. This does three things for you:

- It gives you a marketing advantage over properties which continue to ask for a traditional deposit.
- Prospects are less apt to consider the deposit the equivalent of a month's advance rent. Properties which have used this policy have reported a sharp improvement in the number of vacating tenants who voluntarily pay their last month's rent instead of telling the manager to apply the security deposit.
- If the deposit is minimal, it may be exempted from controls required by current legislation.

These advantages deserve consideration when you establish your security deposit policy. The matter of returning the deposit when the tenant vacates is also important, but this will be discussed under Policies for Better Tenant Relations, p. 96.

Screening Process

Establishing these important rental policies will act as a sort of screen to disqualify prospects who either don't fit or will not accept the limitations you have established. A skilled rental agent can detail these policies in the initial conversation with the prospect without having it sound like a recitation of rules. In prequalifying the prospect, the agent is attempting to save time, effort, and possible embarrassment on the part of both parties. The answers to further questions relating to the prospective tenant will also become known in a controlled presentation by skilled rental personnel. This information will be set out in an application form so the acceptability of the prospect can be determined.

Application Form

In your application form you will be interested in two types of information: that concerning the prospect and that concerning his impending occupancy. The form can be completed by the applicant or the rental agent. It's recommended that the rental agent fill out the form for the prospect and then have him sign it. By asking him the form questions and listening to his answers, the agent will gain valuable insights into the person. The manner in which a prospect responds will often indicate more about the person than the answers themselves.

The document itself can take many forms but certain areas of information must be provided if you are to properly evaluate the prospect. Consider the needs and uses of this information.

1. The name of the applicant, spouse, and all others who will reside in the apartment. For reasons of lease responsibility, you must identify all adults who will occupy the particular apartment. Knowledge of the total number of occupants is needed to prevent overcrowding. Overcrowding is rough on the apartment and too many overcrowded apartments are rough on the building. It causes problems in keeping the place clean and providing essential maintenance services. When move-out time comes, you may have quite a mess on your hands to fix up, probably more than the security deposit will cover.

   For another thing, overcrowding is usually objectionable to other tenants. But this can vary. If a single person living in a studio takes in a roommate, you may hear no objections. But if you crowd a family of six into a two-bedroom apartment, you can expect squawks from neighbors.

   A safe rule of thumb is that an apartment should contain one more room than people. In some cases you may want to stretch this. The following chart is a good guideline:

Occupants Allowed

Unit Size	Normal Conditions	Exceptional Conditions
Efficiency/Studio	One	Two
1 Bedroom	Two	Three
2 Bedroom	Three	Four
3 Bedroom	Five	Six

2. The prospect's age. Check your state law to determine how old a person must be to sign an unrescindible contract. If he or she is under age, get a parent or guardian to sign. A minor can rescind a contract, including a lease; a person of majority can't. A minor who is married, orphaned, or who can demonstrate that housing is a *necessity* is often emancipated from the restriction against minors and can execute a binding contract.

3. The prospect's driver's license number. This will help confirm identity. Most people don't know their driver's license number. When they take out the license to look at it, the rental agent can see if the name on the license is the same as the name on the application. Also the agent can check the birth date on the license to make certain the applicant is of age. The driver's license number will also be valuable in tracking down the individual if he should later skip out.

4. The prospect's Social Security number. Contrary to many managers' belief, the prospect's Social Security number has little value particularly in tracking down skips. One reason is that people not receiving benefit checks rarely report changes of address to the Social Security Administration. In addition, the Social Security people won't reveal what information they have about the person. So don't expect any help from this source.

What the Social Security number is useful for is to help the credit bureau in its check of the person's background. Credit bureaus keep records of people by their Social Security numbers which makes it easier for them to look up information in their files.

5. The name, address, and phone number of the applicant's nearest living relative. This information is helpful in case of emergency and invaluable in tracking down a tenant who skips out.

6. The prospect's past housing record. You need the name, address, and telephone number of the prospect's present owner or agent together with the size of his apartment, rent paid, and length of stay. If the stay has been shorter than two years, you will need information on previous places of residence. A caution flag should be raised if the applicant has resided at more than three addresses in the past two years. There may be good reasons for these housing changes so take the time to understand why. You don't need a new tenant who will move in and then back out in a matter of months.

A substantial jump between the rent being paid and the rent on the unit being applied for can also signal problems ahead. The applicant should be asked to explain how he can handle a large jump in rent levels.

7. Information on the applicant's employment record. The name, address, and telephone number of the company together with the name of the applicant's immediate superior should be included. You will also want to know the applicant's income, occupation, and the number of years on the job. As in the case of residency, you need to know the employment history for at least two years. If this includes more than three jobs in the past two-year period, be alert. Determine the reason. It could be quite legitimate. A highly skilled trim carpenter could very well have two or three employers in one year; skilled craftsmen often move from job to job with little or no loss of time. When the applicant doesn't meet these standard criteria, you must probe deeper. If a satisfactory explanation is not offered, you may wish to "pass" on the applicant rather than take the risk of having problems collecting the rent or regaining possession of the apartment.

The ratio of rent to gross monthly income is very important in determining an applicant's ability to meet rent obligations. As discussed in the chapter entitled All About Rents, when that ratio exceeds 25 percent (30 percent for a single woman) the chances of experiencing rent collection problems increase in a geometric progression. Only regular salary should be considered in this test. Don't include overtime pay even though it is very consistent. Don't count income received from a second job. An applicant who needs this income to qualify for your apartment is stretching and will be a collection problem sooner or later.

Only count 50 percent of the gross income of an applicant's employed wife. This is particularly true if she is in her child-bearing years. Pregnancy could end her career as well as her contribution of income. Working couples with preschool children have higher budget requirements because of child care. The total of both incomes can be used for couples who are past the child-bearing age.

When the rent plus monthly payments on installment purchases total an amount which exceeds 40 percent of an applicant's monthly gross income, watch out. There simply won't be enough money left over to meet all of the other normal living expenses.

8. Information on checking and savings accounts (including account numbers). This can be helpful in judging the applicant's situation. Remember a checking account is a vehicle to spend; a savings account is a vehicle to save. A person with a savings account and no checking account is generally a better risk than one with a checking account and no savings account.

9. Information on both open and closed loan or charge accounts completes the important credit information on your applicant.

The application should also provide information concerning the occupancy of the particular unit for which the prospect is applying. Commonly the information required to draw up the lease document is contained in the application. This includes:

- Address and apartment number
- Term of the lease with beginning and ending periods and monthly rent
- Security deposit
- Information on pets
- List of any optional features or services
- Special conditions including promises of additional improvements, free rent, or special lease provisions

All of these points should be written out and described to avoid any misunderstanding later. A prospect becomes quite wary when these additional items are not committed to writing.

A great many problems arise out of a tenant's failure to insure his personal belongings. Many people believe that the building insurance covers tenant possessions also. Of course, it does not. A way to avoid this confusion and problems in the future is to include in the application form space for the tenant to indicate that he has or doesn't have coverage on his personal belongings. You may even wish to provide him with the names of two or three reliable agencies which can write tenant policies. But in any event, you want to make the applicant understand that his belongings are *not* covered.

Application Deposit

As we will learn in the chapter on Merchandising, a completed application form without a deposit accomplishes very little. Without a deposit, the probability of expending a lot of effort and expense with no result is high. With the deposit comes a decision and a commitment. Without it you have little.

Application deposits should be more than $10 but not more than $50 (if more, you'll discourage prospects). These are recommended conditions for the deposit:

1. If the application is accepted and the tenant takes the apartment, the deposit is applied toward the security deposit. It is important to apply money received first to the established security deposit and then to the first month's rent. The lease agreement will give you rights and remedies to collect rent but seldom provides for collection of a security deposit which was agreed to but not paid.

2. If the application is not accepted, the entire deposit is refunded to the prospect.

3. If the application is accepted but the prospect withdraws, he loses the deposit. Avoid terms like forfeit. People can accept losing things but they don't like to forfeit things. The result is exactly the same; it's just easier terminology to accept.

The final step in your application is to have the adult members of the family or group sign the application form.

Now what is left is for you to begin checking out the listed information and coming to a decision on whether or not to accept him as a tenant for your building.

Checking Credit

You should check the credit of every applicant. It's foolish not to. You're risking rent loss and costly eviction and collection procedures if you don't. Even the best-looking applicant can turn out to be a poor credit risk, while the seediest-looking person can be good as gold. Your check will help tell the tale.

However, a credit check isn't foolproof. You can't beat a professional; he can rig his credit references so you'll never find out. What you want is protection against the casual poor credit risk. He's a person who isn't deliberately seeking to bilk you, but someone whose careless financial habits and credit record will make life tough for you.

The best way to run a credit check is to do it yourself. Don't use a credit bureau to start. It will rarely do more than ask the same questions you've already asked on your application form, to see if it can spot an inconsistency. Besides, new federal laws govern the information that credit bureaus can give out.

Your first step should be *to call the applicant's present owner* or agent, if he has one; if you're dealing with a first-time renter, skip this. If the applicant doesn't want you to call the owner, fearing this will cause bad feelings, identify yourself as a merchant. What you're after is a report from the owner about what kind of tenant the applicant is. Warning: if the owner is trying to evict the tenant, he may give the applicant a good send-off. This is a risk you take. But usually the owner's report will give you something to go on.

Next, try to verify his employment record and salary by telephone rather than in writing. Be aware that the applicant may have given you the name and telephone number of a fellow worker, and set things up so that this friend will give you a good recommendation. This is a possibility but often you can detect it by the person's hesitant manner. If you are really suspicious you can hang up and try again only this time with the Personnel Department. In any event, this procedure is better than writing to the Personnel Department which may take weeks to respond.

As an extra step, you can have the *credit bureau* check the public record for any evidence of bankruptcies, judgments, convictions, divorces, etc., which bear on the applicant's ability to pay the rent. This limited service is generally very low in cost and is well worthwhile.

Further investigation of the applicant's background may be required depending upon the response you obtain in these limited checks. No matter how careful you are, you will make mistakes in judgments. Your best defense is to pay close attention to both the tenant's living and payment habits and to act quickly when something goes awry.

Lease Agreement

Leases traditionally have been written to favor the owner. They are couched in language that not only is hard to understand but is also intimidating to the tenant. Because of their outmoded provisions, leases are becoming harder and harder to enforce in court. The only thing they are really good for is to guarantee the tenant that he has the right to occupy the specified premises for a set rent over a given period. Other than that, leases only aggravate owner/tenant relations.

We can't get rid of the lease concept entirely. We still need a written document to serve as a contract and to spell out terms and conditions. We also need the psychological value gained from the act of signing a document.

The lease document can, however, be revised into a more acceptable and workable form. It doesn't even have to be called a lease. The term *occupancy agreement* can be used, for example, which lacks the sting of the word lease, conveys a more modern-day approach, and can be equally binding. You would be well advised to work on the development of a modern-day version of the lease or occupancy agreement for use in your properties. By eliminating provisions which are no longer applicable or enforceable and by lightening the legal terminology you will provide a fairer, more workable document which will also be valuable both in tenant relations and as a marketing tool.

Lease Terms

Certain lease provisions are more or less standard. Here, we present a brief outline of the important lease provisions for a better understanding.

- **Parties to the lease**. The lease should identify the name of the legal owner of the property. If the managing agent's name is used on the lease, he should be identified as the *agent* of the owner. This establishes that the manager is acting in the capacity of an agent. The owner can be referred to in the lease as the owner, lessor, or landlord. Whatever you choose, use it consistently to avoid confusion.

All adults and emancipated minors who are to occupy the apartment should be listed by name on the lease and should sign it, so that all are held responsible for the performance of the lease. The law generally holds that there is no such person as "Mrs. John Smith." In the case of a married couple, have the wife sign using her given name (i.e., Mary Smith).

If you rent an apartment to two or more people but only one person signs the application and lease, and that person later leaves, you'll have a hard time collecting from the remaining occupants. You can avoid this problem if you have all adult occupants listed on the lease and get their signatures.

This policy will also protect you in the event of death. If a husband and wife occupy the apartment, have them both sign the lease. If one of them dies, the other is still obligated under the lease. If he or she doesn't pay, you can pursue the remedies provided in the lease document. But if the person surviving hasn't signed the lease, you'll certainly have more difficulty in proving your rights.

If you require a *guarantor* or *co-signer*, he should execute a guarantee which is either part of the lease or a separate form which is attached to and made a part of the lease document.

- **Identification of the premises**. While many apartments are known by name, on the lease you should identify the premises being rented by apartment number, common postal address, city, and state.

- **Rent**. See Chapter 4, All About Rents, for a full discussion. If the rent covers more than the apartment—a garage, for instance—the lease should separately state what sum covers the apartment and what sum covers the garage. Also spell out what the rent does not cover, such as the master TV antenna, use of recreational facilities, or whatever is paid for by special fees.

The lease should also state *when* and *where* the rent is due, and require that the *first full month's rent* be paid when the lease is executed and *before* the apartment is occupied.

- **Term or period**. Set down the specific dates on which the lease begins and ends. The lease period can be *any term* acceptable to you and the tenant. You can set a term that benefits your re-rental needs. In most areas of the country, any month-ending date from March 31 to October 31 is a good expiration time. The market is active in these months, in case you have to re-rent. Avoid leases that terminate in cold weather months because fewer people are apartment hunting at those times. In warm weather areas, the reverse policy may be best.

  In a new property, set up your leases so they expire at *staggered* times rather than all at once. This will minimize your re-renting problems. If you're managing an existing complex with a tradition of having all the leases coming up for renewal at once, you can begin staggering them gradually as they are renewed or re-leased.

  Normally, you are under no obligation to renew the lease nor to notify the tenant of renewal or non-renewal. You can renew by including the terms of renewal in the lease or by submitting a new document.

  Be aware of the dangers of the hold-over tenant. Suppose you don't renew the lease. The tenant remains and submits another month's rent. You accept it. The tenant could then become a hold-over tenant and might be entitled to remain in his apartment at the same rent for another year! Local laws vary on this point.

  You can save yourself a lot of trouble and guard against the possibility of a hold-over tenant by having your leases run for a specific period "and month to month thereafter." Then if you and the tenant don't sign a new lease and he remains, he's a monthly tenant and you can terminate his occupancy at the end of any month with 30 days' notice.

- **Security deposit**. It is advisable to acknowledge the receipt of the security deposit amount and to provide for its escrow, use, and return in the body of the lease document. This not only helps avoid misunderstandings, but also alerts a prospective buyer of the property that security deposits exist and should be credited to his account in any sale prorations. The new owner is buying the existing leases as well as the property. He is responsible for performing his part of the lease obligations, including returning the security deposit. Unless the security deposit is noted, he may not know of this obligation or the amount.

- **Other provisions**. Up to now, all of the information sets out the terms as stated in the application form. In addition, you should include at this point special provisions appropriate to the circumstances. These include escape clauses such as:

  Transfer clauses. These permit the tenant to cancel the lease when he produces written evidence from his employer that he is being transferred to another city. But anyone can get a letter from his superior. He may even forge it. So letting the tenant cancel this easily is foolish. He cancels at no cost and you're stuck with an empty apartment.

  Home purchase clauses fall into the same category. It's easy for a tenant to get a cooperative real estate salesman to write a letter saying that the tenant has purchased a home. But why should you be penalized?

  Death clauses may be written for older people who are concerned that the lease may be involved in the settlement of their estate. This clause provides for cancellation, generally 30 to 60 days after the tenant's death, allowing time to settle estate matters and vacate the premises. If you refuse to grant this cancellation privilege, most prospects won't press the matter.

Of course, you can write a lease with no escape clauses and then try to enforce it. That means if the tenant moves out before the lease is up, you can go to court to collect rent as it becomes due. However, the law in most jurisdictions requires you to mitigate or reduce the tenant's liability. You just can't let the apartment remain vacant and sue for what the original tenant owes. You have to try to rent the apartment to someone else. If you incur expenses in renting it again, you can generally include these with what the tenant owes you.

But trying to collect on broken leases in court is a time-consuming and costly procedure. What you want is a policy that will be fair for all tenants, give the tenant the flexibility he needs if he must move, and at the same time protect you against rent loss and extra expense.

What's recommended is that you and the tenant cancel the lease by *mutual agreement* according to one of the following sets of terms:

1. You both agree to look for a suitable replacement tenant. When he is found, you will issue a new lease, cancel the old one, and the former tenant will pay you a fee for administration and advertising.

2. The tenant agrees to pay you a set amount, upon which you cancel the old lease and seek a tenant on your own. The set amount could include a forfeit of the security deposit.

Other possible special lease provisions include:

Renewal options. These should be avoided. They are one-way streets benefiting the tenant. If rents go up and the apartment is now leased at a bargain rent, the tenant will exercise his right to stay for an additional term. If the economy is in a downturn or if vacancies are plentiful, he won't exercise his option and you'll be left with an apartment at a most difficult time. Options represent the worst of all worlds from an owner's standpoint.

Promises of improvements. If you made any such promises in the application, they should be inserted in the lease document to reassure the tenant and to avoid any future misunderstandings.

Pet clauses. This might also be included as a special lease provision but as we've said earlier, a separate pet agreement or license is better.

- **Condition of the premises**. Many old lease forms state that by signing the lease, the tenant acknowledges that the apartment is in clean and safe condition, even when it may not be. But things are changing. In many localities, new ordinances require and courts are ruling that the owner when executing a lease is also guaranteeing that the apartment is in clean and safe condition and that it conforms to all local codes. He can be held liable if it does not.

  A safe recommendation is that you don't put anything in your lease about the condition of the apartment that isn't so.

- **Limitations**. A good lease will specify certain limitations on the apartment. List all the people *who will live there*, with a provision for addition only through birth and adoption. This provides a tool to take action against violators, such as the single person who rents an apartment and then has three or four others move in with him.

The lease should specify who is responsible for *repairs and breakdowns*. If damage is caused by tenant neglect, the lease should say how the owner will recover damages.

How the premises *can be used* should be stated. Apartments are for private residential use, not for commercial or immoral purposes.

Also state the owner's right of *access* and *entry*. The owner or manager should be able to enter the apartment for emergencies at any time and for periodic inspections and routine repairs. The owner should also have the right to show the apartment for re-rental in the last 60 days of the lease as long as he does so at reasonable hours.

- **Repossession**. Include in your lease the provision that the owner has the right to repossess the apartment—and the tenant loses his right to possession—for failure to pay rent, abandonment, and violation of lease terms.

- **Abandonment**. Be careful. Each jurisdiction has its own definition of abandonment. If you violate it, you may be committing a trespass. Check your local law with an attorney, then write into your lease what constitutes abandonment.

  Generally, if the tenant has paid his rent, he has not abandoned his apartment even though he doesn't live there. The test is usually payment of rent; that gives him the right to use the apartment.

  Formal abandonment may have to be declared before you can do anything about the goods that the tenant may have left in his apartment; check your local law for the procedure.

- **Fire and casualty**. The lease should state what happens when the apartment is made uninhabitable by fire, flood, or other casualty. As a general rule, the rent meter stops at this point, and the tenant gets back any unused rent for that month. The owner then has a period of time—45 to 120 days is usual, but the lease should be specific on this—to decide whether he will restore the apartment and continue the lease, or cancel it.

- **Assignment**. Most leases should and do forbid the tenant from assigning the lease to someone else without the written consent of the owner. The reason for this is obvious. It is absolutely essential that the owner or agent know and approve of the occupants in the property. When this control is lost, serious problems will result.

- **Waivers and exculpation**. Most leases state that the tenant gives up his right to hold the owner to blame for property damage and personal injury that occur on the premises. A great many courts have held these clauses to be null and void. The tenant can sue and generally collect for damages if the owner has been grossly negligent. While you may want to include this kind of exculpatory clause for your peace of mind, be aware it's not foolproof.

  Also common are clauses in which the tenant waives his right concerning legal notices, remedies, and procedures. Again, these are rapidly becoming unenforceable. As time goes on, you won't be able to impose contract provisions in which the parties waive or lose most of their rights.

  Traditionally, leases have always discriminated against the tenant. But because of consumerism and the tenants' rights movement, laws and court rulings are shifting to the tenants' side. You can't enforce contract provisions that are against the law.

- **Subordination**. This is a common feature in many leases. The lease gives the tenant a right to the property. The subordination clause simply states that the mortgage holder has a superior right and does not need the tenant's approval before taking certain actions so long as they do not affect the tenant's right to possession.

- **Condemnation or eminent domain.** This clause generally provides that if an empowered authority takes the property through condemnation proceedings, the lease is automatically cancelled without an award to the tenant but with adequate notice, generally 60 to 90 days.

- **Bankruptcy**. Your lease should provide for the eventualities of bankruptcy, insolvency, assignment for the benefit of creditors, reorganization, and even insanity. In each of these situations, the lease should provide for cancellation at the option of the owner. If any of these problems occur, you will be restrained from pursuing claims until the matter is settled. The cancellation provision allows you the opportunity to limit your exposure to further losses.

- **Rules and regulations**. These should be listed, along with your rights to change them. The more up-to-date they are, the better chance you have to enforce them.

- **Signatures and delivery**. Finally, the lease must be executed by all the parties and copies delivered. The validity of a lease which is signed but both copies are retained by the owner or agent is questionable. The lease should be endorsed showing the ownership title as first shown on the lease and the capacity of the person executing the lease on behalf of the owner.

With the lease signed, copies delivered, a full month's rent paid in addition to the full security deposit, the new tenant is ready to take possession. In the next section we will discuss the policies that should be considered to help govern the tenant's stay.

Policies for Better Tenant Relations

If there were no tenants, property management would be a simple business. All the manager would have to do is take care of the physical property, making sure the building didn't freeze up, broken windows were repaired, equipment was in good order, and the grass was cut. It would not require substantial skills.

But tenants are very much involved in apartments; they are the source of the property's income; consequently they must be regarded as a significant responsibility of the property manager, perhaps his most important responsibility.

Until recently, tenants for the most part were a docile group. They leased apartments, paid their rent, and if they didn't like things they either moved out or were told to move by the owner. No one thought that tenants had any rights other than to live in the apartment as long as they paid the rent.

But all of this is fast changing because of the impact of consumerism. A revolution is under way and it may go on for quite a while before the final shape of things to come is revealed. Tenants are demanding their rights, and these rights are being granted by legislation and the courts. If these rights are slow in coming, tenants may take things into their own hands by forming tenant unions, staging rent strikes, and forming embarrassing picket lines. Tenants are becoming adept at the strategy of confrontation. They are learning how to use the press to make their grievances known. All of this can put the property manager under extreme pressure.

Just how far tenants have come in their fight for more rights is seen in recent proposals to establish national landlord and tenant commissions. These proposals state that the owner must deliver and keep the apartment in habitable condition; that security deposits must be put in escrow and interest paid to the tenant; that the owner must give notice if he does not intend to renew the lease; that the tenant may make necessary repairs to his apartment and deduct the cost from his rent; that tenants may withhold rent in certain cases; and that owners may not take retaliatory action against tenants who complain. A system of housing courts would be set up to handle complaints. These kinds of proposals signal a major change in the landlord/tenant balance of power.

Leases have traditionally been written to protect the property with little regard for livability. These practices were established in a bygone era whose conditions no longer exist. We live in a different world. The old saying "Buyer beware" has now changed to "Seller and owner beware!" Property managers today must recognize the tenant as an equal party in the owner/tenant relationship. If a manager persists in the old ways, he will very likely weaken the marketing appeal of his property, antagonize his tenants to the point of high turnover, and reduce the income of the property.

Good tenant relations begin before the tenant ever moves in, in fact before he signs the lease. They begin in the rental office when the tenant, then a prospect, inquires about the apartment from you or your agent. If you have established fair and reasonable rental policies, you will thereby prevent many of your tenant relations problems.

Tenant Guidebook

A good way to set the tone of your property and let the tenant know what you expect of him is to publish a guidebook. It's a good idea to make sure the incoming tenant has the guidebook before he moves in and certainly by the first day he's in the apartment.

The guidebook should be a simple explanation of all the rules, regulations, and policies of your building, along with some practical and useful information. It should be written in plain language. Find a good free-lance writer, advertising copywriter, or publicist to write it for you. The thing to avoid is a list of negative dictates— "you can't do this, don't do that, etc." If possible, illustrate your guidebook with cartoon drawings. Make the booklet lively and interesting, so people will want to read it. Don't mail it or leave it lying around the new apartment; give it to him personally with the suggestion that he look it over as soon as possible.

Here are some of the things the guidebook should cover; add any additional items that are pertinent to your property:

Occupancy limits	Parking
Children	Motorcycles, campers
Pets	Bicycles, buggies
Security deposit	Auto repairs
Decorating	Laundry room
Tenant improvements	Deliveries
Rent payments	Keys and lock-outs
Renewals	Move-in and move-out
Re-leasing	Emergencies
Recreation facilities	Disturbances
Waterbeds	Complaints
Hi-fi, musical instruments	Storage

You may want to add some practical information such as:
Utility companies—name, address, telephone
Nearby churches and synagogues
Nearby schools, public and private
Nearest public library
Nearby public transporation stop
Nearby shopping districts
Nearest post office
Telephone numbers of police and fire departments
Voting precinct number
Names of government representatives—federal, state, local

This guidebook can also be helpful to your rental personnel who may find it contains information they can use in their talks with prospects. But its primary purpose is to help the tenant by making him familiar with your policies and procedures.

Move-in

You need to establish a move-in policy to make certain that an orderly procedure will be followed. This is especially important if you have a number of moves occurring the same day in the same building. The smoother your move-in procedure is, the better impression you'll make on the tenant and the fewer problems you'll cause for yourself.

Your move-in policy should require the tenant to let you know when he will move in so that you can be on hand to welcome him. This notice may also be needed to coordinate the use of elevators. Tenants can quickly become irritated if they arrive to discover that another party is using the elevator and meanwhile, the incoming tenant is faced with mounting hourly charges as his moving crew stands idle.

What if the old tenant hasn't move out when moving day arrives? Get in touch with the new tenant right away and tell him to remain where he is; that's the only thing you can do. If the new tenant is already on his way, you have a real problem on your hands. If the delay looks like it will be a day or more, your best bet is to suggest he move into a motel. Later you will have to work out some means of pacifying the new tenant, even though you may not be at fault.

The tenant may ask about moving in one or two days early if the apartment is already vacant. Although technically they're not on the lease for those few days, it makes some sense to let him in. Earlier occupancy may allow for easier scheduling and you will certainly gain some goodwill at little or no cost.

Before the move-in itself, you should follow a checklist of items to make sure everything is ready for the incoming tenant. The apartment should be given a final inspection; the temperature should be set at a comfortable level; the refrigerator should be turned on; keys, including the mailbox key, should be ready; the tenant's name should be on the mailbox; and the storage locker should be clean and secured.

Finally, you or your agent should be present when the tenant moves in to give whatever assistance is needed, to explain procedures and answer questions, to arrange for a tour of the premises, and to take down and explain to the tenant how any necessary adjustments will be handled.

Improvements

Some tenants may want to improve their apartment by painting it, installing paneling, putting up wallpaper, or laying a new
floor. They may ask you about it first or just go ahead and do it,
which you discover later on.

As a general rule, it's a good idea to encourage the tenant to
invest his own time, money, and energy in improving the apartment. By doing this, he increases his commitment to the apartment
and this adds to his chances of becoming a long-term tenant.

What you have to do is protect yourself against *poor workman-
ship* and the *costs of restoring* the apartment at a later date. So
consider establishing a policy by which you tell the tenant that you
favor improvements but with controls. Those controls are (a) the
tenant must use materials that are removable during restoration,
such as strippable wallpaper, and (b) the improvements cannot be a
danger to others, such as flowerboxes insecurely attached to balcony
railings.

There are some improvements you should forbid and act
against. These include painting entry doors something other than
the original color; using "contact" paper anywhere in the apartment, because it is difficult to remove and leaves a coating which
can't easily be painted over; putting nonslip materials in tubs and
shower floors; and attaching any signs to the property.

Screw and nail holes of ½-inch or less in diameter are a normal
improvement hazard.

The tenant may want to improve the apartment by putting in a
new refrigerator or by adding other appliances and fixtures. Let's
consider these:

- **Refrigerator**. The tenant wants to buy his own refrigerator
  and asks you to store yours. This leads to problems, because a
  stored refrigerator will quickly deteriorate. If the tenant wants
  to put in his own refrigerator, tell him it then must become the
  property of the building.
- **Plumbing equipment**. Unless your building is designed for
  these, don't allow tenants to put dishwashers, clothes washers,
  and dryers in their apartment. You'll have problems with
  vibration, flooding, noise, and plumbing back-ups if you do.
- **Lighting fixtures**. If the tenant wants to take down your
  lighting fixture and put up his own, let him know he must

restore the original lighting fixture when he moves or else leave the replacement as property of the building.

These are just some of the improvements that tenants may request. Think about others that may occur on your property and formulate policies to deal with them.

Service and Tenant Turnover

Some managers may say, "The tenants are not going to tell me how to run my property. If they move out, so what? I can always rent to someone else." That attitude inevitably leads to high turnover which is a drain on net operating income.

In the past 15 years national average turnover rates have risen from 30 percent to over 50. In some communities turnover rates exceed 100 percent each year. Much of this increase has been prompted by the greater choice of available units; and some by the increased mobility of today's renters; but a good part of the increase can be directly attributed to an improper attitude toward the existing tenants by the owner or manager. Turnover is expensive and is a major problem facing owners and managers today.

A common complaint regarding turnover goes like this: "We can't do anything about it. No sooner do we rent 10 apartments than we lose 10 present tenants. We can't improve our position." It's like carrying buckets of water from the basement to fill a second floor bathtub with the drain open. No matter how hard you try, you can't get ahead.

There are two ways to approach the problem of turnover. One is to try by aggressive marketing to get enough new tenants so that you'll exceed the rate of move-outs. But, that ignores the question of why tenants are moving out, and the new tenants then become candidates for turnover in short order.

The second approach is to try to slow down the outflow of present tenants while modestly adding selected new ones. You can't slow the exodus entirely. People will move out for various reasons: a transfer or a new job in another city, a need for a larger or smaller apartment, economic adversity, etc. Another and more important reason for move-outs is poor tenant policies and lack of service. As we'll see, by improving your relations with tenants, you can reduce turnover. Every move-out you prevent is the same as renting a new apartment. Matter of fact, it's better.

Why? First, when you keep a present tenant, you know exactly what you have; a new tenant is always a question mark. Second, new tenants are nearly always of a lower economic status than the ones who move out. When a person leaves your building, he generally moves on to something better; the person moving in is moving up from a lower level. Which would you rather have? Third and most important, keeping a tenant is less expensive than renting to a new one. When you stop to figure it out, the cost of a new tenant is phenomenal. Let's assume you're renting a two bedroom garden apartment and you're lucky enough to have the new tenant move in the day after the old one moves out, so there's no loss of rent. (This is unusual. Typically there's an 18-day lag and consequent loss of rent between move-out and move-in. But for the sake of argument, we'll assume there's no delay.) You still face the following outlays: Decorating, $100; rug shampooing, $35; cleaning (oven, range, tile, cabinets, shelves, glass, etc.), $27; wear and tear on the building caused by moving plus uncollected damage to the apartment, $40; advertising, $60; administrative costs (lease preparation, setting up files, credit checks, etc.), $15. Total: $277.

Now let's go back and add in that half-month's rent you lost because of the lag in renting the apartment. On a $250 per month apartment, the loss is $125. Add that to $277 and the total loss amounts to $402.

In all fairness, it will cost you something to keep the present tenant. You'll probably have to decorate and shampoo the place, but these costs will most likely be spread over a two-year period. So if you spend $100 for decorating and $35 for shampooing, a total of $135, figure your cost at half, $67.50 for a year.

Now subtract $67.50 from the $402 and you're left with $334.50—that's what it costs to rent to a new tenant. That should be convincing evidence that you're better off hanging on to your present tenants.

Assume that you are facing a series of move-outs to newer competition with more modern kitchen appliances, yet you can't afford to make mass replacements. Rather than lose the tenant you can allow him to select a new appliance for the apartment. Let him pick out anything from the catalog—a self-cleaning oven, a self-defrosting refrigerator—and you'll go 50-50 with him on the purchase. The tenant, because he's paid for part of it, will take better care of it and at the same time he has added to his commitment. The tenant is often better off financially to participate in purchasing the desired appliance or improvement than to incur the greater cost of moving and perhaps higher rent payments. You've also protected yourself against complaints from the other tenants, because the same deal can be offered to them as well. By doing something, you will probably *keep him* and *keep him happy.*

Service also means giving the tenant a sense of commitment to the apartment. This is something new in the management business. Tenants rarely have a sense of commitment to an apartment because they never live there long enough; to them it's temporary housing.

But this is changing. Renting is becoming a way of life by necessity as well as by choice for many people. Among the reasons are the high cost of for-sale housing, periodic downturns in the economy, and the growing scarcity of desirable apartments. As a result, tenants are beginning to look at apartments as places they'll stay in for a long time, and they'd like to make it part of their lives. If you can help them, they'll take care of it better and they'll remain longer, reducing your turnover.

Take buying a used car. You don't regard it as really yours until you've waxed it or bought a set of floor mats for it. If you buy an antique ring, it's not yours until you've polished it. An apartment isn't the tenant's until he's put something into it. Look for ways to help the tenant make that all-important commitment.

Illegal and Immoral Uses

How do you deal with a tenant who engages in drug use, gambling, or prostitution in his or her apartment? Most leases state that use of the apartment for illegal or immoral purposes is grounds for eviction. But eviction is a court procedure that is slow, questionable, and expensive. A better idea is to meet with the tenant, let him know his behavior is objectionable, offer to cancel the lease, and return the current month's rent.

But before you take any action, consider whether you want to act at all against the offender. He rented the apartment for his personal use. If what he does within the apartment is not offensive to others, you may be better off ignoring it. For example, the use of some drugs is generally not a matter for the property manager's concern, unless another tenant complains about it.

If you take action, confront the tenant face to face by going to his apartment or asking him down to the office. *Don't write a letter* stating the complaint; if the complaint turns out to be unjustified, the tenant might use the letter in an action against you. When you confront the tenant, you can simply say, "I know what's going on here and I want you to move. We'll give you back your current month's rent. We will expect you to be out by this weekend."

This strategy will work in 99 out of 100 cases. The offending tenant will usually go away, particularly because you've offered his rent back. That removes any excuse he may have of not having enough funds. Have the tenant sign a mutual cancellation agreement and pay him his rent money (and perhaps his security deposit) when the apartment is vacated. If the tenant is suspicious that you won't pay the money once he moves out, offer to put it in escrow.

Tenant Abuses

Tenant abuses that show a disregard for fellow tenants or the property are a source of many complaints and problems for managers. One tenant uses his balcony for storage; another leaves wet goods in the laundry; over there is a noisy family; here's a working tenant who continually wants the manager to let her children in after school; there's one who stacks beer cans in his window.

The offending tenant may not realize his actions are causing problems. The way to deal with the tenant is to show up at his or her apartment door and discuss the problem. Most tenants will agree to correct the problem. Don't approach the problem by writing the tenant a letter; he probably will ignore it. But he can't ignore a face-to-face meeting.

If the offending practice continues, then visit the tenant a second time. This time you tell him that perhaps he should live somewhere else, and you offer to cancel the lease by mutual agreement. That may convince the tenant of your seriousness, and he'll change his ways. If he accepts your offer of cancellation, the problem is solved then and there.

But the tenant may reject your offer and continue the offense. In that case, court action is your only recourse. Be aware that going to court is a long, uncertain process and that the tenant's lease will no doubt expire in the meantime. You're often better off to put up with the nuisance tenant until the end of the lease. You can, however, begin the law suit in hopes that he'll see the light and either change his habits or accept your cancellation offer.

Tenant Damage

Probably your best protection against damage to the apartment caused by tenant neglect is the *security deposit*. It is very difficult to collect in court for damage beyond this amount. Your policy should be to try to collect damages at the time of the occurrence, thus preserving the security deposit amount intact to cover damages which show up upon move-out.

For example, if the toilet in a tenant's apartment overflows because someone has dropped a soap dish or rubber ball into it, let the tenant know that this is not a normal malfunction and that he must pay for the repair. Most tenants will accept this. If he refuses, you must still make the repair for health reasons.

Or suppose your tenant uses an ice pick to help defrost the apartment refrigerator and in the process punctures the refrigerant tubing. In most jurisdictions, you're under no obligation to repair or replace the appliance damaged by a tenant's gross misuse. Point out to the tenant that he misused the appliance and must pay for it. You're better off to purchase a new refrigerator and apply the tenant's damage money toward the purchase. The cost to replace the sealed refrigerant unit is close to the cost of a completely new refrigerator.

As for damage caused by *tenant neglect*—water damage resulting from an overflowing bathtub, or a window left open during a rainstorm, or a waterbed leak—try to attempt collection, but it's rare that you'll be able to collect anything beyond the security deposit. If a fire is caused by tenant neglect, you'll have to rely on your own insurance to protect you. Your own insurance company probably won't pursue (subrogate) the tenant for payment, nor will courts generally rule against tenants in favor of owners.

There are several other possibilities you should consider in setting a damage policy. Broken *windows*, for instance, are generally an on-going maintenance problem; replacing them is a cost of business which you should absorb. Property damage by tenant cars may be collectible by claims against the tenant's auto insurance carrier.

If you rent *furnished apartments*, it's advisable to get a bigger security deposit to cover the added damage risk. Also, make an inventory of all furnishings with a notation of the condition so you'll have grounds to use the security deposit to pay for damages.

Handling Complaints

A complaint that is handled slowly is almost as bad as a complaint that isn't handled at all. You should be geared to react to tenant complaints within 24 hours. Fast action will keep a bad situation from getting worse.

It's important to *keep track of complaints*. Don't try to do it by memory. Every complaint should be written down. If a tenant telephones a complaint, write everything down and then repeat it to him so he knows you understand what he's told you. The tenant should be satisfied that his complaint has at least been acknowledged.

Complaints generally fall into three categories: complaints about others, complaints about the apartment, and complaints about the property.

- **Complaints about others**. "My neighbor plays his hi-fi too loudly," "they're fighting next door," "I think that lady down the hall is in the business of entertaining men"—these are typical of the complaints you may get about tenants from other tenants. Some of these complaints are frivolous, others are serious.

  If the complaint deals with an *emergency* or *civil disturbance*, find out if the tenant has already called the police or fire department. If he hasn't, tell him to do so immediately. If he balks, then you place the call. Be quick to act if life or property are threatened. But be careful about trying to deal with civil disturbances yourself, particularly fights resulting from domestic quarrels. These are jobs for the police.

  If a tenant complains about a non-emergency situation pertaining to others, tell the tenant you'd like his complaint in writing. For every 10 telephone calls of this nature, you'll get only two or three letters. When you get the letter, visit the offending tenant and tell him about the complaint, but *don't identify the complainer*. After settling the complaint, get in touch with the complainer in person or by telephone and let him know what action you've taken.

- **Complaints about the apartment**. These include requests for repairs and maintenance. Take care of these within 24 hours if you can. If you need access to the tenant's apartment, let him know you'll need to get in and you'll take care of things within normal business hours, assuming it's not an emergency.

  Don't delay in taking care of routine complaints. The cost of fixing a leaky faucet, for instance, is never cheaper than on the day the tenant first informs you about it. In fact, the cost may increase if you put it off. What is certain to increase is the tenant's dissatisfaction the longer you delay.

  If your maintenance worker takes care of the complaint while the tenant is out of the apartment, have the worker first put a sign on the door saying that he's inside. This alerts the tenant who returns while the worker is still there. Tenants don't like to be surprised by finding a stranger in their apartment. Some may become suspicious and frightened if they hear the worker and don't realize who he is. They may call the police and cause an unnecessary scene.

  When the worker goes to the apartment, he should take along a *written service request*. When the repair is completed, he should note this on the request and leave a copy with the tenant or in the apartment where the tenant will find it. If parts are needed to complete the repair, this should be noted along with the estimated date the repair will be completed. If there's nothing wrong, the worker should note this on the form along with the request that the tenant call you, the manager, so that you can discuss the situation.

  There may be cases where the complaint stems from the tenant's misuse of the apartment or equipment. If this happens, your maintenance worker should suspend work, notify you, and you in turn should obtain payment from the tenant before proceeding unless you are required to make the repair for health or safety reasons.

- **Complaints about the property**. If tenants complain about the way the property is maintained ("too much litter, the grass isn't cut"), that the laundry room light shines in their apartment at night, or that the recreation hours are too short or too long, pay careful attention. These criticisms of the property in general are important signals of tenant dissatisfaction. They undoubtedly extend to many more tenants than those who are actually complaining. In fact, your very best tenants may be equally bothered but say nothing; then one day they will simply move. So if you start hearing general complaints, acknowledge them and begin investigating promptly.

Tenant Organizations

Tenant organizations are one outcome of consumerism's impact on rental housing. They are the result of owner and management insensitivity to tenant requirements. But customer sensitivity needed to produce the product and service that tenants want must come from management's own awareness of the problem. It is not something that grows out of collective bargaining.

Wherever tenant organizations have grown up, they have had only one effect on the orderly and efficient operation of real estate: bad. You can't manage real estate effectively by committee. If you attempt to satisfy every tenant through a tenant organization, you will wind up satisfying no one. Can you imagine what would happen if every licensed driver had to be consulted on the design of automobiles? The result would be chaos. Consumers can and do exercise a voice when they select a product or a place to live. But to allow them to have a voice in running the affairs of an apartment building is plain foolishness.

Not content to act individually, tenants have realized the power that group action provides. They have seen what labor unions have accomplished and, more recently, what civil rights groups have won. They have taken a cue, too, from condominium associations which manage the affairs of buildings; why not in rental apartments, too? The tenants' reasoning is that if they act together, "the landlord can't throw us all out."

Many tenant organizations start because of nonspecific issues—a feeling that "it's unsafe to live here," or that "we don't like the way this place is run." Very seldom do they focus on specific grievances, such as loose carpeting in the second floor corridor. Once formed, they demand a say in the property's general operations and become a chronic headache for the manager. Because they do not understand—and often have no wish to understand—the need for good business practices, they make decisions on the grounds of emotion and pressure.

Another factor leading to the formation of tenant groups is the idea that democratic principles should rule a community of tenants. Participation is the watchword, an idea promoted by the U.S. Department of Housing and Urban Development in the housing that it sponsors or assists. While democratic action has its place, it can't work in a business enterprise. Once an owner or manager lets a tenant organization tell him how to run his property, he has given up his rights to control and his expectation of maximum net operating income.

The people who become involved in tenant organizations are a varied lot. Some like the excitement of group action. Some have genuine complaints. The leaders often enjoy the ego gratification that goes with a conspicuous position, and this need often remains after the initial cause has long been satisfied. These leaders compel the group to keep looking for new causes, or else the organization's reason for being—and its personal ego support—will collapse.

What, then, should the manager's policy be? You rent to tenants as individuals and you must deal with them as individuals. This means you do not encourage or assist them in the formation of any kind of organization, and you resist dealing with any group they form. Don't even think you're being nice by helping them form a ski club, bridge club, or tenant newsletter, as they can all backfire on you.

In addition, you can stave off the formation of tenant organizations if you adopt the following:

- **Fair and reasonable policies, uniformly applied**. All of your policies should be founded on sound reasoning, consideration of the tenants, and fair and uniform enforcement.
- **Good communications**. If a problem exists, let the tenants know that you know about it and that you are seeking a solution. Don't be mute or try to ignore a problem. You can communicate with tenants through letters or personal visits. Incidentally, management newsletters are not good for this purpose.
- **Prompt response to service requests and complaints.** Satisfied tenants have no reason to band together. Take care of their individual complaints and you will eliminate 95 percent of the problem.

If a tenant organization is formed on your property, the easiest way to deal with it is simply to refuse to respond. Don't answer calls or letters from the group, but be willing to respond to individuals speaking for themselves. Above all, don't attend any meetings called by the group. Even Abe Lincoln couldn't win at a meeting called by a tenant organization. If meetings are necessary—and they may be if you have a major problem—then you call it and you adjourn it. But never make yourself the unwitting victim of someone else's meeting.

Arbitration

You may want to consider arbitration as a way to head off tenant organizations and settle tenant disputes. By including a clause in your lease, you and the tenant can agree to submit any dispute to arbitration. Whatever the arbitrator decides is binding on both of you.

The usual procedure in a dispute is to contact the office of the American Arbitration Association which has more than 35,000 arbitrators across the country. The arbitrator hears both sides and then decides. His fee is $100 to $200 which usually is split by the two parties. If tenants know their complaints will be settled fairly, they are less likely to resort to group action for satisfaction.

Emergencies

Life in an apartment complex goes on 24 hours a day, seven days a week, 365 days a year. While your office hours are established to take care of routine business, you need a policy to provide for emergencies in an orderly manner. Such policies are a guide to your own staff as well as to tenants.

The first recommendation is that you have a listed *24-hour emergency telephone-answering service*. It should be listed as an emergency number to distinguish it from the regular office number which might be used by prospective tenants calling with questions. You may want to have the number printed on a sticker which the tenants can put on or near their telephone.

The answering service can be instructed as to whom to call for various emergencies: the maintenance man for plumbing, electrical, and other repairs; perhaps outside contractors; or the site manager.

The next recommendation is to let your tenants know *what constitutes a real emergency*. If a tenant needs a replacement light bulb, that can wait. But if a water line breaks in his apartment, that's a real emergency. There are six types of real emergencies:

1. **Flooding caused by a plumbing breakdown**. This must be corrected instantly. The longer repairs are delayed, the more extensive the damage will be.
2. **Lack of heat in winter or air-conditioning in summer.**
3. **Damage caused by wind, storm, or fire**. You have to take instant steps to minimize the damage. The tenant should call the fire department first in case of fire; if he hasn't, the answering service should do so immediately before relaying the message to the building personnel.
4. **When security has been breached or is threatened** by burglary, vandalism, or other disturbance. Again, the tenant should call the police first, but the answering service should also be notified.
5. **Back-up of a sewer** or other sanitation facility. This is a health hazard that must be eliminated quickly.
6. **Electrical failures** or short circuits that threaten the safety of the building and the lives of tenants.

You should make tenants aware of these emergencies and whom to call by publishing them on a separate printed or mimeographed sheet or incorporating them into a tenant guidebook. You should also make sure that your answering service knows whom to call in each case and that the service asks tenants to call back during office hours with any non-emergency request.

Disasters are a period of extreme tension for the manager. They often occur at night during the worst weather. After the initial shock of the disaster itself, there are pressures—both physical and emotional—caused by injuries, deaths, loss of possessions, and need to shelter the homeless. Then follow the claims. The manager may be pressed to pay for loss of the tenants' possessions and to provide or pay for interim housing. Just what are his obligations and what should his policy be?

First, the manager has some immediate responsibilities to *protect whatever is left*. This includes boarding up the damaged building, installing emergency lighting and heating, and doing everything else to safeguard the property. Technically, that's where his responsibility ends.

Second, it's a good policy to *stop the rent meter* if the apartment is uninhabitable and to refund or give credit for any unused portion of that month's rent. Then, depending on the terms of the lease, the owner usually has a period of time to determine whether he will restore the apartment and continue the lease, or cancel the lease.

Beyond this, the manager has no moral or legal responsibilities. You may decide that you will make it your policy to move homeless tenants to vacant apartments in your property or pay for their temporary housing in motels or hotels. This action is benevolent, but certainly not recommended. Tenant insurance policies provide for these extra expenses; the property's insurance does not.

Be careful if you move a homeless tenant to another vacant apartment. Your insurance company may deny you any payment on your rent loss insurance policy if you do.

As for paying for loss of the tenant's possessions, your building insurance doesn't cover this. The tenant should have his own household insurance. This is the reason we recommended that the need for individual household insurance be noted on the application form.

Once you have determined your policy concerning disasters, put it in your tenant guidebook so it comes as no surprise.

Personal Injury

If you hear of a tenant or guest injuring himself on your property, it should be a policy to immediately notify your insurance company. Do this even though you've learned about the injury second-hand, from a neighbor who heard that Mrs. Smith fell and injured herself in the lobby. Don't confront the injured person for verification; this may lead the person to expect a high insurance settlement. Let your insurance company do the investigating.

If the injured tenant or guest comes directly to you with a complaint, take down all the information and turn it over to the insurance company. It's their job to follow through.

Property Damage

Your maintenance crew may damage a tenant's car with the project tractor or truck. Make sure your employees report their mishaps to you immediately so you can notify the tenant and the property's insurance carrier.

Keys and Lock-outs

You need policies on keys and lock-outs for several reasons: to reduce replacement costs, to prevent a waste of manpower, and to maintain security.

When the tenant moves in he should receive a fixed number of keys. If he wants more, there should be an additional charge. If he loses his keys, charge for replacements, too. If the tenant wants extra locks on his door, or wants his lock changed because he lost the key, you should have your own personnel or locksmith do this. This way, you can have the new lock fitted to the master key and you'll also gain a more uniform installation.

Lock-outs can be a nuisance. You may have a working mother whose child is always locked out of the apartment when he returns from school and comes down to the management office for the key. Or you'll have an adult who locks himself out and needs a key at one o'clock in the morning.

Regarding the child who locks himself out: If this is habitual, let the parents know you'll charge every time the manager has to let him in. And as for the locked-out adult, have a policy of charging a fee of say $2.50 to let him in during the day, $5 or more if it happens after 10 p.m. Some apartment managers will render no help, forcing the person to gain access on his own and pay for any damages.

One important precaution: *Never lend out master keys.* Some managers, rather than look up the duplicate key for an apartment, will give the locked-out child or adult the master key. This runs the risk of having the master key lost, stolen, or duplicated, thus breaching the security of the property.

You should have only a limited number of master keys, never identified as such. They should be numbered and assigned to only a few designated people such as the manager and the head of maintenance. It may be a good idea to have master keys turned in to the office each night. If a master key is stolen, the manager should have all of the locks re-keyed to a new master, an expensive but necessary procedure.

Politics and Voting

Your property and your management staff should be politically neutral. Common sense tells you that. But you can make meeting facilities available for political purposes, provided they are available to all parties on the same terms.

That's where your political cooperation should stop. You should forbid the display of political signs in tenant windows or anywhere on the premises for appearance reasons except on bulletin boards and again on an equal basis. Political canvassing or distribution of political literature on your premises should be discouraged.

Some complexes are large enough to constitute one or more voting precincts. Where this happens, the local election board may ask to rent polling place space in your building. This is generally a good idea. The on-site polling place is a convenience to the tenant and encourages his participation in the democratic process.

Soliciting

Rules to control soliciting are hard to make. Many communities have laws governing soliciting. Ideally you should prohibit commercial salesmen, to avoid disturbing your residents.

But what about your own tenants doing soliciting? A good policy is to permit this if the tenant is acting in behalf of a recognized nonprofit organization. But if he's going door-to-door selling magazine subscriptions or taking orders for his wife's ceramic figures, that should be forbidden.

Tipping

Tipping can be a problem, especially around holidays. The rents your tenants pay should include the best possible service without tipping. Let your tenants know this periodically, and discourage them from tipping. Let your employees know this, too.

Human nature being what it is, you may not be able to eliminate it entirely, but you can discourage it.

Apartment Transfers

The tenant may ask to transfer to a different apartment during the term of his lease to accommodate a change in his circumstances. Policies covering apartment transfers are difficult and must contain some variables.

Generally, you should discourage apartment transfers because they create added administrative work and they also cause premature wear and tear on the apartments. But be flexible. If the tenant can't satisfy himself in your building now, he'll go elsewhere when the lease is up and you've lost him. This is especially true if there are just a few months left on the lease.

Consider your market conditions to determine whether a transfer is a good idea. For instance, if the tenant wants to upgrade himself by moving from a one bedroom to a two bedroom unit, have him agree to pay for a pro rated share of redecorating his old apartment and make the transfer. This is certainly a good idea if one bedroom apartments are in tight supply and two bedrooms are plentiful. By this means you've rented the two bedroom unit and you should have no trouble renting out the one bedroom to a newcomer.

Move-out

If a tenant moves out of an apartment for any reason, you want him to know what the procedure is and to alert you. You need to know when he's going to move so you can begin searching for a replacement. You also should remind him of the security deposit inspection procedures and arrange to inspect the premises on the day he leaves. Finally, you should be interested in his reasons for moving to help point out deficiencies which exist with your property or your performance.

Security Deposit Return

Having long nurtured a grudge about giving you a security deposit, the tenant who is moving out will now suspect that you are going to cheat him out of it by blaming him for as much damage as you can. Your policy should be to minimize his fears by establishing a procedure that will be completely objective and fair.

It's to your advantage to have the tenant leave the premises in as good a condition as possible, so that you can return his security deposit and not get into heated discussions with him about it. A good policy will accomplish this.

Let the tenant know what the security deposit *inspection* will consist of, and also let him know that you will send him a check within 14 days. When the inspection is completed, you'll give him a worksheet noting whatever damage has been done and the deductions for this, so he'll know what is owed to him.

Knowing that the apartment will be inspected before he moves, the tenant is likely to take extra care to put it in good condition. Without such an inspection, the tenant may feel he'll be cheated and so he may be a little careless. You'll find that your costs will be sharply reduced because of this inspection.

Another good reason for the inspections is that they will enable the tenant to straighten out any misunderstandings about who did what. For instance, you may blame the tenant for chipping a wash basin. The tenant tells you that the wash basin was chipped before he moved in, and he has been putting up with it ever since. If you made an inspection when the last tenant moved out, you'll have a record of this. If the current tenant is right, then you'll avoid the unpleasantness of hassling with him over damage he didn't do.

The inspection may also reveal deficiencies which the tenant will fix on the spot. You may find the oven is dirty and say you'll have to deduct $10. Rather than pay it, the tenant may clean it then and there.

When you make the inspection, be prepared to *make allowances for normal wear and tear*, nail and screw holes, and other signs of tenancy. An apartment is a consumable commodity; it wears out like anything else. You shouldn't expect the tenant to return it to you in *exactly* the same condition he found it. Nor should you expect his security deposit to pay for whatever you'd normally spend in fixing the apartment for the next tenant.

Remember, the fairness you use in dealing with just one tenant quickly becomes common knowledge throughout your property. Fairness is absolutely essential if you're to preserve good tenant relations.

After the inspection is completed, note on your worksheet what has to be done, make whatever deductions are necessary, and *give the tenant a copy*. This will avoid disputes over what has to be done and it also acts as a sort of receipt which helps assure the tenant that he has money coming.

Your last step in dealing with the tenant is to get his *forwarding address* so you can send his check to him, and also get all the *keys* to the apartment and mailbox. Knowing the forwarding address can be a big help if you need to contact the tenant later, and it also lets your marketing people know where people are moving.

You should be able to get your security deposit refund check mailed to the tenant within 14 days after he moves. There is no excuse for taking any longer. If you do take longer, you deserve the extra work and aggravation you'll inherit by following such a policy. Leave the tenant in as good a frame of mind as you can.

Personnel Policies for Better Performance and Service

After all the general, rental, and tenant policies have been formulated, it all comes down to your personnel to make things work. In property management, as in so many other businesses, personnel are often the weakest link. Companies will spend fortunes in equipment, systems, advertising, and everything else related to the business—but it all can be undone by the wrong person or a person with the wrong attitude.

Personnel are particularly critical in property management, because this is a *service business*, with people servicing people. This personally oriented service relationship is basic to everything you do as a property manager, and basic to the work of all of your people, from your rental agents to your maintenance workers.

In keeping with this approach, your personnel policies should provide for three things:

1. Build the idea of service when hiring people. Most property managers rank service behind skills. Can he rent apartments? Can he use a floor polisher? While skills are important, they are not enough. The best maintenance worker is worthless to you if he dislikes people and it shows.

2. Provide for training, because property management is a specialized business. Most apartment employees are not trained or supervised. They are simply put to work, and as a result they are independently solving problems by themselves, without knowing whether their solutions are good or bad. On the management side, a person is told, "You're an agent, here's your desk, now go to work." There's more to it than that.

3. Reward good performance. This requires supervision so you can evaluate performance. It also requires that you know

and use the three basic motivators: ego satisfaction, power, and money. Many managers think money alone is enough. Pay good money, get good people. Give them incentives by offering more money—so goes the theory. But in short order, money loses much of its power. People begin taking money for granted. If they are used to getting regular incentives or raises, they take those for granted, too. When this happens, you need to employ ego satisfaction and power as motivators. Praise for a job well done can be a more powerful reward than money in many cases.

In the sections that follow, we will review the factors you should consider in setting your own effective personnel policies.

Selecting People

Property management needs people whom others will like. That means people who are service-minded and personable. Where can you find such people? Your best source is people you encounter in service situations who are doing a good job—people such as sales clerks, reservations personnel, waitresses, and maintenance people from other fields.

It even means hiring people from other property management jobs. Site managers, especially, begin to grow stale on the same job after two years and a change benefits everyone concerned. This may mean another building for the same owner, or it could be a completely new job working for a new owner.

You can run ads, if you like, or use employment agencies, or ask people to refer job candidates to you. These are less satisfactory than hiring someone you've seen at work.

Checking Out Personnel

Before hiring any management personnel, it's a good practice to check them out to make sure they have the qualifications for the job. These are steps you should consider:

- **Application form.** Be aware of what you can and cannot ask; check federal, state, and local laws governing hiring. In most cases, the standard application form you can get from local stationary or office supply stores will meet current requirements.

- **References**. Talk to the employee's previous employer, if he has one, or a reference who is not a relative of the employee. If the employee has worked in property management before, ask his previous employer what the applicant's *strong* and *weak* points are. Pay particular attention to the answers to these two questions.
- **Credit bureau**. Have the credit bureau check the applicant's record for convictions, judgments, bankruptcy, divorce. It's illegal in most states to refuse employment because of an employee's past, but at least you'll be forewarned that there may be trouble ahead.
- **Bonding**. Any employee who deals with money or is responsible for major expenses should be bonded.
- **Tests**. Some companies require applicants to take a battery of psychological and personality tests. These have their limitations, but they may be useful in giving you another view of the applicant.
- **Lie detector test**. It's a bad practice to tell an applicant that he must take a lie detector test; that lets him know you don't trust anyone. But you can and should let the applicant know that all staff employees, including the manager, will be subjected to lie tests if any thefts occur on the property.

Job Description

Even though most personnel manuals recommend that you have job descriptions, they are not very helpful in property management because they tend to be too restrictive. Management personnel are called upon to perform a variety of duties, some of which can't be anticipated or formalized into a job description. If you must put a description in writing, be sure to make it as broad as possible.

Licensing

Many states have real estate license law provisions which say in effect that persons who *lease or offer to lease* real estate, must be licensed. Often, however, this requirement does not extend to direct employees of the owner of the property. It almost always includes employees of a managing agent. For sure, licensing requirements will become both broader and more stringent. There is a movement under way at this writing which will require the licensing of all site managers. Be aware of the laws in your area and be alert for upcoming changes in those laws.

Compensation

It's not unusual for property management employees to receive several forms of compensation, including salary or wages, free rent, free utilities, and other noncash items. The idea is that the salary or wages can be lower if the other noncash benefits are offered. Thus, as some owners put it, you can hire a site manager for $600 a month, give him a $250 per month apartment, toss in $60 worth of free telephone, electric, and gas utilities a month, and you can claim to be paying $910 a month. Let's see if this works out.

- **Free rent**. The idea of giving a free apartment to an employee came about in the days when apartments were more plentiful than money. When the practice started, it was common for employees not to report the value of the apartment as income. But this has changed. The IRS now includes the apartment's value as taxable income unless the employee is required to live there for the owner's convenience. If the apartment is given for the owner's convenience it can't also be counted as part or full compensation for services rendered.

  In most cases, giving the employee a free apartment is simply a matter of giving him something extra to make up for an otherwise low salary or wage. Under these circumstances, the employee will have to pay taxes on the value of the apartment. So free rent isn't exactly free.

  Now let's look at it further from the employee's standpoint. An employee making $600 a month would normally spend no more than $150 a month for an apartment; that's using the rule-of-thumb of paying 25 percent of gross income for housing. If you give the employee a $250 per month unit, he can only credit you with the $150 he'd normally spend; the other $100 of value is nice but it is needed in cash to pay other normal living expenses.

  There's another disadvantage to giving the employee a free apartment. If he hasn't actually paid for it, he can't appreciate its value. This is not good particularly in the case of a rental agent whose job consists of demonstrating good value. The way to avoid this is to rent the apartment to the employee at its regular value less an employee *discount*. This is the method used by stores for their employees, and it has the result of making the employee *aware of value*. Also in most cases a modest employee discount is not taxable compensation.

- **Free utilities**. These are often offered to employees in cases where utilities are not normally included in the apartment rent. Employees who get this benefit seldom appreciate it as part of their income. Ask them what they earn and they'll reply in terms of their salary or wage, not what the free utilities (and free apartment) are worth. Because they don't appreciate the value, they're apt to waste the benefit. The same holds true of other noncash benefits such as free gasoline for employee cars. It's not appreciated and it's apt to be wasted. Use a mileage allowance instead.

- **Salary or wage**. In summary, you're better off paying your employee a straight salary or wage and forgetting about free apartments and free utilities. As for what the salary or wage should be, set it at a level that will attract the people you want. This level will vary from one area to another.

The property management business has grandly underpaid its people in the past and has paid for it dearly in inefficient operations. In one instance, an owner entrusted a $6 million property to a widow whom he paid $625 per month plus a $225 per month apartment—and then wondered why the property lost $14,000 in one month. The informed owner wants a manager who is worth more. There are no bargains in cheap wages.

Wage and Hour Law

It is absolutely essential that you determine if your company, property, or group of properties falls under the Fair Labor Standards Act. This is frequently referred to as the Federal Wage and Hour Law. The requirements of this law are significant. Likewise, the penalties for failure to comply are also significant. Contact the Wage and Hour Division of the Employment Standards Administration of the U.S. Department of Labor to secure pamphlets and information on the law and its requirements.

The comments in this section amount to a broad interpretation of those provisions. Specific wage and salary amounts have been avoided as they are subject to frequent change. Interpretation of specific situations by various regional Wage and Hour offices vary, making a complete discussion of the subject even more difficult.

A commonly held notion is that if you pay a property management employee by the month, you can work him as long as you want without additional compensation. But the federal Wage and Hour law says this isn't so. The vast majority of apartments are covered by this law which says that *you must pay your employees the minimum hourly wage*—and *you must compensate employees at the rate of time-and-a-half,* with certain exceptions, for all hours in excess of 40 worked each week. So far as the Wage and Hour law is concerned, your employees are all hourly. Even if you pay monthly, the federal agency will simply take the monthly salary, multiply it by 12 months and then divide by 2,080 hours to arrive at the hourly rate.

Consider some implications of the Wage and Hour law. Your objective is to avoid overtime if you can. You can do this by giving compensating time off within the workweek. That means as soon as the employee reaches 40 hours in a week, you give him the rest of the week off. You can't give him compensating time off the following week; the law says each week must stand on its own.

Most workweeks begin on Monday and end on Sunday. If you follow this system and you need your employees to work on the weekend, the time when most emergencies occur, you'll probably wind up paying overtime. You are better advised to declare your *workweek to begin on Saturday and end on Friday.* That means if your employees must work on the weekend, you have the balance of the week to grant compensating time off. This policy can save you many overtime hours. If you do this, it is more efficient to pay your employees weekly or every two weeks, because then your records will conform more easily to a workweek.

How the government figures the minimum wage and overtime is worth your study. First, Uncle Sam will allow both salary compensation and the value of an apartment (less an allowance for profit, and advertising and promotion costs) which are given to the employee for the *employee's convenience.* Remember now that IRS expects taxes to be withheld on the value of an apartment unless it is provided for the *convenience of the employer.* You can't have it both ways.

Test to see that you are meeting the minimum wage requirement. Assume you provide an employee with an apartment for his convenience and that it normally rents for $150 per month. Assume further that a reasonable profit and promotion allocation attributable to that unit is $25 per month. You must then subtract this amount from the monthly rent ($150 − $25 = $125) to arrive at the apartment value which can be added to the monthly wage for purposes of satisfying minimum wage requirements. Carrying the example further, a person receiving a monthly salary of $250 and an apartment with an adjusted value of $125 is effectively receiving $375 per month or $4,500 per year. By dividing $4,500 per year by 2,080 hours (52 weeks × 40 hours per week) you arrive at an hourly rate of $2.16 which is *less* than the current federal minimum wage. You must increase this person's wage at least enough to equal the minimum wage. If your property is in a state which also has a minimum wage, the higher of the two rates prevails.

When computing overtime, the government requires that you use the *total* hourly rate which includes the adjusted apartment value. This figure will be multiplied by 1.5 to arrive at the hourly wage to be paid for all hours worked in excess of 40 during any one workweek.

All of this means you had better keep track of both wage levels and hours worked very carefully. If the government suspects you are violating the law, it will study all of your employees' pay records for the past two years (in some cases, for the past three years) and hold you liable for any underpayment of the minimum wage plus any premium or overtime pay which was not paid during those years. If it can be shown that you acted *willfully* in underpaying your employees, the government can go back three years and even force you to pay double the back wages due.

Your best defense is to have each employee fill out a time card in his own writing each week detailing the hours worked each day. Maintain these cards as a permanent record, and pay overtime when needed.

The Wage and Hour law does provide that certain employees meeting specific criteria can be exempt from the overtime provision. In property management these exemptions come under one of two classifications: Executive or Administrative. The government has published a special booklet dealing with these exemptions (531 Exemption) which is available through the Wage and Hour Division.

In a very broad interpretation of these exemption requirements, a person must at least meet these tests to qualify:

1. The primary duties of the employee must be management-
   related.
2. The employee must supervise two or more employees.
3. The employee must not spend more than 20 percent of his
   time performing manual or nonmanagement-related activities.
4. The employee must receive a guaranteed weekly wage of at
   least a certain amount. This figure has two levels and is
   subject to frequent change. The wage must be guaranteed at
   this level and must not be subject to deductions for sick pay
   or short hours. The test of the wage level *may not include
   any apartment value.* A thorough reading of the government's pamphlet on this subject is recommended before
   determining which, if any, of your employees can be classified as exempt.

Don't take the Wage and Hour law lightly. The law is on the
employee's side and his word will often be upheld against yours. Be
sure you know and understand the law thoroughly and be careful to
document your actions.

Employee Benefit Insurance

Employee benefit insurance, such as a health and hospitalization plan, is rare for many management and maintenance-
associated employees because of the small size of the work force.
Most plans require 10 or more people. This may put you at a hiring
disadvantage, since many employees expect this kind of coverage.
However, even if you do provide it, the employee won't give you full
credit for what it costs you. Again, he thinks only of his wage or
salary, not the full cost of any benefits he may get.

In some areas, *community health groups* have been set up to
provide medical coverage. If your community has one, it might be a
good idea to have your employees enroll on a 50-50 basis. That is,
you offer to pay 50 percent of your employee's premium, while he
pays the other 50 percent. That way he gains a better appreciation
of what the coverage is worth. The employee should also pay any
premium for coverage of his dependents.

Permanent, Part-Time, and Seasonal Employees

Historically, the pattern in property management was to use as few permanent people as possible and work them as long as necessary to get the job done. But the federal Wage and Hour law has changed this. Unless you are a very small operation which does not come under the Interstate Commerce ruling, you can't work your employees more than 40 hours a week without paying time-and-a-half for overtime. In many cases, it doesn't take much overtime to make you realize that you'd be better off with another full-time person.

Overtime in general should be discouraged. If it becomes routine, then the employee expects overtime as part of his regular income and he's disappointed if he doesn't get it. You should seek to streamline your operation to get all routine work done during the regular workweek. There may be certain periods, due to weather, untimely breakdowns, or seasonal traffic, when your short-term needs peak and overtime is justified. But if overtime becomes regular, add another full-time or part-time person to your staff.

Many managers augment their rental personnel with part-time people on weekends. Even if you do this, it's a good idea to assign one of your permanent people to work on weekends, particularly on Sunday, the busiest day, on a rotating basis. The manager or assistant manager should always be on duty on Sunday.

Living On or Off Premises

There are certain advantages in having your personnel, especially the site manager and the chief maintenance engineer, live on the premises. They're always available to serve tenants, even if this means overtime work. Because they see more of what's going on, they can control it better. They have no delays getting to work and no transportation expense. Supposedly they take more pride in their job because it is also the location of their home.

There are disadvantages, too. Overfamiliarity with the project can lead your personnel to overlook certain things. They may tend to spend more time at home during lunch and at break periods than they should. Living on the job may lead them to socialize with tenants. Finally, your personnel lose touch with the outside world.

Consider these things when determining your policy about where your employees should live.

Training

Before you put any employee to work, make sure he understands your policies and procedures. That's the minimum training he needs. Beyond that he needs careful supervision as he goes through his daily routine to make sure he's doing things the right way. It isn't the function of this book to detail employee training aids or methods. Individual chapters, however, would be good reading for employees dealing with rentals, tenants, and maintenance. You should devise your own training policies and methods to suit your needs. The point is, make sure your employee is trained in your ways before you let him go off on his own.

Supervision

Every employee should have *one boss*, no more. It's unfair and unreasonable to have an employee answer to two or more people; that only leads to low morale and confusion. The employee should also have reasonable access to his boss, and should channel all requests, complaints, and wage adjustments through him.

As for the supervisor or boss, he should have no more than *six or seven people* answering directly to him. If he has more, he'll have difficulty providing proper supervision and needed attention. A true supervisor must be able to *hire and fire*. You may want to put some limits on this authority, such as having the supervisor consult with his immediate superior first.

Reporting to Work

Employees are expected to be at work on time. Your policy should read that if an employee is sick or delayed, he should notify his supervisor no later than 30 minutes after the appointed starting time. If the employee must leave his post before the designated break, lunch period, or quitting time, he should notify his supervisor. Three violations of these rules in a month's time is certainly reason for dismissal.

Breaks

A walk through many apartment complexes will find several building employees, but it is rare to actually find an employee physically engaged in productive work. The rental apartment industry has a very low productivity rate. This is caused by lack of proper training and inadequate supervision. A common response from an employee found not working is: "I am on my break." To eliminate this excuse, establish uniform time periods in the morning and afternoon for breaks. Typically these would be from 10:00 to 10:15 in the morning, and 3:00 to 3:15 in the afternoon. You can also establish a set lunch period. At all other times of the work day you should expect to find your employees at work.

Uniforms

Policies on this subject vary widely. Some properties require rental personnel to be dressed in blazers. It's generally a good idea to require your maintenance and service people to wear uniforms while on duty, because that makes them easy to identify and also adds to the well-managed appearance of the property.

If you decide on uniforms, select a *readily available style and color* and provide the employee with two or three sets. He should be responsible for washing and cleaning them. You should be responsible for replacing them when they wear out. Giving the employee a standard *name badge* is also a good idea.

Provide the employee with safety shoes, safety goggles, and a protective helmet if the nature of his work requires these.

Tools

Maintenance personnel should be required to *provide their own tools.* If they are first-rate workers, they will automatically have their own hand tools and take good care of them. Ask to see the tools before you hire the person. If he has proper tools in good condition, you can feel confident that he is a good workman. If you must provide him with tools, expect that he won't take care of them as well as he would his own. The exceptions are specialized or expensive heavy-duty tools which should be provided as equipment of the property.

Guns

At certain times and in certain areas, your employees, especially men, may take to carrying guns for protection. Some may even be constables or deputies.

We recommend that you *forbid your employees from carrying guns* or from having them anywhere on the premises in the course of business. The sight of an employee toting a gun gives your property the wrong image; would you rent an apartment if you saw the manager wearing a gun? Guns can be misused, leading to tragedy and possibly a lawsuit against you and the property. Finally, carrying a gun is not the employee's business, unless he is a bona fide security employee. If the employee can't function without a gun, he should get another job.

Gifts, Kickbacks, Commissions

You need an absolute policy on gifts, commissions, and kickbacks to head off trouble and to ensure that whatever you purchase from vendors is on the basis of price and quality, not favoritism.

Vendors historically have offered management employees bonuses for orders, knowing that the employees' traditionally low pay scale makes them susceptible to this kind of payment. Companies that sell cleaning supplies and chemicals continue to follow this practice. Furniture leasing companies commonly pay $10 to the manager or rental agent for every tenant renting furniture; the companies may then pressure the manager to let the furniture remain after the tenant moves and attempt to re-lease the apartment with the company's furnishings. This practice saves the furniture company money by not having to pick up the furniture. It costs the property owner money in lost rent waiting for a tenant who will accept those furnishings. As stated earlier, a tenant who has his own furnishings is almost always more stable than one who does not.

Commissions, kickbacks, gifts, and bonuses from vendors are bad for several reasons. First, they encourage the employee to order more than is needed to qualify for the gift. Second, the employee may disregard quality. Both of these factors cost the property money. Third, if there are any reductions in price, these rightfully should be credited to the building's account and not go into the employee's pocket.

To make sure that all relations with vendors are on a strictly businesslike basis, employees should be forbidden to accept any kind of money payment from them. They should also refuse any free tickets to entertainment or sporting events and turn down any free dinners or other invitations to socialize. You may wish to permit the acceptance of gifts at Christmas time if they can be eaten, drunk, or smoked in one day.

Gifts or tips from tenants should be refused; they lead to special treatment and unequal service, a source of many tenant complaints. If holiday tipping and gift-giving to employees is a problem, establish a kitty so that all employees share and so that tenants are not identified.

Socializing with Tenants

Don't allow your employees to socialize with tenants. This is particularly hard on employees who live on the site, but it's necessary. Socializing with tenants, becoming personally friendly with them, having an occasional drink with them—all of these are bound to affect the employee's judgment.

Controlling Employee Purchases

It's customary for property managers to establish accounts with local vendors, such as hardware, electrical, and plumbing supply stores. The problem here is that employees may take advantage of these accounts to buy items for themselves. Some property managers attempt to deal with this by setting a dollar limit on each order. But it's a simple matter for an employee to get around this by coming in at different times with smaller orders.

The recommended way to control purchases is to require the vendor to refuse any order that is not *itemized* and *signed* by the manager. This makes it difficult for any unauthorized person to buy for his own use. The same rule also applies to purchases of *capital equipment*.

Pilfering and Petty Theft

Because of stocks of supplies, equipment, rent cash, and coin meter collections on the premises, the property management business is vulnerable to pilfering and petty theft. You should let your employees know that you realize this temptation exists, and that you will use systems to reduce losses. Furthermore, let them know that if they are caught in a theft you will terminate them without severance and with a promise of an accurate reference; that means you'll let the next employer know about the theft. If the theft is a substantial amount, you should prosecute.

These are some steps you can take to reduce the possibilities of petty theft:

- **Keep supplies to a minimum**. Don't order a gross of brooms and expect them to remain; order one or two at a time, as you need them. You can give your vendor a blanket purchase order and have him make drop shipments of small quantities.
- **Buy bulk quantities** rather than small packages. It's easy to steal a gallon can of paint or a quart bottle of household cleaner. But if you buy in larger containers, such as 30-gallon drums, theft becomes more difficult.
- **Bank money daily**. Don't have cash and checks, other than petty cash, in your office for more than eight hours.
- **Keep a log sheet of coin collections** from vending machines. Normally, there is little variation from month to month. If you spot a drop in income, you can suspect theft.
- **Never authorize on-site personnel to sign checks**. They should only make deposits. Exception to this policy recommendation will almost ensure accounting and money irregularities.

Employee Evaluation

The purpose of the employee evaluation is twofold to determine whether the employee is doing a good or bad job and to find out how well the supervisor is performing. Good supervision is a key element in property management, which is why you must constantly seek to get the best out of your supervisors.

We recommend that at least once a year each supervisor be required to submit to his superior a *written report* on the work being performed by each employee in his charge. The narrative report is much more revealing than a fill-in checklist which tends to be perfunctory. In his narrative the supervisor should cover the employee's attitude; performance; relationship with others; job skills; special interests outside of work; personal traits bearing on the job; and future outlook.

These reports are not intended to be reviewed with the employee. However, the supervisor should be aware of privacy laws. At some future time the employee may demand to see his evaluation and if it contains any errors, these could be a cause for action if the employee has suffered because of them.

These reports should be reviewed by the superior to get a picture of the personnel situation. If the supervisor reports many negatives, the superior can logically ask why isn't something being done about them. In other words, these evaluations will force a complete evaluation of all personnel, supervisors included, and indicate where the weak spots are.

Tenant complaints about employees may be included as a part of the evaluation, but they should also be handled when they arise. The recommended procedure, as with all other tenant complaints (see p. 87) is to ask the tenant to put his complaint in writing. Give a copy to the employee and investigate. When the matter is settled, report back to the tenant by telephone or in person, and report to the employee, at the same noting how the matter was handled in the employee's record.

Salary and Wage Adjustments

We recommend a policy of reviewing salaries and wages for each employee not less than once a year. At this time you can determine whether the employee should get a merit or cost-of-living increase. His job performance and local job market conditions will determine your decision.

In keeping with what was said earlier about paying a good wage or salary, your policy should be to reward good performance and to pay your people well in accordance with their responsibilities.

Incentives and Bonuses

Regular incentives and bonuses are self-defeating. Employees learn to count on them and expect them. They become a part of the employee's regular income and lose all value as an incentive for extra effort. For this reason, we discourage any kind of regular bonus, including a Christmas bonus. You seldom get credit for it.

Instead, consider *random bonuses* geared to short-range goals, such as paying employees for renting a certain number of apartments, obtaining renewals, or collecting rent in a short, specific period. Such incentives build excitement and vary the pace of activities. Employees will usually welcome the challenge and respond with extra performance. Bonuses needn't be in dollars; they can be just as effective in the form of merchandise, commendations, and even trips.

Holidays

You need your rental staff at full strength on Sundays and warm weather holidays which are good rental days. Let your rental employees know you expect them to work Sunday hours on those holidays. Thanksgiving, Christmas, and New Year's Day are generally poor rental days and you might just as well remain closed on these days.

The maintenance staff can usually be at skeleton strength on all holidays.

Vacations

The recommended policy is to establish a *vacation year* during which any earned vacation time can be taken. The employee typically earns one day of vacation for each full month of employment, up to a total of 10 days, but he is required to take those within a certain period.

For example, many companies allow vacation time to be accumulated through April 30, a typical vacation year-end date. Employees then have to take their vacation before March 31 of the following year. This prevents employees combining two weeks of vacation at the end of one year with two weeks at the beginning of the next to make a four-week vacation.

Here are some other vacation rules to consider:

- Employees must *schedule vacations* with other employees, so that you are not left shorthanded at any time. If there is a conflict, seniority rules.
- Any vacation *time not taken is lost* forever. It is not carried over into the next year or compensated by money.
- If the employee *resigns*, he loses all vacation time accrued to date.
- If you *terminate* the employee, he receives his accrued vacation pay as severance.
- If the employee *dies*, his heirs will receive any accrued vacation pay.

Death of a Relative

If an employee's immediate relative dies, consider giving him three days off with pay. "Immediate relative" includes spouse, mother, father, son, daughter, sister, or brother. If the employee needs more time, give him an authorized leave of absence. Absence on the death of any other relative is without pay.

Sick Days

It is virtually impossible to set a foolproof sick-day policy. Some companies allow employees five sick days during a calendar year. For each sick day they take, they are paid. For each sick day they don't take, they receive one day's additional vacation up to five days. Any sick days taken beyond five are without pay.

Whatever sick-day policy you establish, be sure to document sick days carefully to avoid disputes.

Education and Tuition

Owners will usually benefit by encouraging their employees to undertake education to improve their skills on the job. This education can include formal day or evening classes, seminars, dinner programs, and short-term training programs. Administrative, rental, and maintenance people should be included in the education policy.

But the policy should be carefully thought out and enforced, or else you may find yourself paying for education that has no relation to the job. Some owners, however, find this acceptable; they feel that anything an employee does to improve himself, even if it's taking a course in modern art, will pay off in better job performance.

The typical education policy requires the employee first to get approval from his supervisor to take a course. The employee then advances all funds to pay for tuition, books, and other expenses. When he presents evidence that he has successfully completed the course, the owner or manager reimburses him for 50 percent of the tuition cost (books and expenses are not reimbursed). This policy encourages the employee to make a commitment of his funds, rather than get a free ride at the owner's expense. It also encourages the employee to be serious about the course.

Labor Unions

In certain situations, particularly in cities, labor unions have made and are continuing to make efforts to organize apartment property personnel, especially maintenance workers. The unions seek out the larger complexes because this is where the most friction between owners and employees is likely to be found.

While unions may promise much, they produce no efficiencies in work performance or morale. From the owner's standpoint, the result is less work and more cost. Some owners think they can get around this disadvantage by replacing all their unionized maintenance and custodial personnnel with a contract service. But this is a loss to the owner, because people on your payroll are easier to control and supervise than contract personnel.

Your best approach is to avoid union organizing in the first place. The way to do this is through fair and reasonable policies uniformly applied, regular salary and wage reviews, good supervision, and communication with your employees. Give them more advantages than they would have as members of a union, and you'll eliminate any need for them to organize.

If a union does approach you with notice of its intention to organize, before you do anything else, *contact a labor attorney immediately*. This is not the time to get tough or make threats. The federal government has strict rules governing union organizing which are best interpreted by a labor attorney.

Chapter Three

How to Get Your Property Ready and Keep it That Way

Earlier in this book, we referred to the five P's of successful marketing: policies, product preparation, price, presentation, and promises. All of them play a role. We cover these five P's in various ways in this book. But if you can remember only one, remember product preparation, because 80 percent of your success depends on that. In fact, you can have all of the other P's in abundance, but if your product preparation is lacking, you can't succeed.

Let's consider why product preparation is so important.

Go to any city in the United States where the rental picture is supposedly bad. You'll inevitably find that there are always a handful of apartment complexes that are 100 percent rented while others are desperately seeking tenants. Look further and you'll discover that the filled-up complexes usually have long waiting lists and are generally charging higher rents than properties with vacancies.

Analyze these successful rental properties carefully and you'll generally discover they have one thing in common: they all look physically superior, inside and out. Professionals refer to this as "curb appeal." This means they have more than better architecture; they have tip-top housekeeping which is evident from the moment you drive through the front entrance.

Now take a look at the properties that have vacancies and you'll almost always find they suffer from the same common ailment: poor housekeeping. They may have lower rents, more amenities, better apartments, but their down-at-the-heels appearance keeps prospects away.

So if your development is to attract prospects, you have to prepare your product; in other words, make it as attractive-looking as you can. This is absolutely essential if you are to capture drive-by traffic, which accounts for the majority of your prospects.

If you doubt this, run a check of prospects visiting a successful development, or any development, for that matter. You'll find that more than 55 percent were just driving by and were attracted by overall appearance. Less than 45 percent were attracted by all other means including newspaper advertising.

Imagine two almost identical apartment developments across the street from one another. The apartments and rents are virtually the same. Manager A invests all he can in advertising to draw prospects but ignores his product preparation. Manager B does no advertising at all, but takes the same amount of money Manager A spends on advertising and instead spends it on product preparation.

What happens? The prospects come out to see Manager A's property, but on the way they notice Manager B's property across the street. They may go in to see Manager A's apartments, but most will almost certainly wind up renting from Manager B. In short, Manager A has handed over his prospects to Manager B who has captured them with a better-looking product.

Manager B is better off in three additional ways, besides having more renters:

- The better-looking complex will attract a better grade of tenant who causes less wear and tear and stays longer with fewer problems.
- Money invested in the property for improvements has a long life and a compounding advantage. The value received from advertising expenditures is very short-lived and rarely exceeds a few days.
- The better-looking property will command a substantially higher rent.

In short, Manager B will rent up faster, attract more qualified tenants, be able to charge higher rents, have fewer tenant problems, be required to do less policing, and have fewer maintenance and record-keeping problems, all adding up to more net operating income for the owner.

Product preparation is important from another standpoint. It helps convey a feeling of status about your property. Remember that prospects are looking for more than a place to live. They are seeking a place that reflects their life-style and their role in life, real or imagined. They don't want to have to make excuses to themselves or their friends about their choice of an apartment. Status is a most important factor in their decision to rent, and product preparation helps to establish confidence in the status your property offers.

These remarks about product preparation pertain to both existing and brand-new apartment properties. A new property, if it is to command the premium rent necessary to pay its way, must be presented as a finished product. The prospect should not encounter all sorts of obstacles: construction litter, partially completed buildings, no landscaping, half-finished parking lots, mounds of earth, mud, and every other conceivable item that can discourage him. The vast majority of new complexes are opened prematurely, causing permanent damage to their economic potential. The more complete and perfect a new development is, the more successful it will be.

An apartment complex has no excuse for not looking its best. If it does not, then the manager is automatically risking the loss of a good portion of his potential drive-by traffic.

Details can make a significant difference in the prospect's perception of your property. Call it nit-picking, but your prospect often has sharper eyes than you do for things that don't look right or are out of place. He is also probably more perceptive of the extra things done to make a building and grounds look sharp.

Consider the case of two used cars for sale, both identical. The dealer gives one a routine wash and polish job to make it shine. The second car gets the same wash and polish treatment, but the dealer does something extra. He has his crew go over all the hidden nooks and crannies of the car to remove dirt and apply polish—the edges underneath the hood, under the trunk lid, and on the inside edges of the doors. They carefully remove any traces of dried polish that may have accumulated between the chrome trim and the paint. They remove any rust spots on the bumpers. They steam clean the engine and shampoo the upholstery. Result: the second car looks better, will probably sell for several hundred dollars more, and will probably move faster than the first car even though they are basically the same car. It's product preparation and appearance that make the difference.

The same thing applies to your property. Make it look better and it will rent faster. Remember that your job is to lease apartments at the best possible rent. Empty apartments mean money lost forever. When an airliner takes off with empty seats, there is no way the revenue from those empty seats can ever be recovered. When a month begins with empty apartments, there is no way you can make time go backward and re-rent those apartments for the month just passed. So everything you can do to see that the apartments are rented when the month begins is money in the bank.

Getting your product ready is half the job. Keeping it ready is the other half. In an existing apartment complex you are constantly in the process of showing and renting units. The tenants you already have are prospects for the next lease renewal period. So you can't afford to let your property run down once you put it in shape. You must work at it constantly.

That is why in the paragraphs that follow we will not only call your attention to the aspects of your property that may need attention but we will also suggest what you should do to maintain them in first-class condition.

If you are relatively new to the property and believe you can still judge with an objective eye, then you can take a tour of the property just as a prospect would. Or you could hire an experienced manager who can be objective and have him go through it, writing down everything he sees that's wrong.

Let us take such a tour in words right now and see what we would look for. We'll start with the outside, which is what the prospect sees first.

Exterior

Landscaping

As the prospect drives by your property, he immediately notices the landscaping, starting with the front entrance and extending back to the buildings themselves. The landscaping covers the largest amount of ground. It sets the stage and immediately tells the prospect a lot about the character of your property.

Landscaping is a relatively unappreciated factor in product preparation. In the days when most apartment properties were city buildings, landscaping was hardly a factor at all; there just was no room for it. A row of perimeter bushes, perhaps a patch of lawn, and that was it. With the advent of suburban garden complexes covering 20 acres or more, developers saw they had more ground so they planted more grass and perhaps a few scattered trees.

In most cases today, landscaping remains the last item in the budget and the first to be cut if the developer runs short in his construction funds. Usually the landscaping budget is inadequate to begin with, and when it's trimmed, there's nothing left.

Another factor to blame is that developers seldom specify what they mean by landscaping, and lenders go along. To many, landscaping is nothing more than grass and a few shrubs, but it must be more than that. In fact, it would be better to sacrifice 90 percent of the advertising budget, carpeting, draperies, and fancy lighting to put in better landscaping—because if you can't get the prospect past the landscaping, you won't get him inside the apartments at all.

We won't attempt to tell you how to landscape, but we will suggest that if your landscaping lacks appeal, you should contact a reputable local landscape architect or landscape contractor and get his advice. There are a number of points to keep in mind:

- The landscaping should look lush, not skimpy. It's better to overplant to compensate for having to put in small specimens. Rather than scatter trees about randomly, group them in clumps. They not only look better, but this makes them easier to maintain and mow around.
- Don't rely on grass to cover the acreage. Grass needs mowing and constant maintenance. In northern climates, vast expanses of grass are drab-looking in the winter. Instead, break up a monotonous appearance with planting beds and clumps of trees. Use ground cover in some areas and in others create accents with shag bark surfacing.
- Use plants that are native to your region. They'll look better and chances are they'll survive better than foreign species.
- Strive for a color effect all year round. Use evergreens at all seasons, plus specimens with gray, yellow, brown, and red bark.
- If you have any natural grasslands, woods, or prairie on your property, leave them that way, with fallen trees and all. Study the nature preserves in your area to see what "natural" really means and try to imitate this effect.
- Use concentrated flower beds for accents. Perennials, including flowering bulbs, inject a note of color just when it's most needed,

at the end of a weary winter. A wide variety of perennials is generally available at low cost. For annuals, you need a substantial budget each year; you also need to spend a lot of effort watering and weeding them. Whatever kinds of flowers you plant, group them in tight masses; scattered blooms look lost and have no visual impact.

- While large boulders are fine for accents, avoid beds of gravel. Gravel is not only unnatural, but it poses many hazards. It can be dangerous underfoot, especially on paved surfaces, and children are tempted to use gravel as missiles.

- Try to determine where people will take shortcuts and then put paths in where the shortcuts will be. Fighting shortcuts is a losing battle.

- Don't use chains and posts as part of your landscaping to fence off areas or to guide traffic. These spoil the natural appearance of your property, and they need almost constant attention because they will be knocked over or broken. Barberry, hawthorne, and other thorny plants are better if you want to fence areas and discourage shortcuts.

- Don't landscape around playground areas. Instead of grass, use sand or shag bark which can take abuse much better.

- Plan your landscaping for easy maintenance. Lay out lawns, tree clumps, shrubbery, and flower beds so that machines can be used rather than costly hand labor. Avoid narrow strips of grass along buildings and walls; these usually require hand trimming.

- Be careful of installing sprinklers. While they make watering easier, they are subject to leaks and freezing damage, and require maintenance. Sprinklers are all right in the South, but seldom in the North because of the frost problem.

The foregoing suggestions can he helpful if you have the opportunity and adequate budget to improve your property's landscaping. If your budget is too low, then try to improve your landscaping gradually. Remember, you need some sort of budget to pay for seeding, fertilizing, and replacing dead or damaged plants. Even with a minimum budget, try to maximize the landscaping's appearance with good maintenance.

Paved Areas

If the prospect is attracted by the lush landscaped appearance of your property, the next element he'll be exposed to is the paved area which covers the second largest amount of ground. What he sees—and feels—can give him another clue to what kind of property he's facing.

The driveways and parking areas should be as smooth as possible. Chuckholes or potholes can discourage the prospect, perhaps even make him turn around and leave. Puddles caused by poor drainage are another discouraging factor.

Often the condition of the paved surfaces goes back to the beginning of the development. The paving is often inadequate to begin with. The base of gravel may be too thin or perhaps it wasn't allowed to settle before the asphalt topping was applied. The asphalt layer may be too thin. Overloaded trucks may have broken down the surface in spots.

Whatever the situation, your job as manager requires you to do the best job you can of restoring the surface and keeping it in good condition. Your on-site maintenance personnel should be instructed how to *patch any holes* that develop. If the surface is worn but still usable, you may want to have it *re-sealed* with a film of liquid driveway coating. When you do this, be sure to alert your tenants and arrange for cars to be moved so that the coating truck has the proper access. Also, be aware that people will pick up the coating on their shoes and track it onto sidewalks and into buildings. It can be a messy procedure.

For paved asphalt surfaces that are beyond surface treatment, you can have a *new layer* applied. This is an expensive process but it should produce a paved surface good for five years or more.

As the prospect drives into the parking lot, what does he see there? Bright *parking stripes* can make a world of difference; these stripes should be painted annually. *Concrete wheel stops* are another asset; they are essential to keep autos in orderly rows and to prevent cars from running onto lawns.

Avoid half-size concrete stops that are intended to halt only one wheel. Sometimes a car can miss the stop and go onto the lawn. If snow covers the half-stop, a small plow can miss the stop, too, and tear up the lawn.

Stay away, too, from asphalt wheel stops. These are less expensive than the concrete kind. But they often have rounded edges which permit a car's wheels to ride over them. The asphalt strips also deteriorate fast and then can be easily ripped off by plows.

Concrete curbing around the parking lot is no substitute for wheel stops. Without the stops, the car's front or rear can overhang the sidewalk next to the curb, which is annoying to visitors and tenants.

Some roadways and parkways have *slow-down bumps.* These are ridges of asphalt which give the car a jolt if it's going too fast. These are very effective in the warmer climates. In the northern climates, however, these ridges can upset snow plows or can be ripped off by the plow's blade. Concrete depressions across the roadside provide an alternative impediment to speeding cars.

Your prospect may be discouraged if he sees a lot of *motorcycles, campers, and boats* parked in the lot. You can counter this by establishing separate parking areas for these vehicles. For motorcycles, make up a rack using $2^1/_2$-inch galvanized pipe and embed the ends of the pipe in concrete; motorcyclists will use this because they can chain their vehicles to the rack.

As for boats on trailers, set aside a distant area of the parking lot for these. The sight of a row of boats lined up neatly will not only solve a parking problem, but will also give your property a country club or yacht club appearance. Do the same for campers and recreational vehicles.

Junk autos and auto repairs in your parking lot should not be tolerated. Check your local laws on junk autos before you do anything, but in general, when you spot a car in your lot that is not currently licensed and drivable, find the owner and ask him to remove it. Auto repair activities going on in your parking lot will attract prospects who like to be auto mechanics, but will turn off the better class prospect. Your rules and regulations should forbid auto repairs, other than washing.

Trash

Now that the prospect has been impressed by your landscaping and paved areas, the next thing that's likely to catch his eye is trash. There's little you can do about trash other than to make it as orderly as possible.

In a large building with central trash-collection facilities, trash is not much of a problem, at least on the outside. Tenants deposit refuse in a chute which leads to a collection bin. There it's collected and stored for the scavenger crews.

But in most garden apartments, tenants must carry their garbage outside to randomly located dumpsters. These receptacles are basically unsightly and hard to keep clean. They are usually dirty, streaked with garbage drippings, and dented by the trucks which pick them up and empty them. Some managers put the dumpsters behind fenced enclosures which don't last long because they're hit by the garbage trucks. To make it hard for the tenant who simply tosses the garbage into the dumpster, a manager may put up a wire fence above the enclosure. But this doesn't stop the tenant; he continues to toss the garbage, and if it hits the wire fence and scatters, that's too bad.

There are other problems with dumpsters and enclosures. The manager may put on a gate to keep refuse from blowing out. Tenants who come to the enclosure laden with two bags of garbage don't appreciate the gate. Neither do the scavenger crews who may refuse to pick up the dumpster unless the manager or one of the on-site personnel opens the gate for them. The manager may also build a tight enclosure that's closed all the way down to the ground to keep refuse inside. This is bad because it could lead a tenant to confront a cornered animal. It's better for the enclosure to be open at the bottom so animals can escape.

Finally, the manager may think a large dumpster is more efficient and holds more refuse without overflowing. But large dumpsters can be child traps. Furthermore, a large dumpster requires a large truck to pick it up, and the truck is apt to make indentations in the asphalt surface.

The dumpster should be *freshly painted* and *cleaned* inside and out whenever needed. If possible, the dumpster should be on a *concrete pad*, so it won't indent the asphalt, and be within a three-sided enclosure, open at the bottom. The dumpsters should be located *away from heavy traffic areas*, including the main entrance to each building, the rental office, model apartments, and recreation area. Most important, the dumpsters should be *policed* by on-site personnel three or four times daily. While dumpsters leave much to be desired, people, including prospects, will accept them if they are neat.

No, don't bother to landscape the dumpster enclosure. Plantings will almost certainly be broken and they'll catch windblown papers. The best procedure is to police this area each day to make sure both the enclosure and dumpster are neat.

Lighting

Moving from the parking lot to the buildings, the prospect will probably notice the exterior lighting, especially if something is wrong with it. In city and suburban apartments, some lighting is used for safety, but a good deal of it is used for accent and beauty. Whatever the use, it's rare that lighting standards and fixtures receive any maintenance other than having the bulb or gas mantle changed when they burn out.

Typical lighting eyesores are parking lot standards that are dented, knocked askew, or broken off altogether. Light poles along sidewalks may have been set in loose earth or with a light concrete ballast and are now leaning over. Fixtures on buildings may be twisted. There is a good chance that the glass in many lighting fixtures will be dirty, broken, or missing. If any of these conditions apply to your property, the answer is obvious: fix them. If lights near parking lots are forever being knocked down by cars, install guard posts or move the light.

Lighting can serve a useful purpose if you locate it properly and take care of it. Landscape lighting, for example, with mushroom-type fixtures and spotlights around plantings and pools can give your property nighttime excitement. But you have to maintain it. To reduce breakage problems, consider using plastic panels and globes instead of glass. The plastic costs more initially but it lasts longer and cuts down on maintenance.

In parking lots, *10 to 15 lumens* is acceptable for residential properties. Your tenants may want the light to be brighter for safety reasons, but don't increase it to a shopping center level of 30 to 40 lumens. The higher level will make your lot look commercial and the safety factor won't be any greater. Also avoid arc, quartz, or mercury vapor lighting. They, too, create a commercial look, they're annoying to people who live nearby, and quartz especially is expensive and short-lived.

Fluorescent lighting is seldom used outside, but is often used in laundry rooms. At night, this light when viewed through windows from the outside can give your property a cold look. Consider ways to shade or screen this light.

Many exterior lighting fixtures are controlled automatically by time clocks or photoelectric cells. The photo cells are generally better because they will respond to darkness regardless of the time of day or season of the year, provided they are shielded from the lights they turn on and off. Time clocks have to be adjusted periodically as the days grow longer and then shorter. If the prospect visits your property and finds the outdoor lights on during the day, he'll think you're not very observant in addition to wasting money. If he visits during the night and the time clocks haven't turned the lights on, he'll think you're skimping. Either way he gets a bad impression of your operational abilities and the property, so make sure the lights are turned on and off at the proper times.

Animal Litter

Good groundskeeping demands that there be no animal droppings on the property. Even if the prospect is a pet-owner himself, the sight of dog droppings is usually offensive to him. And if the prospect is not a pet-owner, the sight is downright disgusting. Your grounds crew should regularly police the property and *remove any droppings*.

Patios and Balconies

The prospect's eye will wander over the buildings as he walks toward your office. Put yourself in his place and what do you see? Are the patios and balconies neat, clean, and orderly? Or do you see a rusty barbecue on one balcony, a pile of firewood on another, bicycles and wagons on a third, and snow tires on a fourth? In one development, a tenant had a soda pop machine on his balcony while another had a barber chair on his.

Patios and balconies should not be used for anything besides patio furniture, flower boxes and plants; *they should not be used for storage* under any circumstances. You have to establish the rule and enforce it. Otherwise the appearance of cluttered balconies is likely to offend the visual sense of many prospects.

Some care must be taken with plants on balconies. They must be well anchored. Flower pots and flower boxes on railings can be blown off or shaken loose with disastrous results.

Fencing

If a fence is to do its job of keeping out intruders, it has to look the part; this usually makes it unsuitable as a decorative element. Split-rail fences, which some managers like because they look natural, seldom are good barriers. *Fencing, in short, is an undesirable element* and should be avoided whenever possible. Especially avoid the "decorative" chain-type pathway fencing that takes away more in good looks than it contributes.

In some cases you must have fencing. Most localities require that swimming pools be enclosed by a fence. When fencing is required, choose a fence that will do its job but one that lacks the concentration-camp look, such as the chain-link-type fence. Then landscape it so it becomes as unobtrusive as possible.

Snow and Ice

Your prospect shouldn't have to carefully pick his way to your office through a snow-covered or ice-laden path. If your property is in a cold weather region, make sure the walks and stoops are *free of snow and ice* as quickly as possible. This should be a routine job for your grounds crew.

Interior

The prospect is about to enter your building. But before he goes in, let's stop and think about why some properties are allowed to run down even when the owner and manager think they are doing a good job of keeping it up. Perhaps it's because they don't realize that a building, like everything else, is a *consumable product with a limited life*. A candy bar may be consumed in three minutes; an automobile may be used up in seven years. Compared to these, the life of a building is long, 40 or 50 years perhaps. Many managers are lulled into thinking the building never wears out because the deterioration or consumption occurs slowly. But a building begins to go downhill from the day the building is completed. That is why maintenance to counteract the effects of deterioration is so important in product preparation.

Another point that many owners and managers may overlook is that the consumption of real estate occurs faster in the *places of greatest use*. These are the public areas: entrances, stairs, halls, corridors, and elevators. The areas of greatest use are also the places of greatest abuse and therefore the areas where wear and tear are likely to be most visible to your prospects.

Entrance Door

The door on the main entrance to your building is used more than any other door in the entire structure. If the building has 50 units, the entrance door will get 50 times the use and require 50 times the repairs of any other door. Therefore, this door should be selected for the heavy-duty service it will be required to give. The hardware should be heavy-duty as well to withstand the constant locking and unlocking it will receive. If the door and hardware aren't heavy-duty, your maintenance job will be greater.

Be sure the door is hung so it opens into the wind. Otherwise a sudden gust can yank the door from a person's hand, and can lead to injury to the person and damage to the door. If the door isn't hung properly, see if you can have it re-hung on the reverse side, or else build a wind screen to shield it. Make sure, too, the door has a *door closer* in working order. These devices go out of adjustment frequently and must be well maintained.

Vestibule

In some apartment buildings, after entering through the outer door you must also pass through a second door, which is locked, before you get into the apartment hall or corridor. A vestibule has certain advantages: it provides *better security* and also enables you to put in a *hard-wearing floor surface* in the vestibule itself. Without a vestibule, the hall carpeting quickly becomes soiled. But a vestibule has to be tended daily to maintain its good appearance. Then, too, the vestibule door *lock is subject to abuse* because tenants tend to open it by pulling on their keys rather than on the knob; in a short time this wears out the lock mechanism. If you have a vestibule, consider putting the keyway in the jamb rather than in the door itself.

Door Glass and Metal

Glass panes in the entrance door and vestibule door are subject to constant handling, fingerprints, smudges, water streaks, dirt, and breakage. Prospects will notice whatever is wrong with the glass, which is why it must be clean at all times. Don't overlook the *transom glass*, too; just because it's overhead doesn't mean it won't be seen. You may overlook it, but the prospect won't.

To reduce breakage, some managers have switched to plexiglass or other sheet plastic. This is expensive and looks good at first. But it is easily scratched and in time it becomes so badly marred that it never looks clean. Avoid it.

Most entrance doors are made of anodized aluminum or painted steel that retain their good appearance with minimum care. But some doors have brass or bronze fittings, hardware, and kickplates that become tarnished. These should be polished first and then coated with lacquer to keep them looking bright for as long as possible. Weathered metal takes away from the sharp appearance of your property.

Lights

Pay attention to lights around the main entrance and in the main hall. These burn out quickly because they are exposed to extremes of temperature as the outer door opens and closes. They also are the last resting place of dead insects. Clean these lights frequently.

Mailboxes

Your prospect will almost certainly encounter the mailboxes near the entrance door. These boxes should be *uniformly labeled* by the management; boxes indiscriminately identified with business cards, plastic tape, hand printing, and stickers only detract from the building's appearance. The exterior of the boxes should be kept neat and clean.

One problem you'll discover with mailboxes is that *handbills* aren't allowed to be placed in them. In fact, only items sent through the mail can legally be put in mailboxes. That means that handbills will be dumped on the floor beneath the boxes. Handbills are a fact of life. You can't get rid of them, but you can provide a special box, rack, or shelf where the handbills can be placed.

It's a good idea, too, to have a small *waste receptacle* near the mailboxes, and a *shelf* below the boxes. Tenants will find the shelf handy when sorting their mail and the waste receptacle is a convenient place to toss junk mail; otherwise this mail may wind up on the entrance or hall floor. Daily pickup of this material should be a part of the maintenance schedule.

Directory

If your building has a directory—and generally these are found only in the larger buildings—be sure the directory is up-to-date and has the names arranged *alphabetically* for the convenience of visitors.

Furnishings, Plants, Artwork

Not too many suburban garden complexes have lobbies spacious enough to accommodate furnishings, but you'll often find such lobbies in large buildings. The furnishings should be *built in* or *permanently fastened* to prevent theft. To discourage lounging, the furnishings should be backless and scattered, not grouped for conversation. Fabrics should be chosen for high wearability and easy maintenance. And, of course, the furnishings should be spotless. Whether you have furnishings or not, you should have wall-mounted or weighted *cigarette receptacles* in the main entrance hall and also at elevator doors.

Plantings can add decorative interest, but use them only if they can be *secured.* The same applies to paintings and sculpture. If you want to have art in your lobby, consider having it *painted on the wall* in the form of a mural or graphic. Otherwise you'll have theft problems.

Doormat

To keep your entrance lobby and halls clean, you may want to have a doormat near the door where visitors can wipe their feet dry in bad weather. The ideal mat is a *cocoa mat in a floor inset* in the outer lobby. The inset keeps the mat from being moved about and preventing the door from opening; it also eliminates a tripping hazard. The cocoa mat itself absorbs moisture and cleans shoes better than a rubber mat. If you use a rubber mat, the inset should have a drain, or else it will collect standing water.

Corridors and Stairs

Now that the prospect is in the hallway, he'll notice the carpeting which is subject to heavy wear. You should start by installing a *high-quality carpet* which has a closed-loop tight weave for maximum life. Since it will be difficult to match the carpet when replacement time comes, select a color that either *complements* or *contrasts* with carpeting elsewhere in the building. That way you can make a replacement without an exact match.

Some managers get extra economy by moving carpet from less-traveled areas of the building—say the second floor—down to the entrance lobby, rather than replacing the entrance lobby carpeting with new goods. You may devise your own method, but the point is to keep all the carpet looking good.

Daily attention is essential for good carpet care. This requires that you set up a schedule, train your people, and give them the right equipment. Remember, you may be unaware how the carpeting looks because you see it every day and it's hard to detect the way the carpet is wearing. But the prospect sees it through fresh eyes, and if it looks worn, shabby, or dirty, he'll downgrade your property accordingly.

Stair carpeting also gets heavy wear, especially where the carpet passes over the nose of the tread. Usually the carpet installer leaves enough material at the end of the stairs so that you can lift the stair carpet and shift it the length of a tread. This moves the worn portion into the crevice of the stairs where it can't be easily seen and doubles the life of the carpeting. Stair pads, which fit over the nose of the tread underneath the carpeting, are another way to extend carpeting life. They're expensive and you can get most of the same benefit by simply doubling the regular carpet padding.

Your building may have a breezeway or external stair system which you may be tempted to cover with *indoor-outdoor* carpeting. This material looks good when first installed, but it quickly loses its good looks because of weathering, stains, and spills. It's better to leave the outdoor stairs and landings in their natural condition.

Before you leave the stairs, check the *handrails* to make sure they fit tightly and are not loose. Examine the *balustrades;* they are prone to collect dust. If the stairways are the open kind, with no riser between the treads, check the *floor* beneath the stairway for litter that falls between the open spaces.

Elevator Cabs

Elevators are where you'll find more wear and tear than any other area of the building because of the concentrated use the elevator gets. The figure "1" on the first floor button may be worn off. People have a tendency to steal the inspection certificate, to stick gum wrappers in openings in the walls and ceiling, and to write on the walls. The carpet gets intensive wear. Because of the flue effect in the elevator shaft, there will be a layer of dust on the frames on each floor and on the edges of the elevator doors. One or more of these deficiencies will be spotted by your prospect.

Arrange for proper maintenance of elevators. *Daily cleaning* is a must. Worn elevator *carpets should be quickly replaced.* Whoever cleans the elevator should be instructed to *look for papers* stuck in the most unlikely places. *Graffiti should be removed instantly;* if you leave it, it will attract other writing as one clever person tries to top another. The people you want—people of substance—will be repelled by graffiti and will avoid your building. If the graffiti is carved into a wall panel, then replace the panel—this is easier to do than attracting a prospect or replacing a tenant.

Many managers will protect elevator cabs by hanging *move-in pads* when tenants are moving furniture in and out. Be sure these pads are removed when the moving is over. If you leave them, two things will happen: (1) The pads will destroy the residential character of the elevator, and (2) they'll be stolen.

Corridor Lighting

In many corridors you'll find uneven lighting because different sizes of bulbs have been used or because bulbs have burned out. You may also find that the globes are dirty and that there are dirt marks on the ceiling caused by faulty venting of the fixture. All these take away from the good appearance of the corridor.

You can avoid this by following a system of *replacing all bulbs periodically.* First, determine what size bulbs are needed for your fixtures. Second, learn what the rated life for bulbs is. Third, just before the bulbs are scheduled to burn out, have your crew replace all of them. By doing this, your crew can gear up by having the right-size bulbs and the right cleaning equipment on hand. If they replace bulbs piecemeal, they're apt to put in whatever size bulb is handy, leading to an uneven appearance.

You can stretch the period between bulb replacement by using 130-volt instead of 120-volt bulbs. The 130-volt bulb has a filament that lasts almost twice as long as a 120-volt bulb. However, the 130-volt bulb gives only about 60 percent as much light as the 120-volt, so you have to order a higher-wattage bulb to get the equivalent amount of light. For example, you need a 100-watt 130-volt bulb to equal the light of a 60-watt 120-volt bulb. The price of the 130-volt bulb is only slightly more than that of the 120-volt. The major cost is in the labor to install the bulb.

Cleaning the fixture, by the way, is an important part of maintenance. Fixtures tend to collect insects, dirt, and burned-off pieces of labeling. Globes should be cleaned every time the bulbs are replaced.

Some fixtures are poorly ventilated; this causes the bulb to burn out faster. Other fixtures have vent holes that are poorly placed and cause hot air currents to spill out on the ceiling, leaving dirt marks. You may want to try drilling extra holes in the fixture to relieve this condition.

Odor

The sense of smell is the most easily fatigued of all the senses. In other words, it's very easy for the manager to get used to unpleasant smells and before long he doesn't notice them. But the prospect who is hit by a bad smell notices it immediately, and he's apt to remember it.

Mildew is one of the most common odors, especially in humid areas. *Cooking odors* are also common, especially in buildings where kitchens back up to the corridor wall. The odor from backed-up *sewers* is another annoyance. Mildew and sewer odors are especially common in cheaply built garden apartments with poor sewer systems and leaky construction.

Most corridor odors can be dealt with by opening the exterior doors periodically so the corridor can air out. If necessary, turn on a window fan in the doorway to speed up the exhaust. If bad odors are a chronic problem, consider putting a ventilation system in the corridor. Don't use deodorants; they add an odor of their own which is a sure sign to the prospect that you're covering up.

The best course is to *correct the source* of the odor if you can. Badly designed sewer systems should be fixed. Seepage around windows, doors, eaves, and overhangs should be eliminated so that wood components will not mildew.

The odors caused by fire and dead bodies need special treatment. Local exterminators usually can apply a foam that will absorb the odor in a few days. The smell caused by water-soaked carpet padding can be corrected only by removing and replacing the padding.

Exit Signs

Most localities require corridor exit signs in apartment buildings. Some of these signs must be lighted. Unfortunately, exit signs are much in demand for decorating, so they have a habit of disappearing from halls and doorways. You then have a problem of ordering a replacement which may be difficult to do because of varying sizes. Your best strategy is to *order a quantity of replacement signs* at the same time and keep them on hand, because you'll certainly need them.

You may find it makes sense to replace glass panels with ones made of plastic. If you do, you can make your own plastic panel by cutting sheet stock and then spraying on red paint through a stencil.

Fire Extinguishers and Hoses

Another thing your prospect may notice as he proceeds through the halls are signs of missing fire extinguishers. In the days when soda acid or water extinguishers were common, they were seldom stolen because of their bulky size. But the modern kind of compact pressurized ABC-type extinguisher is adaptable to use in the home, car, and boat, which is why they vanish so quickly from apartment corridors.

Some local ordinances will permit you to *put the extinguisher in a cabinet* behind a glass door; this discourages theft. Extinguishers that are simply hung on the wall will most likely be stolen and should be replaced. If you put the extinguisher in a wall recess, make sure the recess is kept free of litter which it's almost certain to attract.

Fire hoses in corridors should be checked to make sure they are neatly hung. Like extinguishers, the brass nozzles on hoses are often stolen. It's up to the manager to replace them quickly.

Numbering

You may wonder why numbering is included in a chapter on product preparation. The reason is that people need a sense of *personal identification and status* which the right number can provide and the wrong number deny. The numbers your prospect sees on your building and your apartment doors can say a lot to your prospect's ego.

You should identify your buildings either by their addresses or a special name, never by a project number. Apartments should be identified by numbers that refer to their floor. Consider the difference between a person who says he lives in Apartment 302 at 415 Park Terrace and the one who says he lives in Apartment 14 in Building 10. The first person is proud to give you a residential address, while the second may feel he's giving you a cell block number.

In general, the first number of an apartment identification should refer to the floor, and the second to the specific apartment, with numbering starting at the northernmost or easternmost apartment and going clockwise. Apartment 302 refers to the second apartment on the third floor; Apartment 2112 means the twelfth apartment on the twenty-first floor.

Numbers should be applied uniformly to apartment doors, or they can be part of the door knocker. Check the numerals to make sure none are missing. Don't let tenants put anything else on the corridor door. Stickers, hand-lettered names and numbers, and signs will detract from corridor appearance.

Foul-Weather Gear

In many areas it's common to see corridors lined with galoshes, umbrellas, boxes, and doormats outside individual apartment doors. These contribute nothing to the neat appearance of the halls. One thing you can do is provide uniform doormats for all apartments. Another is to let your tenants know that all foul-weather articles must be kept *inside the apartment*, not out in the hall. If tenants say they don't want these wet articles inside, let them know that putting them in halls is a violation of fire laws. If a tenant persists, remove the offending articles to your business office and have the tenant claim them there.

The Apartment

If you have skipped over everything else in getting your product ready, the one place you shouldn't neglect at any cost is the apartment that you're going to show the prospect. It should be absolutely perfect. This is the rule: *When there's no further reason to enter the apartment to make any improvement, then and only then should you show the apartment.* More prospects are lost by violation of this rule than any other.

Picture what often happens. The manager shows the prospect into the apartment and immediately steps on a stack of literature that has been slipped under the door over the past few days or weeks. The apartment itself is musty, dirty, and either overheated or chillingly cold. The carpet is stained, and the walls are full of holes and marked with dirt where pictures have hung. In the kitchen, the refrigerator has food stains, the stove is encrusted with baked-on debris, the sink is rust-streaked, and there's insect poison in the cabinets. The bathroom has a tub with dead spiders, a toilet bowl that's dried up, and a medicine cabinet with rusty shelves and a de-silvered mirror. To cap it all off, bulbs are missing from the light fixtures or the power is off, and the manager has to show the apartment by flashlight.

This may sound like an exaggeration, but a good many of these faults are present in most vacant apartments shown. The standard response of the manager is to say: "We'll fix it before you move in."

This approach seldom works. Prospects judge by first impressions. You can never get the maximum rent for an inferior product. If you ask for and get the rent you want for a product that isn't in the best shape, then you automatically know that you could have received more if the product was in perfect condition. *The prospect responds on the strength of what he sees, not on what you promise.*

If you don't accept this argument, then ask yourself: What kind of person is this prospect if he'll move into an apartment that's not first-rate? Prospects who are moving in are generally "moving up" in status. If a filthy apartment means "moving up," just how bad is the place the prospect is moving from? Again, do you want this kind of person in your building?

In short, if you don't make improvements before showing the apartment, you'll have trouble getting the highest possible rent and attracting the best-quality tenant. Instead, you may be compelled to lower the rent and accept a lower-grade tenant.

It's vitally important that you make your apartment as perfect as possible before you show it. If you do that, you'll get a better rent, attract better tenants, and your property will be competitively ahead of almost everyone else.

In addition, the closer to perfect your apartment is, the more confident you'll be in setting and asking the maximum rent (see Chapter 4 on setting rents).

Let's state the rule again: *When there's no further reason to enter the apartment to make any improvement, then and only then should you show it.*

Ready-Ready Checklist

There's no need to get all of your vacant apartments ready at the same time for showing. Instead, have a meaningful assortment of every type and kind of apartment in what you can call a "ready-ready" condition. How many you need to keep in this condition depends on the pace of the market at any particular time. Under normal conditions, three or four of each type will provide an adequate inventory.

For your guidance, here is a list of the things that should be checked to make sure an apartment is "ready-ready":

1. All walls and ceilings should be freshly painted. Don't overlook closets or the shelving.
2. Carpeting should be freshly shampooed. If there are any stains or burns, these should be removed or else the carpeting replaced.
3. All windows should be washed both inside and out.
4. Window sills, the tops of double-hung sashes, ledges, and shelves should be wiped clean of dirt and dead insects.
5. Light fixtures and switches should be in working order. Fixtures should be clean—no dead flies inside globes.
6. The apartment temperature should be set at the level appropriate to the season. On moderate days open the windows to help air out the apartment.
7. The kitchen should be immaculate with all appliances clean and working. Make sure the refrigerator has the proper number of ice cube trays and that the cabinets are clean inside and out. Pay particular attention to the undersink

cabinet. There should be no stains in the sink and no
dripping faucets.

8. Bathrooms should be spotless. Watch for dripping faucets,
stains or worn-out enamel in the tub, and dirty toilets. The
medicine cabinet should be freshly painted and empty, with
no leftover razor blades. Tub and tile grout should be tight
and without stains.

9. Watch out for the typical apartment starter kit: that's a few
bent hangers in the closet, some half-used soap bars in the
bathroom, and a few sheets of toilet paper left on the roll.
Get rid of these.

To aid in getting the apartment ready, we recommend that you
make up a *checklist* of all the items to be inspected in getting an
apartment in "ready-ready" condition. This checklist can be on a
card that the manager himself *personally signs* and posts in the
apartment in a prominent position, testifying to its perfect condition. The card shouldn't be dated; you wouldn't want the prospect in
February to see a card dated last November. This would indicate
you're having trouble renting the apartment.

The supervisor should check to see that *only the manager's
signature* is on the "ready-ready" inspection card, and that the card
is never placed in an apartment that isn't ready. This operation is
critical because it forces the manager to inspect his apartment and
put his reputation—and his job—on the line.

Daily inspection of "ready-ready" apartments is essential to
make sure they stay that way until they are rented. We strongly
urge that every day, before the start of business, the on-site
manager—never the rental agent—personally inspect the apartments. This procedure accomplishes several things:

1. Because the manager must visit the apartment, he must
first obtain the key. This ensures the key is available. It's
surprising how often the key is missing when the manager
or rental agent wants to show the apartment to a prospect.

2. This procedure eliminates the possibility of showing an
apartment that isn't ready.

3. The inspection will reveal deficiencies that may have happened since the last inspection, such as leaflets slipped under
the door, a dead insect falling into the sink, or a window leak
that has stained the carpet.

4. The manager is then reminded to turn on the lights in the

apartment and adjust the heating or air-conditioning.

5. Finally, this procedure compels the manager to walk the property in the course of which he may discover other things that need attention.

In summary, getting the apartment ready, inspecting it to make sure it's perfect, and inspecting it daily to make sure it remains perfect are the three steps to preparing and maintaining the apartment for showing.

Drapes

Drapes and carpeting merit special consideration as part of product preparation.

Drapes are almost always included in suburban garden apartments as a marketing aid. Some city apartments provide them, too. Uniform drapes can give the building a better appearance from the outside. Drapes can also help the tenant who is short on his furnishings budget.

However, drapes can present a problem. Generally, the quality of drapes that come with the apartment is not of the highest. They don't hang well after awhile. The higher-quality tenant knows this and would rather have his own drapes. He may resist renting an apartment because drapes are included, an example of marketing in reverse.

Meanwhile, the transient-type tenant who likes the drapes neglects to care for them, because they're not his. He leaves the windows open, exposing the drapes to dirt, soot, and rain. As a result, the drapes need cleaning all too often and certainly every time there's a tenant change in the apartment. Because of their poor quality to begin with, drapes seldom last more than four years.

Nor do drapes accomplish the uniform outside look that many managers want. Even with drapes, some tenants will put tinfoil against the windows to reduce heat in the summer, and others will put up newspapers, especially on bedroom windows, to make the room darker. In many garden complexes, the drapes can't be seen from outside because balconies interfere with the view. So the effect on appearance is nil.

All of this suggests that if you can *avoid including drapes* as part of the apartment, do so. You'll eliminate high initial cost as well as high maintenance costs. In addition, the tenant who will install his own drapes is generally a more desirable tenant than the one who likes the drapes included. Local market conditions may dictate that you include drapes, but if not, avoid them.

One thing you should provide is *traverse rods* at the windows. If you don't, people will put up their own and take them down when they leave. The constant installation and removal of rods by tenants will damage the wall. You can avoid this by having your own rods installed. Use the *double rods* that provide for liners.

As for *liners* themselves, they're desirable for a uniform outside appearance, but there is no realistic way you can enforce their installation and use. At the time you take the prospect's lease application, you can point out the requirement for liners. But if the tenant later refuses to purchase a liner, or refuses to draw it in front of the drapes, there's not much you can do about it. Chances of evicting the tenant on these grounds are very weak.

Floor Covering

In most suburban complexes, wall-to-wall *carpeting* is standard in all living areas (living room, dining room, bedrooms, and halls). Carpeting gives the apartment a strong marketing advantage. Except for tenants of luxury high-rises, few people want to spend money to buy apartment carpeting of their own, so if the carpeting is included, they can move in at less cost than otherwise.

Carpeting also is a fine sound absorber and buffer, but only if it's wall-to-wall. Some apartment managers don't provide carpet but require that tenants put their own carpeting on at least 80 percent of the floor. This is hard to police. It also falls short in reducing sound transmission. Furniture legs resting on the uncarpeted surfaces, usually around the edges of the room, continue to transmit sound caused by vibration and by the furniture's moving back and forth.

Carpet *styles* change with fashion trends, so what is "in" today may not be suitable tomorrow. Generally, shag carpeting looks better than it really is and is easy to repair, but it doesn't wear well. Don't make the mistake of buying high-priced long-wearing carpeting for apartments. It will show wear patterns regardless, and is just as apt to suffer from stains, burns, and spills as a lower-grade carpet. A reasonable life for carpet is five years and rarely more than six.

The best carpets are neutral in *color* and salt-and-pepper, or tweed in *patterns*. Neutral tones can fit into any decorating scheme. Salt-and-pepper and tweed patterns conceal wear patterns, soil, and burns more easily than solid colors. Avoid yellows and celery tones. These look good at first but they show wear and dirt quickly. Also avoid bright reds, blues, and oranges, because they are difficult to decorate around.

Carpeting must be *shampooed* with every tenant change or no later than every two years. If the carpet is badly stained but not worn, consider having it dyed; this usually costs one-third the price of replacing the carpet. Call in a carpet expert before you decide. Be aware that if you have the carpet dyed, the dye may get onto the baseboard woodwork, necessitating a repainting job. The dyeing should be done in the apartment with the carpet in place. If the carpet has to be taken to the plant, it will undoubtedly shrink. The costs of picking it up and re-laying it will add to the total cost, reducing the difference between dyeing and replacing the carpet altogether.

Tile and *hardwood* are other floor coverings which are less common than carpeting. Tile is a good alternate in buildings with concrete floors. Some buildings provide asphalt or vinyl asbestos tile as standard; others may have resilient sheet goods installed.

Hardwood flooring is common in many older buildings and may be installed in some newer wood-frame buildings. But good oak flooring is expensive to buy and install. It also shows scratches and stains easily and needs to be sanded and varnished to remove these mars. Sanding takes away $1/16$-inch of floor surface each time. After three sandings, the flooring nails may be exposed. At this point, no more sandings are possible. Based on the extra wear and tear a hardwood apartment floor gets, it would have to be sanded every three to five years which means the normal lifetime would be only nine to fifteen years. For these reasons, carpet is a better choice.

Amenities

Your product preparation should also cover the amenities of the building, those features the prospect will use if he becomes a tenant. If these areas are properly maintained, they are assets that are well worth showing. If maintenance is disregarded, you will not be inclined to show them and thus lose the chance to impress the prospect. In addition, poorly maintained amenities will discourage existing tenants and you may lose them.

Laundry Room

This room will get a lot of use, and with use comes abuse. It must be checked and cleaned regularly, with particular attention paid to floors, appliances, ventilators, dryer vents, lighting, and waste receptacles. (See p. 47 for a description of what equipment and facilities you should provide in the laundry room.)

Storage Locker

At least twice a week one of your maintenance crew should inspect the storage locker room to check for leaks, theft, debris, and the possibility that the room has become a gathering place for youngsters. Lockers should be clearly identified and secured. Light bulbs should be checked to make sure they're not burned out. If possible, the lights should be controlled by a handy switch near the door so you don't have to grope in the dark while the prospect waits in the hall.

If your storage room seems to accumulate junk endlessly, here's an idea you can try on your residents. Have them stage a "flea-market" once or twice a year to sell unwanted items. This gets rid of many still usable items, and earns some money for the tenants at the same time.

Garbage Chute Room

Don't count on the prospect ignoring the garbage chute room which is a common feature of larger buildings. Too often tenants will pile garbage behind the door or leave it stuffed in the mouth of the chute. The chute door and wall beneath may be streaked with accumulated garbage drippings. The only way you can deal with this situation is to have your maintenance crew *police the area regularly.*

If your locality or your building requires that cans and bottles be separated and not put into the chute, then you need a container for this in the chute room. The container should be kept clean at all times.

Recreation Features

Whatever you have—be it a simple hospitality room or a swimming pool and clubhouse complex—your recreational amenities must receive the same kind of intensive maintenance that you give to the apartments you show. If your facilities are regularly used, maintenance becomes all the more important so you can take care of the spills, stains, cigarette burns, rips, and scratches that accompany heavy use.

On a daily basis, your maintenance crew must make certain that furniture is arranged, equipment such as pool cues neatly put away, ash trays emptied, floors vacuumed or swept, and furniture dusted. If there was a big party in the hospitality room the night before, make sure that there's no sign of it when the prospect comes through.

Around outdoor facilities such as tennis courts and playgrounds, be sure that all equipment is present and in good order; don't tolerate frayed or missing nets, hoops, chains, etc.

Pay particular attention to the swimming pool and the deck. Outdoor furniture should be in first-class order and neatly arranged during the season or stacked out of sight at other times. The pool water should be clean. If the pool is closed for repairs, display a professionally lettered sign that says as much, including the estimated time of reopening. In the off-season, your best procedure is to cover the pool to prevent debris from accumulating.

Real vs. Mental Walk

Now that you've mentally "walked your property" as we have described, how do you think your property shapes up? If a prospect walked into your office this minute, could you show him around with full assurance that everything is in "ready-ready" condition? Or would you have to start making excuses followed by promises to fix things up after the prospect moves in?

Don't guess. Instead of relying on a mental image of what your property looks like, go out and examine it right now, starting with the front entrance, moving through the parking lot, into the building, through the vacant apartments, through the laundry and storage locker rooms, and winding up with the recreational amenities. Chances are you'll find enough to do to keep your maintenance people busy for quite awhile. Get them started on it immediately.

Maintenance—Crisis or Planned?

So far we've discussed the challenge of getting your property ready. Now let's turn our attention to keeping it that way. Most properties suffer physically and economically from crisis maintenance, the kind that waits until something goes wrong before anything is done about it. The manager delays until a condition is really bad or until a piece of equipment breaks down before he takes action. For example, a light post begins to lean. It will never right itself and will very likely lean further until it topples over all together. At this point a major repair or replacement job is in order, whereas if the pole had been straightened earlier, the cost would be less. Or perhaps the manager ignores maintaining a piece of equipment whose life is predictable. Tending to it at scheduled intervals involves a small cost; replacing a broken or burned-out piece of machinery almost always involves a major expense.

Many breakdowns occur because the manager fails to maintain equipment according to the *manufacturer's instructions.* Fans and motors may need regular oiling. Pumps may require periodic disassembly and cleaning. Perhaps the manager doesn't know what's required because the instruction booklets have long been lost. If this is your predicament, you can often correct it by writing to the manufacturer for a replacement booklet and setting up a permanent library of these manuals. Most manufacturers will gladly send you extra booklets because they're anxious for their equipment to operate properly. Some manufacturers will even offer to train your people in proper maintenance procedures.

In the paragraphs that follow, we are going to outline a program of planned maintenance that you can use to avoid a continuing stream of crises and to keep your property looking as sharp as possible. You'll discover that planned maintenance can be done with fewer people and will inevitably lead to lower operating and maintenance costs. Again the payoff is in more net operating income for your owner.

Inventory Mechanical Equipment

Every piece of mechanical building equipment should be inventoried, identified, and located. The manager should know first-hand what equipment he has on the property and where it is. The way to get this information is to go through each building looking for the equipment and making a list as you go along. Your custodial engineer may accompany you. In some larger structures, you may want to hire a mechanical engineer, preferably the one who was involved in the design of the building, to go along with you. But you personally must know where the equipment is.

The equipment you're seeking includes fans, motors, pumps, door checks, ventilators—anything that moves and needs maintenance. As you go through the building, make a list of what you discover, identifying items by their *general name, the manufacturer,* and the *model number.* Generally you'll find this information stamped, printed, or engraved right on the equipment. You may also discover that the maintenance instructions are on the equipment, too.

Back in your office, draw up a maintenance *schedule* that shows each piece of equipment and when it needs attention. This is where you'll need the manufacturer's instruction manuals. When you have all of this down, you can determine who will do the maintenance work on each item: your own people, a factory representative, or a service contractor.

Now give each piece of equipment a *code number*, and put a large legible sticker or tag on each item that shows the code number clearly. You can then refer to the code number on a check-off list. The sticker or tag on the item should be large enough so maintenance workers can write down the date of last maintenance.

Your maintenance schedule should cover an entire year, and should be conveniently located so that you and your custodian can tell at a glance what has to be done and when. Following this calendar diligently, you can then take care of mechanical equipment at the proper time and avoid breakdowns that interrupt the orderly operation of your building and cost you extra money.

Guarantees

In setting up your maintenance program, find out what items are protected by guarantees. This may be indicated by labels on the equipment, in the manufacturer's instruction booklets, by separate guarantee certificates, and possibly on invoices. You'll generally find guarantees for the roof, heating and air-conditioning equipment, pumps, and apartment appliances.

You need the guarantees for two reasons. First, the guarantee may still provide service coverage for the item if it needs repair or replacement; there's no sense paying extra for this if the guarantee takes care of it. Second, many guarantees are valid only if service is performed by the manufacturer's people. If you tinker with the item yourself or have an unqualified serviceman do it, you may void the guarantee.

Inspect the Structure

While your building's mechanical equipment needs the frequent attention, you must also pay attention to many of the structural components of the property. Wear and tear on these items usually takes place so gradually that you hardly notice it, but it takes place nevertheless. At least twice a year you should have the following inspected:

- **Roof:** Leaks are apt to develop at points where the roof surface joins something else: stacks, chimneys, parapet walls, flashings. The roof inspection should be done by a skilled person who knows what he's doing, not by a casual laborer. Roof work is dangerous and an unskilled person may actually do damage by walking carelessly on the roof surface.
- **Windows**: Caulking around windows should be sound. Missing or loose caulking can lead to water leaks which are the greatest cause of apartment damage.
- **Brickwork and Siding**: Examine brickwork for any undue cracking or settlement, usually indicated by loose or missing mortar. This can usually be repaired by spot tuckpointing. If the problem persists, call in an expert to analyze what's needed. Wood and composition siding can develop problems at joints, allowing moisture to enter and damage the rest of the material and interior wall surfaces as well. Caulking is needed to prevent further deterioration.
- **Eaves**: Look for mildew, an indication of poor venting. Mildew means dampness is present which can lead to serious damage, and in the meantime it is unsightly and can cause annoying odors.
- **Slabs and Balconies**: As the building settles, these can shift position. Balconies can work loose. Cracks can develop in slabs, or the slabs may pull away from foundation walls. Pay particu-

lar attention to slabs beneath air-conditioners. If these slabs aren't level, the bearings in the air conditioners will wear unevenly, leading to an early breakdown.

- **Stairs and Railings**: Settlement can cause these to shift and lean. See that the railings are tight.
- **Paint**: South and west elevations get the most exposure and show the earliest paint deterioration. Many managers find they can reduce the paint bill by painting the north and east exposures half as frequently as the other two.
- **Gutters and Downspouts**: Joints can pull apart, seams split, and the channels themselves can be clogged. Often the concrete splash blocks at the bottom of downspouts are dislocated, permitting the water to collect around the foundation.
- **Screens**: Pay particular attention to patio screen doors which cover a large area and take a lot of abuse.
- **Paved Surfaces**, including walks, driveways, and parking lots: Look for settlement cracks, heaving, spalling (pitting and flaking of the surface), and chuckholes. Some may be fixed with minor repairs, others may need major work.
- **Sewer Clean-outs**: Know where the clean-outs are located. If you have problem lines, rod these out more frequently than others to avoid trouble later on.

Apartment Maintenance

There are many items in the apartment which should be on the maintenance schedule, too. For example:

- **Plumbing**: Periodically, without waiting for leaks to develop, arrange to have faucet washers and seats replaced. Inspect the ballcock and Douglas valve in each toilet tank. Have spare parts on hand to make quick replacements.

The quickest and best way to make plumbing repairs is before you have to, when you can select a time that's best for you and for your tenants. It's better to shut down an entire building for one day to replace all of the worn plumbing parts before they fail, than it is to shut down repeatedly for short intervals to take care of emergencies. Repairs never get any cheaper if you wait, but waiting runs the risk of even greater costs and wider damage later on.

- **Tub and Shower Caulking**: As the building settles, the caulking or grout between the tub or shower floor and the wall tile will work loose. Unless the caulking is replaced, water will eventually seep into the cracks and damage the walls. Replace caulking or grout as soon as you see cracks develop.

- **Fans**: Many apartments have ventilator fans in the kitchen and bathroom. Unless these are permanently lubricated, they may need periodic oiling.

- **Filters**: There is no excuse for not changing the filters in the heater or air ducts of the apartments. A dirty filter causes the furnace and air conditioner to work harder. This runs up the fuel bill unnecessarily. If the building is paying the bill, you're losing money. If the tenant is paying the bill, he's undoubtedly disgruntled because he's paying too much money.

- **Cannibalization**: For several reasons—emergencies, economy—a manager may take parts from one apartment to repair another. This is a bad practice. For one, it doubles the work; you must take out both a working part and the defective part. Sooner or later you will have to replace the working part which you cannibalized. For another, the tenant feels he's being shortchanged when he sees used parts being installed. Once cannibalization has begun, it's difficult to stop. The manager begins with taking a relay, then takes the toilet bowl, and before long it takes a major overhaul to restore the apartment. It's not unusual as cannibalization becomes evident that the apartment becomes a storeroom or that workmen begin to strip other parts and take them home. All of this reduces the chances of ever restoring the apartment back into the income stream.

  Cannibalization should not be permitted. You should have a stock of frequently needed parts on hand or know where they can be obtained quickly.

Performing scheduled preventive maintenance work in apartments requires that you enter the tenant's apartment. Notice should be provided to the tenant several days in advance of the work to be performed. If your crew makes repairs while the tenant is out, make sure they (1) post a sign on the door to alert the tenant if he returns while the crew is still inside and (2) leave a notice saying what maintenance work was done. This will keep the tenant from becoming upset if the crew has left anything behind (which they shouldn't).

Painting

The subject of painting deserves some discussion because it's something the manager will deal with constantly. Every vacant apartment will need painting before it's put on the market. In addition, occupied apartments will need redecorating as determined by your policy or the lease renewal terms.

It's generally best to use *off-white colors;* these are easy to integrate into any decorating scheme the tenant may choose. Select a basic color and stick to it. Buy that color in bulk for economy's sake and to reduce pilferage. These days manufacturers can control the paint shade exactly so it's easy to match one lot against another. This means that in some cases you don't have to paint an entire room just because one wall is bad; you simply paint the wall that needs it and the blend is perfect.

Whether you use your own staff to do the painting or hire an outsider, you should establish a *painting norm* for each apartment through experience. This will let you know how much paint and how much time is required.

Here are a number of suggestions to help you get the best possible painting job:

- The manager rather than the painter should *purchase the paint.* That way you can control the color and the quality of the paint.
- Latex paint is almost universally used today. It wears as well as other paints, is easier to clean up, and doesn't produce odors which can be most annoying to other tenants in the building.
- Don't spray paint; use rollers or brushes only. Spray paint is messy and you run the risk of overspraying and damaging apartment components.
- Have your painters *use drop cloths* and make them responsible for all *spillage.* Painters should also be responsible for unclogging drains if they clean their brushes and rollers in the apartment sink or tub.
- *Use semi-gloss paint* in kitchens and bathrooms and on painted doors and woodwork. Semi-gloss is more resistant than flat paint to water, dirt, and stains. It's easier to clean and wears longer.
- *Don't paint any baked enamel surface* in the apartment, including grilles, ventilators, or convectors. These surfaces attract dirt and once painted they can't be washed as easily. Leave them the way they are.

- *Don't paint acoustical ceilings.* These surfaces not only soak up vast quantities of paint, but in addition, they lose their acoustical properties once painted. If the ceiling is stained, it's better to re-apply the acoustical coating than it is to paint it.
- Your painter should not paint any *electrical outlets*, telephone jacks, switch plates, master antenna outlets, window and door hardware, tile, Formica surfaces, or plumbing fixtures. Insist that he *remove switch and outlet plates* and *window* and *door hardware* before painting, then replace these afterwards.
- Natural-finish doors, windows, cabinets, and other woodwork should be *oiled* or *varnished*, not painted. Note that you will not need to varnish as often as you paint.
- Remember to *paint all closet walls*, shelving, the inside of bathroom vanities and the bottom of the medicine cabinet. These areas are easy to skip but the prospect will surely notice them.

Exterminating

Insects and other vermin are distasteful to prospects and tenants alike. Roaches and rodents are among the most common invaders. Roaches are rarely in the building to begin with but generally enter in grocery bags and boxes. Once in, they thrive where they find darkness, dampness, and food. Rodents, too, need food to survive and prefer darkness. If these pests are a major problem, suspect an unclean situation and take steps to correct it.

When you exterminate, *do the whole building*, not just one apartment. Otherwise you'll simply drive the pests from one apartment to the others.

Unless local laws require that you use a licensed exterminator, you can train your own staff to do the work.

Grounds Maintenance

Maintenance of your grounds, particularly the landscaping, depends largely on what region of the country you're in, the climate and season of the year, and the type of landscaping you have. Obviously you need a regular schedule for *fertilizing, weeding, spraying*, and *disease control.*

Your county extension agent is a good place to start. In many states either he or the state agricultural service will analyze soil samples you send in and tell you what you need. You can also work with a local landscape contractor to map out a program.

Seasonal Maintenance

Snow and ice removal are the major seasonal maintenance problems in many areas of the country. You need to determine who is going to do the work—your own crew or an outside service—and where to stack the shoveled and plowed snow.

Most apartment complexes aren't large enough to justify the cost of a regular snowplow. Trying to do the job with plows mounted on smaller vehicles leads to early transmission burn-outs. You're better off contracting for plowing service and having your own people take care of the walks and stoops.

Be careful in your use of *snow-melting chemicals.* Rock salt is the cheapest and most commonly used, but it can do a lot of damage to pavements and plant materials. Rock salt won't work at all if the temperature is too low. If tracked inside, it can also damage carpeting.

Snow-melting pellets cost more than rock salt but do less damage and work at all temperatures. But these pellets can't be stored for long periods or they lose their effectiveness. So if you use pellets, buy only what you can use up in a short time.

Shoveling is better than using snow-melting chemicals. For traction, ice can be handled with sand, salt, or chemical melters.

Standard vs. Custom Checklists

Many of the foregoing points are contained in standard maintenance checklists available from the Institute of Real Estate Management, your apartment association, or your local real estate board. These checklists are good guides, but since every building is unique, we recommend that you *develop your own checklist* that has everything you need to know about your property.

There are only two answers possible on an inspection and maintenance checklist: O.K. and Not O.K. If an item is "O.K.," then it's in perfect condition and needs no further explanation. If it's "NOT O.K.," then an explanation is called for. So leave room on your checklist for a narrative report. Whoever performs the inspection—and this should be the manager in most cases—should write down whatever is wrong. Don't use terms such as "Good," "Fair," or "Poor." These tell you nothing. The narrative explanation will tell you what needs to be done.

Deferred Maintenance

If you set up your program carefully, most of your maintenance will be routine. Emergency maintenance will be at a minimum. There is a third category: deferred maintenance. These are items which need care sooner or later but which may not require immediate attention.

You must keep a sharp eye out for deferred maintenance items because they have a tendency of building up and then suddenly causing breakdowns. For example, if six water heaters fail in one year, then you can expect that the 22 others installed at the same time will fail very shortly, too. You ought to be prepared for this and have money enough to pay for their replacements.

Deferred items can also be noticeable to prospects who will downgrade your property accordingly. Most apartment complexes have long lists of deferred maintenance items, such as cracked concrete sidewalks or curbing, dead shrubs, worn patches in the roadway or parking lot, and clogged water heaters. Some of these items, such as the dead shrubs and the holes in the pavement, should have been taken care of by routine maintenance.

The point of deferred maintenance is to avoid surprises to the owner. You do this by laying aside money for repairs or replacements that will be necessary. As we noted earlier, practically every component and piece of equipment in an apartment building has a predictable lifespan. Knowing this, you can plan for replacement and set aside reserves to cover this. You can also sometimes act to extend the life of a component. For instance, if you recoat a tar and gravel roof in its sixth or seventh year, you can extend the life of that roof another seven years. But if you wait until the ninth year to do anything, the felt fibers will have disintegrated to the point where a completely new roof is necessary. Water heaters are another example. You can sometimes extend their life and cut replacement costs by installing a water-treatment facility.

At least once a year, right after one of your inspections, make a list of all of the items on your checklist that can be classified as deferred maintenance. This is where the narrative inspection report is so valuable. If you find that the roof is going, your inspection report should carry a note to that effect with an estimate of how much longer it will last. Make these notes alongside every item on the checklist. Then take whatever action is appropriate on deferred maintenance now, to prevent things from getting any worse, or advise the owner of how much money he must set aside to take care of eventual replacement or major repair.

Staff Requirements

If you follow the recommendations we have made for programed maintenance, you should be able to reduce your maintenance staff and costs. One man doing his job on a planned, programmed basis can usually accomplish much more than several men working on a crisis program. As a rule of thumb, you will need one full-time maintenance employee for each 60 apartment units. The chart below shows how many supervisory and maintenance personnel are needed for various sizes of developments:

| Employee Classification | Number of Units | | | | | |
	80–120	120–180	180–240	240–300	300–400	400–500
Maintenance Supervisor					1	1
Maintenance Personnel	1	1	2	2	3	4
Custodial/Yardmen	1	2	2	3	3	4

Note: Includes all normal repairs and maintenance performed by staff personnel including apartment cleaning and lawn and ground maintenance. Seasonal work has been adjusted to a man-year (2,080 hours = 1 man-year). Apartment and common area painting is not included.

In-House or Outside Personnel?

Once inspections have been made and the maintenance calendar drawn up, there's the question of who is going to do the work, your own maintenance people or outside organizations? This question is hotly debated at practically every gathering of management people.

Contracting your work to others has certain advantages. At peak periods you can get extra hands without adding permanently to your payroll. You can minimize your employee record-keeping. Often you can fix your costs. You can get specialized skills you don't have yourself. And you may escape union pressures if you deal with outsiders.

The disadvantages are that you lose control. Given two crews, both equally able, one your own and the other belonging to an outsider, your crew will do the job for less. The outside organization's reaction time is slower; you can't often get it to work as fast as you want. You can't give direct orders but must work through a designated supervisor. Most contracts provide for specific services at specific terms with no provision for extra duties. Finally, using an outside service is an easy way to avoid training your own people; you are simply spending the owner's money rather than trying to maximize his net operating income.

In general, we feel you are better off if you can do the work yourself with your own labor. You have better control of the work and, if you have proper supervision, it's cheaper.

However, there are certain maintenance tasks in apartment operation for which outside service is advisable. These include:

- Central air-conditioning. At the very least you need an expert to start up the system at the beginning of the season and shut it down properly at the end. Failure to do this the right way can mean interruptions and costly repairs during the season. You can generally have your own crew take care of individual apartment air-conditioners.

- Elevators. Service organizations are geared to preparing elevators for the annual inspections required by most localities. Never attempt repairs or adjustments yourself; the risk to human life and safety is too great. If the elevator breaks down between inspections, be prepared to pay stiff hourly charges.

- Swimming pools. Like central air-conditioning systems, swimming pools need experts to prepare them at the start of the season and close them down at the end. Routine pool maintenance between these two times can generally be done by your own people.

- Master antennas. The new systems are solid-state and virtually maintenance-free. If you have the old type, you'll probably need a specialist to take care of it.
- Exterminating. Check local laws to find out if this job must be done by a licensed exterminator. Some states forbid the sale of exterminating chemicals to any but license-holders.
- Refilling fire extinguishers. Local laws may regulate who may do this.
- Sewer rodding. Generally, you can train your own people to rod up to 500 feet. Anything beyond this requires an outside contractor.
- Window washing. Windows in tall buildings or in places that require special equipment to reach are better serviced by outside contractors. Most garden apartment windows can be handled by your own crew.

In general, outside service is recommended on the basis of the complexity of the machinery to be serviced, the need for special equipment or skills, and the requirement of licensing.

Service Contracts

Whether you should purchase outside services when you need them or sign a contract for them on a regular basis will depend on your analysis of your needs and what the contract provides. A good contract that provides for preventive maintenance can save you from big bills later on.

Before signing a contract, examine it to see what it covers. Does it pay for everything, or is there a deductible amount? Does it cover parts and labor? Are emergency calls as well as routine maintenance included? The more the contract covers, the more it will cost.

You also have to determine whether you should deal with a manufacturer's service organization or an independent contractor. Manufacturer service may cost more, but the manufacturer's organization knows the equipment better and has quicker access to parts.

Supplies and Parts

Having the right supplies and parts on hand is an essential part of a maintenance program. As noted earlier, if you run out of

100-watt bulbs and start using 150-watt replacements you'll create a spotty appearance and also need to replace bulbs faster because of the heat build-up. Not having the right parts and supplies means your program won't be effective.

What you need will be dictated by your property. A walk-through inspection of the property as we've recommended plus "ready-ready" preparation of apartments will help you produce a list of what should be on hand.

The following recommendations should be useful to you:

- Keep your supplies and parts in a central place, not scattered. This will enable you to keep an eye on what's there, what needs replacing, and what is disappearing because of pilferage.
- Balance your inventory so that you can take advantage of quantity discounts while at the same time you avoid having too much on hand. Some chemical supplies may deteriorate with time, so it doesn't pay to buy large quantities. *Large quantities always invite pilferage.*
- Buy in bulk lots to discourage theft. Paint especially disappears fast. Instead of buying it in one-gallon cans, buy it in 15- or 30-gallon drums and pump or pour it off as needed into open pails which thieves are not likely to put in their car trunk. Chemicals can also be purchased in bulk and then dispensed into smaller containers.
- Avoid aerosols. They're expensive and easy to steal. You can buy the same chemicals inexpensively in other forms.
- Anticipate your needs and program your purchases so you order as few times as possible. Gang your orders and arrange for delivery instead of having your staff waste time by making individual trips to the hardware store. If these trips are a necessity, limit them to twice a month.
- All orders should be authorized and signed only by the manager. This will reduce the chances of the staff buying too much, buying what isn't needed, buying personal items, and getting kickbacks from suppliers.

Maintenance Equipment and Major Tools

You need a complete inventory of all the maintenance tools owned by the property plus a specific location for each piece so you know exactly where it is. If the article is assigned to someone, you should also list this. Your equipment requires maintenance, too, and this should be regularly scheduled, preferably in the off-season when the equipment is not in heavy use and when you can get good service at fair prices.

To reduce pilferage, consider painting your equipment a special color or putting on a distinctive marking so it can be readily identified.

Getting the Right Start

Many managers who attend seminars on property maintenance come away fired up with enthusiasm and the determination to set things right in their apartments. But soon their enthusiasm wanes and the maintenance program bogs down. Why? Because in most cases the manager attacks the problem all at once. That seldom works. There is just too much to be done at one time for the staff to accomplish. Resistance builds up, discouragement sets in, and it's back to business as usual.

But programmed maintenance can work if you *divide the task into manageable segments* and then finish one completely before proceeding to the next one. Consider this approach:

Take a site plan of your property (or a building plan if you have only a single large building) and divide it into areas or zones. Label them A, B, C, and so on. Then take Area A. List everything that needs to be done to make Area A perfect. Determine the equipment and staff needed.

Gather the staff together and explain what needs to be done in Area A. Give each person a calendar and list of the tasks. Don't simply say, "Maintain it." Instead give detailed instructions: "The grille must be removed, the filter taken out and washed, then replaced and the grille put back once every two weeks." That's an instruction that few can misunderstand.

Then put your people to work on Area A. Watch them as they do the job. If they do something wrong, correct them. If they do something right, tell them so. Evaluate the work as you go along. While you may have a supervisor in charge, you personally must be involved so the supervisor knows what you expect and so that both of you can set the standards of quality, establish time frames, and determine if any other tools are needed.

When Area A is in first-class order, then and only then proceed to Area B. Meanwhile, set up a continuing maintenance program for Area A so it won't slip back again. In this way you proceed through your entire building or development, piece by piece. By the time you are finished, you will have put your entire property in top condition and you will have a sustaining maintenance program in operation.

This kind of program is possible if you, the manager, do your job of scheduling, supervising, and evaluating. If you have done your homework, you know what has to be done and when. You know how many people are needed, what kind of supervision is required, and what tools and equipment must be provided. Finally, your regular inspections give you the feedback needed to evaluate and make corrections.

If you think all of this will cost extra money, think again. As we've noted, a good product preparation and maintenance program will cost less than one based on crisis management. Experience shows there is little or no difference in the operating cost of a first-class development and a run-of-the-mill one. The difference is in the daily attention and supervision.

There is also a difference in the occupancy and turnover rates. The better-maintained property will attract better tenants faster and keep them longer than the run-down property will. That difference makes a lot of sense to the manager who wants to see net operating income at its maximum.

Chapter Four

All About Rents

If you want to be a better property manager but you only have time to read one chapter on the subject of property management, this would be it. The subject of rent is the least discussed and least understood subject in property management. The reason may be that common sense tells you that rents are due the landlord and must be paid. But there is much more to the subject of rents than the obligation to pay them. Rent is the lifeblood of the investment real estate business and it is a subject which must be understood thoroughly if the industry is to continue.

Most tenants who sit down every month to write out a $250 rent check understand only one thing: they know that they are $250 poorer and it only stands to reason that someone must be $250 richer. They write this check with somewhat of a defensive feeling. They feel deep down that if they had managed their finances properly or if they had been as energetic as they should have been, they could have been on the receiving rather than the giving end of rent. Even to people without a desire for home ownership and its accompanying burdens, paying rent rather than making monthly payments which build equity has a sort of second-class ring to it. The largest number of property managers managing real estate today were or are renters themselves and not homeowners. Thus, their feelings are much the same as the tenant who writes that check each month.

What is Rent?

In our study of the subject of rent, let's first look at what rent is. When rent payments first began, most rents took the form of a *ground rent.* The lord who acquired or inherited parcels of land let them out to people to work the land, usually as a farm. Their rent was generally a share of the crop. The landowner had little invested outside of his raw land and therefore the rent, for the most part, was a return on the value of the land being used.

That beginning has fostered the myth of rent which exists today. Payment for the land itself in multiple-family housing makes up a very small percentage of the total rent dollar paid. The portion of the rent dollar attributed to the investment in the brick and mortar improvements, plus the land, accounts for about 50 percent of the rent dollar. If you were to take the investment an owner has in the real estate—the land—and the improvement upon it together with the cost of borrowed capital (interest) needed to produce this housing and add to it a reasonable rate of profit, you establish the *investment rent.* But we must be concerned with more than repaying the original investment, the cost of the borrowed funds, and a reasonable rate of profit. We must not only collect for these items but also for a variety of *services* and *charges* which relate to this housing. Real estate taxes, insurance, utilities, and decorating are just a few of the many items of cost which must be added to the investment rent in making up the *chargeable rent.*

This becomes clearer if we use the purchase of a condominium as an example. Let us assume that you intend to purchase a condominium apartment for the purpose of renting it out as an investment. You pay $30,000 for the unit with $6,000 cash and $24,000 in borrowed capital at $8^{1}/_{2}$ percent interest for 25 years. The investment rent that you would need to charge would add up something like this:

	Year	Month
Return on cash invested $6,000 @ 10%	$ 600	$ 50
Repayment of borrowed capital $8^{1}/_{2}$%, 25 years	2,316	193
Investment Rent	$2,916	$243

(You choose 10 percent as a return on your investment because it is a few percentage points better than you can receive on a top-grade stock or bond. You need the extra return to offset the greater risks involved in real estate investment.)

If your prospective renter was to pay all other obligations and costs associated with this unit (heating, utilities, maintenance, insurance, etc.) you could be well satisfied with this investment rent with some allowance added to cover periods that the unit was vacant and for collection losses which might reasonably be expected. A net rent such as this would appear as quite a bargain to an uninformed renter.

But now include all the costs and obligations associated with the unit and the rent breakdown begins to look like this:

	Year	Month
Return on cash invested $6,000 @ 10%	$ 600	$ 50
Repayment of borrowed capital 8¹/₂%, 25 years	2,316	193
Vacancy and collection loss factor	180	15
Real estate taxes	600	50
Maintenance assessments	780	65
Interior maintenance	300	25
	$4,776	$398

This rent does not appear to be near the bargain our first example offered. The rent being charged in most apartment complexes includes many more items than those included in just the investment rent. A substantial part of the tenant's monthly payment is for services due to occupancy. The rental housing industry is remiss in not having properly explained the ingredients of the total rent bill.

Continue this study by comparing two different housing types, townhouses and high-rises. The rent paid by a townhouse renter is often a truer example of what rent really is than the rent paid by an occupant in a high-rise apartment complex.

If you managed a row of townhouses with individual water

meters, heating plants, and separate tax bills, the rent you are charging is more representative of the investment rent. Let's assume that our arrangement with the tenant provides that he pays the light bill directly to the utility company and that he does the same for water and heat. It could even be provided that he is responsible for the particular unit's tax bill and escrows money each month the same as a homeowner would. Finally, our townhouse tenant is responsible for minor maintenance upkeep, including grounds maintenance. The monies that we would charge this tenant now more closely resembles true rent. With the exception of a few dollars for an insurance allocation and a reserve for replacement for major repairs, his rent payment is almost entirely for the use of the property plus a fair return for the investor.

The high-rise building tenant, on the other hand, includes virtually all of his housing-related expenses in one rent payment. Most of his utilities, his share of taxes, repairs, and even Christmas tree decorations are included. The owner prorates each tenant's usage of utilities, services, and needed repairs and adds them to the investment rent. The owner acts as a junior tax collector, collecting small payments from each tenant each month and forwarding that money to the local tax collector.

The best way to secure a complete list of all the things included in rent is to ask a renter who has recently purchased a home. The new homeowner very quickly becomes acquainted with the hundreds of extra costs associated with operating and maintaining a housing unit. He can recite the cost of a bag of fertilizer, the hourly charge for a plumber, the cost to dispose of garbage, and even the cubic foot cost of water. When he made his decision to become a "first-class citizen" and to purchase a home, he generally grossly underestimated the cost, comparing only his monthly payments and his insurance and real estate tax escrows to the monthly rent which he was paying. All of the other expenses in the operation of housing were forgotten or minimized. Had the rental housing industry been unified as some industries are, the story of rents and what's included in them would have been told. Or had property owners itemized their rent bill, listing the various charges which were included each month, there would be a much greater understanding and less antagonism toward rent. Of course, this hasn't happened nor is it about to happen, so the payment of rent continues in the minds of many as a "waste payment."

Ways Rents are Charged

Monthly Rent

For the most part, rents are in the form of a monthly charge. This is particularly true of unfurnished apartment buildings. Historically rents are due and payable in advance on the first day of the month. A few owners make the mistake of dividing the year into twelve 30-day increments and charging rent beginning on the day that occupancy takes place. This practice is wrong because it works against tradition, is confusing, and terribly complicates bookkeeping matters.

Weekly/Semi-monthly Rent

In some furnished units, rents are expressed monthly, weekly, and sometimes as a semi-monthly rate. This practice had its start in apartment hotels which are designed for a more transient trade. These rents, as in the case of unfurnished apartments, were to be paid in advance.

Payment in Advance

Sooner or later a tenant or a group of tenants will ask why rents are not payable after delivery of the service or at least during the middle of the month, but not in advance of the month. Their argument is that you pay for your meal when you leave a restaurant, you pay for a rent-a-car when returning the car, not when you take it out, and you pay your room bill when you leave the hotel, not at check-in. Most tenants who bring up this argument do not expect you to take them seriously and really don't expect to change tradition. But there is an answer. Rent amounts to a *purchase of time* for the use of the apartment. Time is not reversible or recoverable; once it's gone, it's gone forever. A tenant who does not pay his rent on time deprives the owner of any chance to rent that apartment for the past unit of time. Court action to recover the amount due is slow, costly, and not always certain, and this can cause even greater losses to the owner. So the landlord is fully justified in asking for advance payment to make certain that this period of time is covered. This is a bit of tradition that favors the landlord. It probably began with the landlord looking for a financial commitment by the tenant before turning over his dwelling unit. This commitment took place in the form of an advance payment of rent, and therefore you pay before you receive, the same as you would at a theater or sporting event.

Aggregate Rent

Many apartment lease agreements provide for an aggregate or gross term rent which is payable in monthly installments. This is almost a standard procedure in office and commercial leases. The reason behind it is to obligate the tenant for the entire rent amount in one lump sum rather than installments. These leases usually contain an acceleration clause which provides that if an installment is late or missed, the entire sum becomes due. The purpose is to avoid having to sue each month as another rent payment becomes due. Courts take varying views of this type of provision. The courts' tendency with apartment leases is not to enforce the acceleration provision and to rule on rent claims as if they were the standard lease with a fixed monthly rent.

Extra care should be exercised when using aggregate rent leases. If, for example, a lease is written for a two-year term but an aggregate rent amount for only one year is inadvertently inserted, you have granted two years of occupancy in return for only one year's payment of rent. It's doubtful that the court will give you or the owner much sympathy.

Graduated Rent

Use of a graduated rent provision is a common method used in leases particularly when the term is longer than one year. To avoid confusion and possible later argument, make certain that the beginning and ending dates for each rent level are clearly spelled out.

It is generally easy to negotiate a lease with a rent which is graduated on some periodic basis. Tenants are usually more concerned with the immediate future and will agree to higher charges at some distant date.

A different form of graduated rent is often found in college towns. Such housing for students will often have two rates. One rate will be for a 10-month term, followed by a much lower rate for the two-month summer term. The two-rate system works better than averaging the rent for the entire 12 months. This way, the tenant is required to pay the first 10 months of the year at a higher rate. If he remains for the summer, he can take advantage of the two discounted months.

Head Rent

In college towns and in developments looking to attract young unmarrieds, it is not uncommon to find rent being charged by the "head" rather than by the dwelling unit. This is more true in furnished units than in unfurnished. In these types of housing, the owner or manager establishes a rent by first determining the number of people who could comfortably occupy the apartment. For example, he may decide that a two bedroom, two bath apartment could accommodate four adults. He then offers the apartment to four adults, each of whom would pay, say $70 per month. The unit can then be rented to four persons unrelated or unknown to each other at the $70 per month head rent. One of the roommates can leave without affecting the rent of the remaining three. While they enjoy this benefit, they also face the prospect of not knowing who their new roommate will be. Generally, when this type of rent program is available, the owner may lease the unit to a family or a smaller group of people who will accept the responsibility for the entire rent payment for an amount less than the individual four rents; for example, $250 per month instead of $280. This method of rent charging is unique and is not recommended unless you find yourself in a very difficult or specialized market condition. Bookkeeping and collection problems are dramatically increased when head rent is used instead of the standard unit rent.

Seasonal Rent

Seasonal rents are common in vacation areas, with the heaviest rent charge made during the short period of greatest demand. If you owned an apartment building in Aspen or Miami Beach, you would find that you will need to collect about 80 percent of your rent dollar during a three- or four-month period of the year. Once out of season, demand for this type of housing falls back to the year-round residents, who, of course, are much fewer. Seasonal rents are, for the most part, paid in advance. For example, a person renting housing for the season which normally lasts six months can be expected to pay as much as 50 percent of the total season rent prior to taking occupancy. He would then be expected to pay his rent the first of each month for the first three months with his advance payments making up the last three payments. There are a variety of systems for seasonal housing rent payments, but you will find that most of them involve substantial advance payments.

In both seasonal and student housing, owners adjust their rentals to produce the needed gross rent dollars. The majority of operating costs go on with or without tenants, so the rents are adjusted to collect these costs during times of heaviest market demand. In addition, the rent must also reflect the transient nature of the tenants. A high turnover is common in seasonal and student housing, perhaps twice that of a normal unfurnished apartment. The use and abuse by transient tenants are greater and the cost to re-prepare the apartment occurs more often; thus the rent charge must be higher.

Structuring Rents

Rent and the Economy

Rents, just as all products and services in a free competitive market, are related to cost, supply, and demand. Housing, being a necessity and in limited supply, should be capable of producing steadily increasing rents in a progressive economy. The cost to build and maintain a rental apartment building is constantly increasing. Therefore, rent should be increasing proportionately. Rents, however, have not increased at the same rate as all other commodities. In the past several years, according to the Bureau of Labor Statistics, wages, consumer prices, and direct operating expenses have risen at rates far greater than rents. While rents can be expected to lag somewhat, the margin between the economy and rent levels must be maintained to preserve the viability of investment real estate.

Rents are not as instantly responsive to changing economic conditions as other costs are. Because rents are locked in for a year or more, they are not subject to day-to-day fluctuation and often maintain themselves over small dips in the economy. Even during periods of major economic depression, rents hold their levels for many months. Likewise, however, in an upturning inflationary economy, increases in rental rates lag by the same several months. Everyone needs housing, so even during economic downturns, housing, particularly rental housing, maintains its balance.

The economy plays an important role, however, in increasing and decreasing the demand on various unit types. This was briefly pointed out in Chapter 1 under the discussion of unit mixes. There we noted that in a downturn economy or one in the early stages of recovery, efficiency, studio, and other small apartments with relatively low rentals are in the greatest demand. People who need or could use a second bedroom find themselves making do with a small apartment at a lesser rental. The larger three bedroom apartments, particularly those with moderate rents, maintain strong demand for two reasons. First, they are traditionally in short supply and second, they are being sought by families hoping to purchase homes when the economy shows strength.

As confidence in the economy increases, demand for larger and more luxurious accommodations will increase. The auto industry experiences similar shifts in demand from the small, stripped-down compact to the powerful, luxury models. The taste levels of Americans tend to the newer, bigger, and better, thus making periods of austerity adjustment rather short.

Demand for the larger apartments and townhouses is also affected by the supply and availability of home mortgage money. As the money supply grows scarce, the demand for larger rental units increases.

In recent years, most parts of the country have experienced a growing trend toward condominium ownership. Apartment managers were facing move-outs at rates much faster than they were used to due to this new housing type. When the availability of mortgage money for both condominiums and single-family houses slowed, sales immediately fell off. This, in turn, increased the demand for the larger rental apartments.

When the economy is doing well, the newer, more expensive apartments do the best. The studio and efficiency apartments show signs of weakening in their market position, while the newest one and two bedroom apartments find themselves in greater demand. The larger three and four bedroom apartments, particularly those in newer complexes, lose some of their market appeal as their former occupants move on to home ownership.

A skilled property manager can predict with reasonable accuracy the current general position in the economic cycle by simply studying the tenant demand for various-size apartment units.

You should be aware of these shifts in market demand as the economy changes. The housing business is seasonal. The effects that the market will experience in relationship to the economy depends to a great degree upon the season in which it occurs. For example, in a northern city, economic swings in the midwinter season usually have little effect on housing because most people are oriented to make housing changes in the spring and summer months. Short periods of ups and downs will often go unnoticed in the rental housing market, with only prolonged changes in the economy affecting rental housing.

The Manager's Role

Establishing rental rates in a new apartment project is an important part of the property manager's work. Setting those rents either too high or low can result in financial disaster to the developer. Unfortunately, most initial rent schedules are established using rates set out in the mortgage application. This application may have been filed months or even years earlier when costs were much lower. Typically, these rates bear no relation to conditions when the building is finally ready for renting. The property manager is often given these old rates and these become the prices without any further market study or adjustment. Ideally, the property manager should be permitted to produce a rent schedule for the owner's review independent of any previously decided rental rates. Establishing the correct rental rates involves a great deal of study. First of all, you should be thoroughly familiar with the rent being charged in your area of operation. If you are marketing a new garden-type apartment development for the first time, you should look at all similar projects in your immediate area as well as in other communities which have the same appeal as the community where your development is located. In most metropolitan areas there are several middle-income areas to live in, with approximately the same access to transportation and quality of community facilities. Although they are not adjacent to each other geographically, they enjoy equal appeal from a prospective renter sitting at home reading the wantads in his Sunday newspaper.

Market Feel

In making this study, make careful note of just what is included in terms of convenience and amenities for the rent being charged at each location. Don't rely on hearsay. Get your information first-hand; you will be making some important decisions, the outcome of which will depend on the reliability of the information that you have secured. It is easy but wrong to speed up your market study by relying on the telephone, real estate brokers, and other supposedly informed sources. Getting reliable market data generally takes several days but is essential if you are to be successful. When you begin to feel comfortable that you have a "feel" for the market and you find that you can reasonably predict the rent of a unit that you are studying before it is quoted, you are ready for the second step in establishing your own rental rates.

The next step is actually to set the rates. Rental rates cannot be established uniformly or with some formula. For example, it is not uncommon in a high-rise apartment building to find a printed rent list or printed rent roll with the apartments increasing in price as you go up each floor. Granted, the view on the top floor is superior to the view on a lower floor, but there are limits as to what a view is worth. In a garden development, it's very common to find one set of rents being uniformly charged on the ground level with another set of rents being uniformly charged on the second level. Both of these pricing techniques are the result of conveniently establishing prices in the quiet and comfort of an office and not the result of studying each individual apartment unit being priced.

Identify Most Desirable

Experience shows that initial rents should be established beginning with the best of each type of apartment in the building. The way to do this is to tour each apartment unit in the complex or development. You may prefer to group the various unit types and layouts together and inspect only a particular layout at a time; this is perfectly acceptable. On your visit to each apartment, make note of its features and drawbacks. You are looking for the very best apartment of a particular unit size or type. Using one bedroom units as an example, find the apartment with the best combination of qualities, such as the nicest floor plan, the best exposure and view, and the best access.

Next ask yourself: "What is the highest possible rent that I can get for this very best one bedroom apartment?" Forget about how many apartments you must rent. Set this first rent as if it is the only apartment. With the knowledge that you have gained during your personal market study, you will have some definite feelings about what that rent should be and how this apartment stacks up with competition. Your answer to this question should now be put down as the rent rate for that particular unit.

Now identify the next most desirable one bedroom apartment. Determine what less desirable features this apartment has compared with your very best and establish a rent rate for it which will be something slightly less than your very best apartment. If the differences are negligible, you may decide not to discount the rent. Continue this procedure through each and every apartment down to your worst one bedroom apartment on the ground floor between the elevator shaft and the boiler room or the apartment overlooking the trash bin and an old tree stump. Repeat this process for every unit size and type that you have in the development.

By setting your rents in this way, two good things happen: first and most important, you have done just what the public will do. Chances are your prospects will have seen many of the comparable units that you have seen and they will be looking for an apartment with the best exposure, nicest floor plan, etc. Second, by finding the best apartment and pricing it the highest and then working down rather than following the typical method of finding an average and going both up and down, you will normally increase your rent roll by more than 5 percent over traditional methods of pricing.

Status and Rent

In your study of setting apartment rents there are a number of other lessons to be learned. Remember first of all that housing is very much a status symbol. There was a time when housing was just one of several ways that an individual could establish and demonstrate the degree of success attained. Clothes and automobiles were popular status symbols. In recent years, however, clothes and autos have lost much of their appeal as status symbols for a variety of reasons, leaving housing as the principal method of indicating personal achievement.

Luxury high-rise buildings with their impressive entryways and lobbies, as well as amenities such as doormen, are employed to answer the need for status identification. Garden complexes in the suburbs satisfy the same needs with their pools, recreation buildings, tennis courts, and such. These facilities receive their greatest use by tenants not through use or participation, but during "grand tours" of these amenities with their friends. If the need for status identification were not involved, housing requirements could be solved with functional, sterile cubes. You should understand this fact before you begin the pricing of any housing units.

Partly because of status but primarily because of American tradition, the American buying public believes that if it costs more, it must be better. If you price your rents to be "competitive" or cheaper than most other developments, you may lose more than needed revenue; you may also lose the status appeal which is a part of the subconscious decision-making process of a prospective renter.

Some examples might help to prove and impress upon you the importance of these principles. The first example has been successfully used for a number of years with positive results. If you manage a high-rise building (10 stories or more), take the top floor or even the top two floors. Install carpeting and wall covering in the public corridors that are obviously superior to that which is used on lower floors. Add some dramatic improvements such as a marble wall or rich paneling around the elevator doors. Install expensive-looking corridor lighting and maybe expensive ashtray urns. Finally, use woodgrained doors with superior hardware and a distinctive door knocker on each apartment entrance. These improvements, even though they are only in the common corridor, will permit you to charge and receive some $20 per month more for each apartment. The apartments themselves are the same in size and equipment as those on lower floors. They will not only command this premium rent but will also be in the greatest demand. Why? Only because of status identification: a person's need to show superiority over his fellow man. When his friends come to visit they will understand that this bit of extravagance costs money. They will also understand that one who makes more money (i.e., is more successful) can and will spend some of it just to have things a little nicer.

The importance of impressing others is demonstrated in anoth-

er way. You won't work in property management too long before you
realize that tenant requests for service pick up dramatically just
before major holidays. They want to correct problems and make
improvements to their apartment. Why? Because their friends and
relatives will be visiting and they want things to look right. Their
home reflects their achievements and they won't look like much of
an achiever if they are living in a broken-down apartment. Your
sensitivity to these needs will make you more effective in both
setting and achieving maximum rents.

Views and Rent

Sometimes we just misjudge the desires and needs of prospective tenants when establishing rents. In Chicago, for example, it
was generally thought that apartments with a lake view were far
superior to apartments with any other view and therefore should
command the best price. A study of the occupancy rates of the
various exposures of lakefront buildings showed substantial vacancies in apartments with lake views. This happened because the
tenants discovered that at night a view of a lake as large as Lake
Michigan offered nothing but black with an occasional light. Meanwhile, a view of the city offered endless changes of beautiful
sparkling lights at night when most people are home to enjoy their
apartments. The warmth and glow of the city lights and their
outline of the city's silhouette were far more appealing to a tenant
and therefore in much greater demand. When the rent for these
units is less than others (those with lake views, for example) the
demand is just that much greater. The manager who prices his units
from his office finds it difficult to explain the vacancies in what he
believes are his choice units.

Other misconceptions about pricing apartment units have become apparent over the years. For instance, it has long been
assumed that a person who takes a higher apartment gets a better
view. But generally in a high-rise building as you get above the
midpoint of the building, the benefits in improved view become so
subtle they are almost impossible to detect. To test this, let's say you
go with someone to the fifteenth floor of a high-rise building and
look out the window—after taking note of what you've seen, your
companion blindfolds you and moves you about the building on the
elevator in an effort to confuse you as to whether you are above or

below the fifteenth floor. He takes you to an identical apartment on the nineteenth floor. Without the help of a relatively significant landmark or other measure of datum, you will find that you cannot detect that you are four floors higher. So if the difference in the view from these two apartments is undetectable, the only way you can tell you are higher is by the apartment number on the door. Therefore the rent differences between these units should be slight as there will be little or no discount for loss of view, only a discount for the loss in status appeal for not being higher in the building.

Floor Pricing

By studying the two illustrations we can see the effects of the typical pricing method as compared to the "best-of-type" method we are suggesting. The building used in our example is 25 stories high with 24 typical apartment floors containing 12 apartments each, or a total of 288 units. The four corner units are two bedroom apartments; the balance of the units are one bedroom apartments. For ease of demonstration we will only concern ourselves with the two bedroom apartment tiers on the front two corners. The front of the building faces a wide boulevard and similar buildings on the opposite side of the street. One side of the building is next to an old 9-story stone building just 25 feet away. On the other side there is a picturesque church set in a large park area. Assuming that the mortgage application calls for an average rent of $270 per month for the two bedroom front apartments, we could expect a rent structure similar to that shown in our first example. Rents would rise from the midpoint of the building starting with the average rent of $270 using a $3 per floor increment with two $5 raises on the top two floors. Descending from the midpoint, rents drop at the $3 per floor rate down to the first typical floor which is $5 less. The tier facing the park and church is $5 more than the tier facing the old building. The figures at the bottom of each tier represent the total monthly rent of each apartment in that tier. (See illustrations, pages 174 and 176.)

Best-of-Type Pricing

Now let's put the new system to work and observe the difference. First of all, we used a different numbering system. This example is the same building with its 24 typical floors; we just

Typical Rent-by-floor Method

Tier A	Tier B	
315	310	24
310	305	23
305	300	22
302	297	21
299	294	20
296	291	19
293	288	18
290	285	17
287	282	16
284	279	15
281	276	14
278	273	13
275	270	12
272	267	11
269	264	10
266	261	9
263	258	8
260	255	7
257	252	6
254	249	5
251	246	4
248	243	3
245	240	2
240	235	1

Total $6,640 $6,520

changed the numbering system to reflect higher floors. Remember apartments on higher floors have greater status appeal and that means more rent dollars. Because the lobby level is about $1^1/_2$ stories in height, we begin our numbering sequence with the third floor. We have also skipped the thirteenth floor as many people avoid that floor because of superstition. Our top floor now carries the number 27 rather than 24 as seen in the earlier example.

Next, after thoroughly studying the competition, we begin our search for the best two bedroom apartment in the building. We make the decision that it is the top apartment overlooking the church and park. We also decide that with our knowledge of the market, $305 is the highest rent the market will bear for that apartment. Before we set that price, however, we decide to make our "penthouse improvements" to the top two floors and therefore add $20 to our $305 rent, making it $325.

Checking the opposite corner on the same floor and the two apartments on the floor below, we find virtually no change in view and price them the same. Both corner units on the next three floors also enjoy the same view so we set their price at the same $305, omitting only the $20 for "penthouse improvements." Our inspection reveals that the view suffers slightly on the next three floors when compared to our best unit and our status appeal is slightly less, so we deduct $2 from our rent. Further reductions are made in blocks of units to adjust for loss of view and the appeal of height.

The principal differences in the pricing techniques thus far are that we are maintaining a higher rent average and we have yet to make an adjustment for the side overlooking the park and church versus the roof of the adjacent building. Why? Because in our inspection we note that this view does not become a negative influence until we reach the fifteenth floor. There its presence is clear and we adjust accordingly.

In the first example, we established and maintained a $5 differential between the two tiers. It wasn't needed on the higher floors as the view was not affected by the 9-story building. Now as we approach this building's roof and go below it, we find that a $5 differential isn't enough to overcome this building's undesirable effect. Because we didn't discount the rent when it wasn't needed, we now have room to make a substantial discount to counteract the negative effect of the view from lower apartments.

Again in the first example, what would probably happen in the

Best-of-type Method

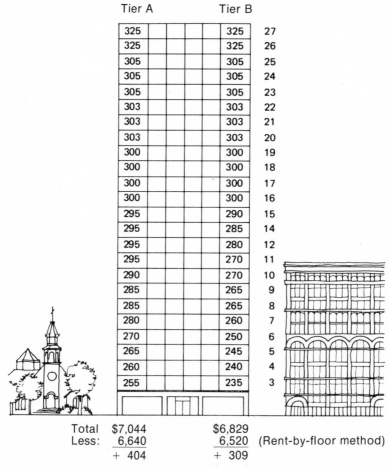

Tier A					Tier B	
325					325	27
325					325	26
305					305	25
305					305	24
305					305	23
303					303	22
303					303	21
303					303	20
300					300	19
300					300	18
300					300	17
300					300	16
295					290	15
295					285	14
295					280	12
295					270	11
290					270	10
285					265	9
285					265	8
280					260	7
270					250	6
265					245	5
260					240	4
255					235	3

Total $7,044 $6,829
Less: 6,640   6,520   (Rent-by-floor method)
         + 404   + 309

Best-of-type method yields 5$^{1}/_{2}$% higher rent level.

initial rent-up is that prospective renters would choose the church and park side and pay the $5 premium up through the fifteenth or sixteenth floor. Then the renting progress would switch to the opposite corner to take advantage of the $5 discount with no appreciable difference in the view. The lower apartments facing the 9-story building and the more expensive units on the opposing upper corner will be slow to move until the others are rented. This procedure is wrong. Your pricing should equalize desirability. What renters don't receive in view, size, amenities, etc., they should receive in a discount in rent.

Don't make the mistake so many managers make of letting bargain apartments exist. What happens is your bargains will be snapped up leaving you with the most difficult to rent. A produce manager in a supermart doesn't put good and bad apples out on the same shelf at the same price. He doesn't because shoppers pick through the good and leave the bad. He will either separate the apples and price them differently or bag them together, giving you an assortment of both good and bad.

Getting back to our examples, we can readily see that in both we have the same $235 price for our "leader." In the "best-of-type" example, we have made substantial adjustments for the less desirable units and have still managed a rent schedule which is more than 5 percent greater than our first illustration. Even more important is the fact that you will undoubtedly rent up faster using the latter rent schedule. While the first example looks good on paper, the second simulates what the prospect does: namely, matching price to value.

You may wonder if many different rental rates on similar-size units aren't confusing to prospective tenants. The answer is yes. Most complexes today use little variance in their pricing structure so you will face some problem when establishing a proper pricing system. That confusion will also exist among your rental agents. You should prepare printed or mimeographed rent schedules detailing the rent for each unit. This eliminates much of the confusion and at the same time reassures the prospect that your rents are firmly established and are not subject to negotiation on an individual basis.

The same principles we used in setting rents in our large high-rise building will work equally well in smaller buildings or garden-type housing. Differences exist in every housing type for the very same reasons: view, layout, access, size, and floor. Your pricing procedure remains exactly the same.

Some owners and property managers dispute the value of the best-of-type pricing method. They argue that it is best to fill up the building quickly at minimum rents, and then adjust rents when leases are renewed. This is foolish. If rents are established below what the market will bear, you will simply lose immediate income in favor of quick occupancy. When you are forced to raise rents at renewal time, you will prompt an excessive number of move-outs. Moreover, in the interim, your operating costs will probably have risen, and those costs will also have to be covered by the rent increase.

Adjusting Rents

No matter how careful you are in your initial pricing, you will make mistakes. You will under- or overestimate the desirability of certain units. Constant review and adjustment is needed to keep these mistakes from becoming costly problems. Unfortunately, the unskilled manager doesn't recognize these mistakes for what they are but instead considers them as assets. Ask a manager what units are in the greatest demand. More often than not you will get a quick response that the "H" units or the corner one bedrooms or the units overlooking the park are always full. He doesn't realize that if they rent too quickly, or if the demand is heavier, then they are priced too cheaply and that too much value is being given for the rent charged.

Assuming that you have a good product and you present it well, the speed of your rentals will be controlled by your rent rate. It becomes the gas pedal which dictates just how fast or slow you rent the whole building or any particular unit type. If you discover that certain unit types have "sold out" overnight, you have given away your best units at bargain prices. The prospective tenant, who is the rental market, has found something in that particular unit type that makes it more desirable than the other apartments of the same size. You have priced it too cheaply. Maybe the renting public gave more credit for a larger kitchen, extra closets, etc., than you did. Or, maybe renters know from experience that the city view from a high-rise is better than a lake view, which maybe you didn't know. Whatever it is, when an apartment type begins to move out at a faster rate than others, it is more appealing to the prospective renter than the other units they've looked at. Yes, it is important to rent as many apartments as quickly as possible, but it is equally important to ensure a relatively even flow of rentals. Each unit type should rent at approximately the same rate. As we discussed earlier in this chapter, the present state of the economy will play a role in the amount of demand for different unit sizes and this should be allowed for. A runaway rental of a particular layout or unit type indicates faulty pricing.

Upward Adjustments

With the gas pedal being the rental rate, you can make the fast-renting units less desirable by raising the rent. This makes the slower-renting units more desirable because of the wider gap in rent. Reaction time is most important. If you react too slowly, you will not be able to raise the faster-moving units in time, as they will all be rented, but you must also allow enough time to identify a trend.

If you can't determine why a unit is renting faster than others, make your raises small, in $2 and $3 increments to find the proper point of balance. Often you can determine the reason by simply asking the tenant at the time of application why he chose that particular unit type. Your new tenants will readily provide you with the answer. Don't be surprised if apartments with layouts similar to those in your decorated models rent faster than others. Prospective tenants often choose the same layout hoping to duplicate the ideas and to create a mood similar to the feeling of the model. Generally you should anticipate this extra demand and increase the rents for layouts which are the same as your model units. Add this increase after finishing your initial rent schedule. Typically a premium of $5 or more per month can safely be added to these units.

You should review your rental progress and your rental rates each week. If you are renting quickly, a daily review is not unreasonable. Your job as the property manager is to maximize rental income. This requires your constant attention and review if you are to ensure that outcome.

To summarize:

● If certain apartments are renting much faster than others, raise the rents of the best-sellers to increase the desirability of the slow-movers and to produce a more even flow of rentals.

● If the entire property is renting much faster than the competition, consider raising all rents to the point where you encounter resistance. Remember, your task is not only to rent out all the units, but also to achieve maximum rental income.

There are comparatively few problems with rent adjustments when the adjustments are on the upside. The difficulty in rent adjustments is always associated in a weakening market when downward adjustments are indicated. There is little complaint or even comment from tenants when new tenants are rented similar space for more money but the complaint grows louder and more vigorous when new tenants pay less rent than that being paid by the existing tenants.

Downward Adjustments

Just as upward adjustments in rent are made in response to market changes, there will be times when a downward adjustment in rent is needed. When you are assured that your product is correct, and that you are making a good presentation, yet some or all of your apartments are not moving, a downward rental adjustment is in order.

This can be done in a variety of ways. Let's say, for example, your initial rent-up of two bedroom, two bath apartments is moving very slowly. Let's assume that all together you have some 240 apartments, of which 80 are two bedroom, two bath and of those 80, you have only rented 10. You check the market to find that your competitors are experiencing pretty much the same problem. You can rationalize slow rentals in the two bedroom, two bath apartments because everyone reports the same problem. But you know that price is the gas pedal and determines how fast or how slow an apartment rents. You experienced good success in renting your two bedroom, one bath apartments and found resistance only in the two bedroom, two bath apartments. If you were to reduce the price of the two bedroom, two bath units to the same as you asked for the two bedroom, one bath, you should again rent with the same progress you rented the two bedroom, one bath apartments. You know there are people who are willing to occupy and pay for a two bedroom, one bath apartment and you know what they will pay.

What has happened is that you have miscalculated how much

more they will pay for the extra bathroom. The guesswork is removed when you price the two bath apartment the same as the one bath apartment. Actually the answer lies somewhere between what you've been trying to get and what you have successfully gotten for the one bath apartment. When errors are detected, adjust your schedule accordingly. In our example of the building where we rented only 10 of 80 apartments, an adjustment obviously is needed. Determine what that adjustment is and then make it.

Please note that adjustments do not necessarily have to be in the form of rent reductions. Rent reductions have a direct negative effect on the value of the property and should be used when other choices are not available. Before you make a downward adjustment in rent, ask yourself this one question: "Is there a way that I can improve the apartment that I am offering so that it is worth the rent I am asking?" If the answer to that question is yes, then you should make the improvement rather than reduce the rent.

Valuation of Investment

Rental property is an investment, and its value as an investment is related to rental income. A common method of ascertaining the value of an apartment building is by using the income capitalization approach. In this method, you estimate value by dividing a desired capitalization rate into the net operating income. "Cap" rates are established by investors in the market and vary between communities as well as with type and age of the building. Assume for the moment that the desired capitalization rate is 10 percent. In other words, knowledgeable investors are looking for a 10 percent return on their investment. For every dollar you reduce rent, you reduce the value of the building by $120 ($1.00 × 12 months = $12.00 ÷ .10 = $120). A hasty and unsupported reduction in rent can cause a serious decline in value. It is therefore necessary that you exhaust every available avenue in finding ways to maintain the rent schedule even when it involves costly improvements.

Sometimes the rent reduction may prove to be your only alternative. This is particularly true in brand-new complexes where it is difficult to further improve the property. When you decide to reduce rents, your reduction must extend to those people who rented at your earlier higher rents. In our example, the 10 people who already rented should receive the same reduction in rent as the 70 apartments which haven't rented. Ideally these people should receive a refund for the excess rent they have paid. This is particularly true in a new complex which has been open only a few months. (A retroactive reduction is not recommended when rents are reduced in older established developments.)

If you fail to pass similar reductions on to your existing tenants you cause problems. You guarantee poor tenant relations. The bad-mouthing will cause more harm than the few dollars you will lose in reducing their rent also. Remember, the need for the reduction in the first place is probably because of your mistake in pricing. Don't accentuate that mistake by making your early tenants continue with your faulty pricing.

Concessions

When downward rental adjustments are discussed, the word concession pops up. Concessions have been used for many years as a device to pep up slow rentals. Concessions had their biggest day back in the depression era when property owners who were anxious to sell would fill up their buildings by giving generous concessions. This enabled owners to maintain a fictitiously high rent schedule which, of course, brought higher sale dollars.

Many unsuspecting purchasers found themselves in financial ruin when they discovered that they did indeed collect a high monthly rate but they could only collect it for ten months of the year. To protect purchasers from being bilked, most states passed laws requiring the seller to identify any concessions which were granted. In some states this identification process involves a stamp which must be affixed to the lease in large letters stating that a concession has been granted. While these laws continue to exist, little attention is paid to them. You, as a property manager, should use extreme caution in granting concessions without properly making the fact known.

Particularly during periods of weak market acceptance, concessions are still the most commonly used inducement to rent an apartment without making a downward adjustment in the rent.

Admittedly, concessions have many tempting advantages: the offer of one or two months' free rent attracts many tenants. The building maintains a rent rate which is higher than the market will currently bear.

As the new tenants get their reduction up front in terms of free rent, the existing tenants go on paying the higher rate, without the benefit of the concession.

Tenant backlash is supposedly minimized as managers granting concessions hope the tenants won't compare notes and discover that concessions are being offered. Even when a tenant faces the manager on the inequity of the existing tenants not receiving concessions, the manager often says that the new tenant moved in earlier than he was supposed to, and that it was an unauthorized concession. Finally, when a tenant who was given a concession renews his lease, he is expected to do so without requesting another concession.

While concessions sound good, have worked for years, and seem to be just the thing to bridge short economic downturns, we should look at their drawbacks. As we've said earlier, in many states they are illegal or highly regulated. The thought that everyone does it and enforcement is weak in no way makes this practice correct. It is a method in which the owner fictitiously upholds an unrealistic rent schedule. When a building is sold on the strength of leases with unidentified concessions, it amounts to fraud. The practice of granting concessions does not go unnoticed by the existing tenants. While they may tolerate it, as they have learned to do with so many things today, they do not like it. The practice of granting concessions in a community plays a major role in increasing turnover rates. There are individuals and families in some cities in this country who travel from apartment complex to apartment complex taking advantage of the concessions offered. The added wear and tear of these moves finds their way to your expense journal. Many building operators try to stop this apartment jumping by spreading the concessions out over the term of the lease. For example, they might offer the third month and the last month of the lease as free. To perpetrate their fraud and to minimize the chance of tenants comparing lease documents, they fail to put these provisions in the lease.

Often the tenants are expected to accept this concession as an oral promise; sometimes they are given coupons or a letter they can present at these later dates. These are poor business policies, bordering on the illegal. They are certainly not recommended.

Rent concessions sometimes come in a more subtle form. Rather than give away a month's rent, the manager may credit the tenant's account for a security deposit, but forego actual collection of that amount. The tenant saves the outlay of cash for the security deposit which typically equals one month's rent and which is not refundable until the tenant successfully completes his term and vacates the apartment unit. This may be a little better approach but it still has the taint of supporting an unrealistic rent schedule.

Deficiency Discount

The *deficiency discount* is a different form of concession in which the tenant is given a reduced rent in return for accepting an apartment with a real or imagined deficiency. The theory is that if a tenant is willing to move in to an apartment with a stain in the carpeting or a burn hole in the formica countertop, why shouldn't he get a break? Isn't the owner saving money on repairs? By reducing the rent, the manager is not only reducing the net operating income but he is also lowering the value of the building. Eventually the repair will have to be made, and the cost will never be any less than it is today; chances are it will be greater. On top of it, if the tenant is willing to live with a deficiency, he may not be the kind of tenant the building wants.

Deficiency discounts shouldn't be permitted. Repair the deficiency and rent the apartment at market value.

Exchange for Service

All the arguments against concessions apply to renting in *exchange for service.* This is the renting of an apartment at a reduced rate to a tenant who promises to perform needed services for the building. Often a policeman will provide part-time security service to the complex in return for all or part of his rent. Tradesmen, such as air-conditioning repairmen, will provide their skills for rent. In college towns the use of hall monitors is common practice. In exchange for all or part of their rent obligation, the hall monitor provides custodial and supervisory services to one or more buildings. The most common form of trading for rent occurs with assistant managers or rental agents who provide their time and service for the rent allowance and perhaps a small salary.

All of these practices are bad. On a sustaining basis the complex rarely gets full value. It is an unprofessional approach that takes away from the quality of the development. The practice started in developments that had more vacant apartments than money. It is also used to avoid withholding taxes, thereby giving the recipient a form of tax-free income. Income taxes on the value of the apartment are not due *only* when living in the on-site housing is required as a condition of employment for the benefit and convenience of the owner. When housing is traded for services, the value of that housing is taxable. Social Security contributions are also due. Failure to pay either of these is illegal.

If your complex is large enough or comes under Interstate Commerce Regulations, you also risk violations of the Wage and Hour Act with regard to the Minimum Wage and premium pay after 40 hours. Granted, the services you trade for are needed, but trading is the wrong approach. Hire and pay for the needed services just as you do with your other obligations. Rent and collect full value for your apartments. Following this method you will come out dollars ahead with a better quality of service.

Concessions, deficiency discounts, and trading rent for services are all defensive devices conceived to artificially build occupancy and avoid cash outlays. They are all bad business practices and should be avoided. Managers should develop *positive programs* to improve operations.

Raising Rents

Our discussion so far has dealt with structuring rents in a new apartment complex and the necessary up-and-down adjustments to achieve the proper pricing. Next we must investigate the methods and timing for increasing existing rentals in *existing rental properties.* This is a most unpopular subject but is probably one of the most important concerns we have in the operation of multi-family housing. It is unpopular, of course, from the tenant's standpoint because he doesn't wish to pay more money than he is currently paying, particularly when it is for the same apartment he has been occupying. The apartment manager finds the idea of raising rents of existing tenants to be most unpleasant and therefore he resists rent raises as much as he possibly can.

Generally the conversation about whether or not to raise rents begins after the owner has spent time with his financial records or with his accountant. During these sessions the owners of most multi-family rental housing find themselves with a spendable return or "cash-on-cash" return of something like 2 percent or 3 percent of their invested dollars. This is a very small return in contrast to the 9 percent to 12 percent returns which are commonly associated with the real estate industry.

The investment community has long considered multi-family rental housing as one of the most stable and one of the best growth potential investments available. This notion is often unfounded and has led many to disappointment. The primary reason for this disappointment is the inability of multi-family housing today to produce a fair return, considering the risk and managerial effort necessary. The cost to construct, finance, operate, and maintain rental housing today is far greater than it was in the past. Costs have skyrocketed, yet rents have moved upward in a very shallow curve as we noted earlier. It is not uncommon to find communities where the cost to operate an apartment project has risen almost 45 percent in the past five years while rents have only increased some 15 percent to 20 percent.

Our industry's inability to maintain rent levels at least consistent with increased construction and operating costs will soon, if allowed to continue, be the principal reason for the lack of interest and investment in the rental housing business. Unfortunately, owners have kept property managers and site managers in the dark about the actual cost of operating an apartment complex. Without understanding the full picture, the manager, in effect, operates without knowledge of the principal goal: profit.

Secondary goals such as occupancy, turnover, and expense cutting can't make up for the loss of the primary goal. It would be like being taught the game of baseball with only an explanation of first, second, and third base without mention of home plate. While most managers are familiar with the operating costs that they are responsible for, namely, the repairs and maintenance, the advertising budget, supplies, payroll, and the like, they are not familiar with many of the larger expenditures such as real estate taxes and principal and interest payments. These managers do not see the urgency to increase rent rates to cover all of these costs. They can often only see the potential move-outs that an increase might prompt.

Manager's Resistance

Before we can successfully begin a program of achieving rent rates which are at least in the same proportion as increases in operating costs, we must overcome two obstacles; first, the resistance of the property manager or site manager who is responsible for the particular project, and second, the objections of tenants presently occupying apartments in the project. The manager is actually the most difficult of the two to convince that a rent raise is necessary. Property managers must be schooled in the economics of real estate and must be made to understand where the rental dollar goes and why rental housing today is not the good investment that many people think it is. The manager must be taught to understand basic pricing and how it is handled in other industries. For example, if a car maker is faced with a new government regulation for an improved antipollution device, the exact cost of that device will be reflected in the next year's model. The salesman of that particular auto will not be questioned as to whether or not the market will bear such an increase. The increase is simply added to the price tag. In no other industry does the salesman or clerk who is in charge of selling the product play a role in the pricing of the goods which are being sold. A shoe clerk is not involved in the pricing of the shoes he sells. The price of those shoes is a combination of the cost to produce and the company's idea of what the market will bear.

In the rental housing business, however, the site manager does play a role. Talk of rent raises is rarely initiated by the manager but he is invariably consulted. During such a meeting the manager, burdened with the problems of the day, usually recommends against any rent raise. He dislikes rent raises almost as much as the tenants who must pay them. He knows that a raise will prompt some move-outs. He knows that raises mean more work and louder complaints. Chances are good that his performance as a manager is judged on the occupancy he maintains, not the dollars collected. A rent raise will, at least temporarily, adversely affect his record.

All too often the owner will back down on his request for higher rents when the manager expresses his fears of mass move-outs. Should the owner persist and demand that reasonable though substantial raises be invoked, the manager is still the one who must put them across. If he doesn't believe raises are actually needed, his attitude and the results will both be bad. Often rent increases passed on to the tenant fall short of what is actually needed to offset rising costs. It is unfortunate that a manager frequently doesn't understand that he faces the same problems with a $5 to $8 per month raise as he does with a raise of $12 to $15.

Raising Rents on Vacant Units

The outcome of the owner's need for more rent and the manager's reluctance to raise rents often ends in a compromise. That compromise goes something like this: the manager agrees to raise rents the needed amount but those raises will only be applied as units become vacant. The existing tenants will be allowed to remain at the old rate. This eliminates the manager's fear of mass move-outs from existing tenants. The new tenants are expected to pay the premium rent because they are new and therefore ignorant of rents which have been charged. The manager expects that if the apartment complex experiences a 40 percent turnover each year, in some two and a half years a 100 percent turnover will have been accomplished and that all of the rents will have reached the new level.

This technique is wrong. First of all, if an apartment project is experiencing a healthy rate of rentals of its existing vacant units, it is being selected by prospective tenants who make up the active rental market as being a good investment of their rent dollar. Existing tenants, when they are not actively seeking new housing, do not make up the active rental market. This market is made up of the people who are spending their Saturdays and Sundays visiting various apartment complexes looking for the best value for their rental dollar. Therefore, if you are experiencing a normal amount of new rentals, your rental rates are competitive in the market place.

Raising at Turnover

The idea of raising all of the apartment rents over a period of two and a half years, assuming a 40 percent turnover rate, is also faulty. Some 60 percent to 70 percent of the turnover will occur in only 30 percent to 40 percent of the units in a particular complex. The remaining residents who stay on for years and years will soon be paying a rent far less than the new rent for new tenants which will only prompt the old-timers to continue in the apartment to take advantage of the bargain rates which you are offering them. So you will never achieve 100 percent of the rent raises you expected.

If a supermarket by mistake grossly underpriced a product on its shelves, that product would sell very quickly until either the error was detected or the supply was exhausted.

The fact that some people received an unreasonable bargain through a mistake does not and will not increase the loyalty of the customer to that particular store. The same holds true for rental property. If you are giving your apartments away at a bargain rental rate, you can expect that the people will flock to your doors to gain that bargain. But when the time comes that you can no longer stay in business at the bargain rates, these tenants will move with the same lack of loyalty as they would had they been paying the higher competitive rental rates all along. In fact, there will probably be a higher rate of turnover because these tenants have become unduly spoiled by the lower rent rates and move out as an act of spite.

Ability to Pay

The manager may think it's the size of the increase that prompts the move, particularly when he gets an initial series of move-out notices after the raise is announced. The manager tends to overreact when these notices first arrive, to lose perspective on the value of the product that he is offering, and to become conciliatory and inclined to back down. But if this manager were to follow up on tenants who were moving, and who stated that the increased rent was the reason, he would find himself in for a rather shocking surprise. Almost without exception the people who move from a particular apartment complex because the rent has been raised will promptly go out and rent a similar apartment at a higher rental rate than they were paying even with the rent raise. For example, a tenant who objects to having his rent for a one bedroom apartment raised to $180 from $160 will often go out and rent a similar new apartment for $200 per month. The answer is that the tenant has the ability to pay increases in rent just as he can pay for increases in all the other costs of living. Costs of food, clothing, transportation, and education have gone up sharply since the 1950s. Each time they rise, people say they don't see how they can pay. But they do, because incomes have gone up, too. No one likes paying more, but they do it. Tenants have the ability to pay more rent, or will soon earn the ability to pay more rent, but they will not *offer* to pay more rent. The property manager must be trained to see this, and use this knowledge in the process of raising rents.

Even more important than learning that the tenant has the ability to pay more rent is the lesson of why that additional money is needed. In recent years the cost to construct, finance, and operate multi-family housing has set new highs. Rents have not kept pace.

The need for manager understanding of the profit-and-loss aspects of multi-family housing is vital if he is to play a role in rent increases. Most managers have heard that it is virtually impossible to produce any cash return on invested capital or the energy needed in the development of multi-family housing, but find this difficult to believe. To demonstrate this fact we will put together an example using figures which are both conservative and real. Our example is very similar to the actual economic analysis being struggled with by developers across the nation.

A Typical Example

Let's begin by assuming that we know of some property available and zoned for multi-family housing. We decide to construct a 200-unit garden apartment complex with ten, 20-unit apartment buildings. Our unit mix is one hundred 700 square-foot, one bedroom apartments and one hundred 900 square-foot, two bedroom apartments. The apartments are to be of typical construction quality found today with conventional interior appointments and the usual amenities. In addition we plan laundry and storage facilities in each building and a swimming pool and perhaps a tennis court.

Next we set out the cost, income, and expense figures that can reasonably be expected. These figures are based on experience in actually operating properties in more than 100 cities.

These figures can be found to be typical in the majority of rental markets in this country. They will not work in cities like New York or others facing unusual land and construction costs. For the most part these figures are conservative, reflecting efficiency in construction and effective property management.

BUILDING DATA

100—1 Bedroom	700 sq.ft. Net Rentable Area =		70,000 sq.ft.
100—2 Bedroom	900 sq.ft. Net Rentable Area =		90,000 sq.ft.
			160,000 sq.ft.
Halls, corridors, common area	16%		25,600 sq.ft.
Total building area			185,600 sq.ft.

COST

Building: 185,600 sq.ft. @ $16 per foot	$2,969,600
Land = 200 units @ $1,500 per unit	300,000
Indirect: construction and financing @ 15%	445,440
Total cost	$3,715,040
	or say $3,700,000

SOURCE OF FUNDS

First mortgage proceeds	$2,850,000
Sponsor's cash investment	850,000
Total project cost	$3,700,000

As our annual projection shows (see page 192), we end not with a surplus but with a deficit. The owner in our example has invested $850,000 in addition to substantial time, energy, and risk only to lose $13,000 during a stabilized year. Even if he was able to save 25 percent in the total construction cost he would still face a loss. Assume a 100 percent mortgage with no cash investment and he would be responsible for a cash shortage each year of some $85,600. Our example shows a mortgage rate which in the mid-1970s was impossible to get, an occupancy level seldom maintained, real estate taxes at 15 percent of gross income, and an efficient set of operating expenses. Even with these optimum conditions the property is not an investment which produces a return but a monument which needs yearly support.

Some critics will attack the reserve for replacement. This category of expense is unheard of to many. The reason is that as properties have become less and less profitable, reasonable reserves have been forgotten or hopelessly minimized. This thinking is

CASH FLOW PROJECTION

INCOME	Month	————Year————
100—1 Bedroom, 700 sq.ft. @ 30¢ = $210	$21,000	$252,000
100—2 Bedroom, 900 sq.ft. @ 30¢ = $270	27,000	324,000
Gross Rental Income	$48,000	$576,000
Sundry Income	400	4,800
Gross Total Income	$48,400	$580,800

Less: Vacancy Loss		$29,000	
Collection Loss		2,900	
Apts. Out of Income Stream*		8,300	40,200
Total Estimated Collections			$540,600

EXPENSES

Real Estate Taxes (15%)	$86,400
Utilities	32,400
Payroll and Related	34,000
Services	5,400
Insurance	8,100
Repairs & Maintenance	32,400
Supplies	5,400
Management	21,600
Advertising & Promotion	2,700
Miscellaneous	2,700
Reserves for Replacement	47,000

Total Expenses Including Reserves	−278,100
Net Income Before Debt Service	$262,500
First Mortgage Debt Service	−275,595
($8^{1}/_{2}$%, 25 years = 9.67% constant)	
Cash Flow to Owner	(−$13,095)

*Assumes rent-free apartments for manager, maintenance chief, office. Models are not included.

foolhardy. Now more than ever before with new innovations coming on the market each day those reserves are necessary. If they are not available, the useful life of the property will be dramatically shortened. Review how the reserve figure was created and decide for yourself if it is unreasonably high:

---

200 Appliance sets (stove, refrigerator, disposer, hood fan, and dishwasher) @ $500 per set	
200 × $500 = $100,000 ÷ 10 year life	$10,000
24 oz Shag carpeting (estimate $500 per apt.)	
200 × $500 = $100,000 ÷ 5 year life	20,000
FHA minimum required replacement reserve on structure and mechanicals of 6/10 of 1% of total construction cost	17,000
Total annual reserve allowance	$47,000

If this same property is to pay its bills and to return even a 6 percent return on the owner's investment, the income must rise at least $64,000 or 11 percent. Rents must average $233 for the one bedrooms and $300 for the two bedroom units. This assumes of course that all of our operating expenses remain constant. This minimal 6% return will only remain if we continually compensate for cost increases with yearly rent raises.

Tenant Resistance

Tenant's feelings toward rent raises would also mellow somewhat if they knew that increases were due to today's high costs and not to make a fat cat fatter. The image of the landlord in the minds of most tenants makes this an even more difficult task.

How then do we go about correcting this imbalance in the budget without bringing out the wrath of the tenant? The answer is—*carefully.* The first step is to begin letting them know what is included in their rent bill and how much it costs.

Property owners are not organized as an industry, thus a major public relations effort is not possible. We must rely on the individual efforts of owners and managers to get our story across. We can save, reproduce, and distribute local news articles which announce price increases. We can furnish tenants with statistics on construction, financing, and operating costs today as compared to previous years. In addition, we can chart their rent rate to demonstrate how rents have failed to keep pace with other costs. There are many, many ways to inform the tenant that rent raises are needed and will be forthcoming. After years of remaining relatively silent on the subject, we owe an explanation before setting out on a major rent-raise campaign.

Ways to Raise Rents

If every manager were to raise rents in the same proportion on the same day there would be little risk. The oil and steel industries seem to act uniformly and at the same time when they raise prices. Unfortunately, property managers are not so united and must face the question individually. That means there will be an element of risk. When raising rents we risk being higher than our competitors, at least temporarily. Rest assured that your risk is only temporary as virtually every multi-family development suffers from the same problem of diminished or nonexistent profit. With just the slightest encouragement they, too, will join in and the risk begins disappearing. Actually the risk you run applies more to your occupancy level than to your monthly collections. Consider this true story:

The tenants of a 490-unit garden complex were given an across-the-board rent raise of approximately 7 percent. This property had maintained nearly 100 percent occupancy levels for about two years. The effect of the raise increased the average rent from $250 per month to $267. As a result, notices to move came from almost 20 percent of the tenants. Many of those tenants later rescinded their notice and, in addition, many of the units which were to be vacated were leased to new tenants. On the day the new rent rates went into effect, 30 units were vacant. The manager was very upset and made his feelings known. He complained bitterly about how his almost perfect record of 100 percent occupancy had been ruined, and how a once fully occupied complex now suffered with a vacancy problem. This happened because he was trained with occupancy levels as his primary goal. He did not understand the importance of collections or bank deposits. As his supervisor, I asked the manager to take his calculator and multiply 490 apartments by his previous average rent of $250. He did and the answer looked like this: $490 \times \$250 = \$122,500$. I then asked him to multiply the now 460 occupied apartments by the new $267 average rent. It looked like this: $460 \times \$267 = \$122,820$. The point he now saw was that we were not only collecting $320 more per month, but that we also had the potential of renting and collecting from 30 vacant units. Granted, 94 percent occupancy doesn't appear to be as good as 100 percent occupancy, but we don't pay our bills with occupancy rates. We pay them with the cash collections. Incidentally, that same manager achieved 100 percent occupancy again in just a matter of a few months. His monthly collections then totalled almost $131,000 or some $9,000 more each month.

This example is not unusual. Long experience gained while implementing rent raises indicates these results:

A rent increase amounting to approximately 7 to 8 percent of current rent levels will prompt a "notice to move" from 20 percent of the tenants. A number of these notices will be withdrawn and some of the units will be pre-leased prior to the move-out date. On the day the new rents go into effect, the vacancy rate will be 6 percent greater. For example, a 2 percent vacancy rate will increase to 8 percent; 16 percent will go to 22 percent; 70 percent will rise to 76 percent. Even though the occupancy is less, the total income from these units will be more. Within 90 days the occupancy level will return to the point where it was prior to the raise.

Your measure of success in effecting a rent raise should be a comparison of your bank deposits before and after the raise has been accomplished. Don't let a temporary loss in occupancy trouble you or lead you to back down.

Discriminatory Pricing

When raising rents you can use the same technique used for initially structuring rents. In other words, there is no reason that rent raises need be equal in either amount or percentage. Use discriminatory pricing to stimulate renting. If you enjoy good occupancy in your one bedroom units and poor occupancy in two bedroom units, you would be correct in raising the one bedroom units by a higher rate. The same holds true for your "best sellers." If they are in greater demand than others, it means they offer too much value for the rent charged. You can equalize this demand or desirability when you raise rents. Visiting each apartment the same as you did in the brand-new building will help you understand how to proceed. There will be a temptation to judge the apartment's value on how well the tenant keeps it or has decorated it. Try to disregard this, as it would be unfair to penalize a good tenant for investing his time and money.

Avoid Divided Raises

One substantial raise is better and easier to effect than two smaller raises in a period of a year. Small nuisance raises reduce the chances of move-outs, but when repeated at close intervals they aggravate tenants and prompt an even greater turnover.

Once-a-Year Adjustments

When you go through the turmoil of a rent increase you hope to forget it for awhile. That won't work. With costs increasing as they have, you will need rent adjustments at least once a year. If you have gotten behind on adjustments, raises every nine months may be required.

Tax and Utility Pass-Throughs

This is not really a rent raise but a method of passing on major increases in real estate taxes and utility charges to the tenants. This provision started when the energy shortage caused utility costs to soar. While these raises were steep, they represented only a fraction of the total operating expense statement. All of the items of expense including payroll, insurance, repairs, and maintenance were increasing at almost the same rate as taxes and utilities. To limit rent raises to only two items of expense is foolish. Some courts have even held that if a tenant has agreed to a tax and utility pass-through and makes these extra payments, he is safe from further rent increases. The theory is that had the owner expected additional money for other increased operating costs, he would have included these in the original pass-through provision.

Escalator Clause

Raising prices to cover increases in operating costs should be a routine act of management as it is in all other industries. But so long as the site manager continues with the primary control over rent levels, there will be lengthening delays between cost increases and rent increases. A way to lessen the delay is available by making rent increases somewhat automatic. Leases can be modified so that the rent will increase as expenses increase. This is accomplished with an escalator clause like those in wide use in office buildings for years. Office buildings typically establish a base year for both real estate taxes and operating expenses. As these costs increase they are billed to the tenant as additional rent. Because office building leases are written for longer terms, five to ten years, they need the rent adjustment protection that an escalator clause provides.

The same technique can also be used to solve a problem with rental apartments even though their leases are written for only one- and two-year terms. The problem is one of *applying an automatic device* that will let the apartment manager and tenant know that a rent adjustment is needed to keep pace with changing costs. An index is needed that reflects price increases, is readily available, and possesses accepted reliability. Utility charges and real estate taxes come to mind because of their alarming increases in recent years. They are probably too erratic and too political to meet the test of sustained reliability. Both of these expense items as well as all other items of expense which we are faced with in the operation of multi-family housing can be found in one index: the Consumer Price Index. This index is published monthly by the U.S. Department of Labor, Bureau of Labor Statistics. It reflects changes in the cost of living not only nationally but in most major cities as well. Because of its source and proven reliability, it receives front-page attention in most newspapers every month. Property owners and tenants can receive these statistics through a free monthly subscription just for the asking.

Adopting this type of lease provision will allow the owner to preserve a margin of profit in an inflationary economy. Its primary design is not to make a losing investment into a positive one but simply to maintain an equal level. Actually you will improve your position inasmuch as debt service payments are usually fixed, thus allowing all of the increased revenues to be applied to cost increases and improvements in cash flow.

At first blush you may think that the concept of an escalator clause providing for automatic rent adjustments would have a negative marketing appeal; tenants won't like it. But just the opposite can be expected. Because the rents will be tied to an impartial well-known government index, apartment renters are more likely to accept it and will have no grounds to complain of so-called gouging.

It is important, though, that renters be told about the escalator clause. Managers and owners cannot assume that just because the tenant has signed the lease containing the clause, he has read and understood it. Courts no longer assume that the tenant has read and understands lease provisions, so you must take steps to call the escalator clause to the renter's attention. One way to do this is by including a legend on the lease form title page: "This lease contains a rent escalator clause; please read it carefully." Another is to affix a sticker with similar wording on the lease. It also helps to personally tell the tenant of the escalator clause. In other words, do all you can so that the tenant can't say he was never told about the clause, or that he assumed he was signing the conventional lease form.

Can the escalator clause work in apartment leases? All signs suggest it can. The concept is well established in office leases. Escalator clauses are a part of Social Security benefit payments and are also the basis of most wage contracts. In the case of leases, the goal is one of fairness to owner and tenant alike. The escalator clause can offer you an excellent way to reduce or eliminate the gap between cost increases and thus help you preserve a margin of profit.

Now is the Time

You can and should choose the timing for effecting a raise. In most parts of the country the early spring is best. It allows you the full summer to recover from any vacancies that develop. Of course, for seasonal or student housing, rental raises should begin with the season or term. Surprisingly, January 1 is also a good time for raises. Most people are preoccupied with the holidays or reluctant to go apartment hunting in inclement weather. Because of the unpopularity of the task and the tendency to procrastinate, maybe the very best time to raise rents is *now*.

Rent Payment

Handling the payment of rents encompasses some aspects which should be carefully thought out and understood. These include where and when rents are to be paid as well as in what form they are to be paid.

A Matter of Habit

The payment of rent is traditionally and by contract due on the first. Payment of rent is a matter of training and habit. If you don't establish yourself firmly on this subject, you will not enjoy prompt or complete payment. Tenants will test you and stretch you just as far as you will allow. Understand that tenants spend what they have each month. If you allow them to get behind once, you will find it most difficult to get them current again. A knowledgeable owner put it this way: "If a tenant can't pay one month's rent, how is he going to pay two? And if he can't pay two month's rent, he will never pay three." Those words are so very true.

Make Your Policy Known

Your policy on rent collection should be made known when the tenant first completes the lease application. It won't affect your sales presentation because tenants expect that rent is due on the first. Your policy should be reiterated when the same party executes the lease. In doing this, you firmly establish the collection policy and eliminate 90 percent to 95 percent of the potential problems.

Rent Bills

Should a tenant be billed for his rent each month? This is a commonly asked question, and the answer is NO. Rent is usually a fixed charge each month, the amount of which is known exactly by the tenant. He also knows that it is due on or before the first of each month. What then is the reason for billing? In a luxury building with variable charges added to the rent, or in a condominium with owners, not tenants, a monthly billing might be useful. But rental property for the most part does not need the extra cost and problems associated with billing rent. If the mails are delayed or an error exists in your billing, you provide an easy excuse for the tenant to be late.

Site Office

You gain maximum control over rent payments when they are collected at an on-site office. Granted, from an efficiency standpoint, more rents can be collected and posted in a single day when they are mailed to a central location. The loss of control at the project level, however, is more than enough to offset this advantage. Convenience to the tenant and the benefit of personal contact each month are further advantages to be gained when collections are handled on-site.

Computers and Lock Boxes

In recent years tenants have been given an additional excuse to be late with their rent: the computer. Many companies and complexes have incorporated computer service bureaus or bank lock box systems for the collection of rent. These systems often provide the tenant with an excuse. The delay in processing the information back to the manager is frequently called the "blackout period." During this time, the site personnel are out of touch with just who has actually paid. Depending upon the system, this period can extend to as long as 20 days. The tenant, when approached about his delinquent rent, learns to reply: "I sent it in." The need for computer accounting in larger firms is obvious. But those systems must be designed to give the site manager complete knowledge of the rent status of each tenant.

A more effective electronic system allows rent payments to be paid to the building office. Prepunched data cards are processed through a small terminal device and then through telephone lines to the computer. A daily bank deposit is made at the same time balancing the amount on the data cards. Many such systems are available. Only as a last resort should the actual collection of rent be taken away from the site office. When daily control is lost, delinquencies will increase.

Forms of Payment

Rent payments can take many forms: money orders, cash, personal checks, and even third-party checks. Some consideration and policy decisions are necessary with regard to the form in which rent is paid:

- **Money orders and cashier's checks** offer the best method of payment from an owner or manager's standpoint. They are convenient to process, recoverable if lost or stolen, and safe in terms of cashability. To a tenant they lack convenience and are expensive to obtain. Your policy should be to gladly accept them but not to require them.

- **Cash** should be, but isn't, a welcome form of payment. Many managers and even the FHA either discourage or refuse to accept cash rent payments. They do this because of the risk of robbery when large amounts of cash are known to exist on the premises. Cash also means you must make trips to the bank; checks can be deposited through the mails. Use caution in establishing a "No Cash Policy." Cash is legal tender in this country. Your refusal to accept cash in payment of rent may very well void your legal claim to that debt. You can certainly request that the tenants pay by check or money order and most will accommodate you. But think twice before refusing a cash payment. Most of the major thefts of rent money are caused by the managing offices' failure to make daily deposits. With the extra work volume around the first of the month, several days' build-up of deposits makes a robbery an even greater loss. Solution: bank money daily.

- **Personal checks** account for the vast majority of monthly rent payments. They offer convenience to both the tenant and manager and can generally be replaced if lost or stolen. The problem arises with "NSF" checks which are frequently delayed several weeks in being returned.

- **Third-party checks** should be avoided. Even though these are frequently company payroll or Social Security checks and can be termed "good as gold," they present problems. To cash these checks you may need to make change for the tenant if the check exceeds the rent amount. When a third party check "bounces," it causes enormous problems in identifying the tenant, making bookkeeping adjustments, and getting a replacement check.

Advance Payments

Occasionally a tenant will offer to pay rent for a number of months or even a year in advance in return for a discount in the rent. Advance payments are fine, discounts are not. Even though the additional cash would be helpful in meeting your current bills, you would be ill advised to accept this money if it meant discounting the rent.

Collecting Rent

Collecting rent is almost as painful to many managers as raising rents. We are not speaking of the rents that show up in your office voluntarily but the ones that don't. A manager's ability to keep the rents collected is an important measure of his performance. A poor manager will rarely have a good collection record. Long hard experience suggests that this should be your policy toward the collection of rent: "It is due on the first; it is late on the second; and I am going to evict you on the third." This recommendation brings very vocal arguments from managers. When presented with this policy, they quickly say that local laws won't permit eviction on the third day, which may be true. The same manager, however, when asked to list what tenants he expects to be outstanding in their rent on the tenth of next month, can do so with uncanny accuracy. The point is, if he knows who they are, why isn't he doing something about it?

Enforce on the First

If the rent fails to arrive in your office during the very first few days of the month, you must begin enforcement, preferably in person. Telephone calls or a personal, hard-hitting letter are not as effective. Reminder notices and final notices are not worth their paper value much less the stamp required to mail them. It doesn't take a tenant long to discover your complete rent collecting procedure. They quickly learn the steps you follow: reminder notice, final notice, five-day notice, letter, phone call, attorney. They will make their payment just before the nasty personal letter or phone call. Knowing this, why waste time with the preliminaries?

Spotting Trouble

There are some rules of thumb which will help in spotting potential rent collection problems. When a tenant's rent goes beyond 25 percent of his gross income, pay attention. The risk of having a collection problem dramatically increases with each dollar his rent exceeds the 25 percent mark. The warning flag is also up when the combination of the rent plus the tenant's monthly install- ment payments reach 40 percent of his gross income. When these rules are broken there won't be enough income to go around and somebody will come up short. Another early sign of trouble is the "insufficient funds" check. When the first check comes back, that is the time for a personal visit. Get the check replaced with either cash or a certified check and make it clear that trouble will begin with the next bad check.

Penalty Charges

When delinquencies begin occurring, some managers like to impose a late or penalty charge. This is a bad practice. First, it implies that rent can be late; it just costs more. A tenant who is late with rent and incurs the penalty assumes he has paid for the privilege of paying as late as the last day of the month. Such a policy adds a "bend" in what should be an inflexible rule. Second, a penalty is not usually collectible in a court of law. By changing the term to "service charge" you may be able to collect your extra charge but you will be required to demonstrate how your costs went up because the particular tenant was late. Don't use this as an alternative to your requirement that rent be paid promptly.

Discounts

If you insist on providing flexibility in your rent payment policy, consider this suggestion. Increase your rents by the amount you would use as a "late" or "service charge," then allow a discount of that same amount if paid by a certain date. Your claim for rent will then be the gross rent beyond a certain date which is both acceptable and legal. Many utility companies use the gross/net system and most tenants are familiar with how it works.

Excuses

When a tenant who is behind in rent is confronted by the management there is usually a variety of excuses. Very seldom will you hear the real reason: "I don't have the money." Instead, you will be told about the deficiencies in his apartment and how he is withholding payment until things are corrected. *Don't* trade repairs or improvements for rent. If repairs are needed, they should be made in your regular manner. Understand that this is a ploy to buy time and save face. The rent is due and payable on the first. When a tenant can't meet it, the excuses begin. The imagination used in some of their stories is something to behold. After a year or two, though, you will have most of them down pat.

Payment Program

Once a tenant admits to being short of the money needed to pay the rent, he may offer you a payment program. Don't accept it. The great majority of these programs fail. The very reason the tenant is behind is because his expenses exceed his income. If that is true, then how is he going to get ahead again? Usually it's the Christmas bonus or the tax refund he expects. How many more creditors are waiting for that same check? Remember, the rent meter registers another rent charge each month. There are businesses that exist for people who need temporary money. They are called banks and loan companies. Property managers are not in the business of making loans and therefore shouldn't do it.

Some will argue that it is better to be receiving something than to have the unit empty and receive nothing. That theory is totally wrong. You are far better advised to enforce your policy on rent payments to the limit. A vacant apartment is far superior to one occupied by someone who hasn't paid for it. A merchant would rather have unsold goods on his shelf than to have "sold" the product but failed to collect. The weaker the market, the stronger your policy on rent collections must be. Throughout this book we discuss policies and recommended procedures. Of those policies *the rent collection policy should be the most inflexible.* Your failure to accept this principle will cost thousands of dollars each year.

Damage Deductions

A tenant may send in his rent minus deductions for what he

considers damages: his oven is broken, the refrigerator went out and $100 worth of food inside spoiled, or the air-conditioning didn't work so the family had to sleep at a nearby hotel. Don't allow such deductions. Insist that the rent be paid in full. Payments for damages are another and separate matter. Use your judgment. If you delayed in getting the stove or refrigerator fixed, then pay for the damages separately, not as an offset against the rent.

Test Your Skills

You can test your skills as a rent collector with the following chart:

Excellent =	$1/4$ of 1% of Gross Income Delinquent
Good =	$1/2$ of 1% of Gross Income Delinquent
Average =	1% of Gross Income Delinquent
Poor =	More than 1% of Gross Income Delinquent

Collecting the full and proper rent is to a great degree what this business is all about. The problem areas we discussed point out where most managers go astray. Maybe this happens because the amounts are large and seem somewhat unreal to the novice property manager. In any case, take the time to understand what is in the rent charge, how it is structured, the constant need for increases, and the methods used to collect it. Regardless of the type, size, or location of the housing these principles remain constant. With the application of these principles, you are well on your way to becoming a professional property manager.

Chapter Five

Product Presentation: How to Merchandise Your Apartments

Of all the elements of successful marketing—policies, product preparation, price, presentation, and promises—presentation is the only one that has little residual value once your apartments have been rented. The sole purpose of presentation is to *attract prospects* to your apartments and show them what they can expect if they rent. Once that's done, product presentation has done its job.

Of course, this is a mighty important job. Unless you get prospects to rent apartments, you won't have much of a management task to perform. There's no trick to managing an empty building. The real test of a property manager is whether he can *fill apartments and keep them filled.*

To attract prospects who will become renters and fill your apartments, you need an effective merchandising program. Before going further, we should make a distinction here between merchandising, which is what this chapter is all about, and selling.

Selling vs. Merchandising

A salesman is someone who *creates a need and fills it.* He's the vacuum cleaner salesman who knocks at your door, sprinkles dirt on your carpet, and then convinces you that you need a new vacuum cleaner to clean it up. Or he's the encyclopedia salesman who convinces you that your children are being culturally deprived and that a 24-volume set of the Encyclopedia Universica is the answer.

Or he's the pitchman on the late night television show who shows you all the wonderful salads you can make with the Super-8-Chopper. Where you didn't have or know of a need before, you have one now, because the salesman has created it, and he has just what you need to satisfy your wants.

A merchandiser is someone who helps you *fill a need or a desire you already have.* He doesn't come to you. You come to him. People who visit rental apartments don't come because someone sold them on the need to move; they come because they have the need or desire and now they want to find out if you can fill it. That is why *it is virtually impossible to "sell"* a rental prospect. You're not only wasting effort if you do, but you're creating a barrier to closing the deal. Let's consider why.

People today are more sophisticated than they used to be and they are wary of selling efforts. This is especially true of the younger people who are better educated, more suspicious, perhaps slightly cynical, and less amazed by superlatives than their elders. Perhaps this is because today's younger market, and many older people as well, have been so inundated by selling messages from TV, radio, newspapers, and magazines that hard-sell techniques have lost their effectiveness. When they are used, they are almost always quickly discounted.

Perhaps that's why many of the largest users of TV advertising no longer use hard-sell messages but are content to get their name across with entertainment or information. Very few TV commercials today wind up with, "Go out and buy some today!" Instead, the name is repeated without the command to buy in the expectation that when you see the product in the store, you'll recognize the name and buy it.

A second reason selling doesn't work when it comes to renting apartments is that the *landlord is automatically starting from a minus position* simply because he's a landlord with a centuries-old tarnished image; that also applies to the property manager as his agent. People tend to discount a salesman; they doubly discount the landlord who's trying to sell because they know all he's doing is trying to satisfy his interest. So the task becomes one of trying to win the prospect's trust rather than meeting him head-on in a sales confrontation.

It's important that the property manager and his rental agents understand the distinction between selling and merchandising. The novice agent who thinks selling is required will almost automatically begin to use high-pressure techniques in dealing with the prospect and will generally lose him. The more experienced agent will recognize that his job is to help the prospect determine if the rental apartment will meet the prospect's needs. To do that, the agent will have to identify those needs. That's what the presentation is designed to do.

If you'll clench both fists and then push one against the other in front of you, like two bulls meeting head on, you'll get the picture of a typical sales situation. One fist represents you trying to sell, the other represents the prospect countering your arguments with objections. This is a tiring posture and one that the prospect will resent. He'll most likely walk away from you because he doesn't want to be sold.

Now put your fists alongside one another, symbolizing you and the prospect working *side by side.* This is more indicative of the climate we are trying to create in our product presentation, making it possible for you to work along with the prospect in satisfying his needs. This is the kind of relationship the prospect wants and will welcome. Keep this attitude in mind as we go through this chapter and as you work out your own product presentation. Ask yourself: "Am I trying to sell the prospect something?"—head to head—or "Am I helping the prospect satisfy a need?"—side by side.

All of this requires that you be genuine, warm, likable, and sincere in your presentation. Avoid phoniness and superlatives. Present your wares in a straightforward, honest manner. Do the best job you can of preparing your product, and then show it in an honest light. Stress helpfulness, not pushiness. Recognize that you can't sell an apartment to anyone, but you can help them recognize its merits on their own, with a little help from you and the product presentation.

Selecting a Theme

If yours is a new apartment complex or one undergoing a major change, you have an opportunity to *establish a theme that should be carried through your entire presentation.* If your apartment development is well established, the theme may not be yours to change. But don't regard an established theme as untouchable; if it is out of character with the development, it may need changing.

By a theme we mean a *name and symbol* that typify the development and help to identify the market. Many times a theme is suggested by the architecture or surroundings of the property. Perhaps it's Spanish or Western, suggesting a relaxed way of life. If the architecture is traditional, a more refined life-style is suggested. Then there are nondescript architectural styles that lend themselves to almost any theme.

The presence of lakes and streams on the property provides thematic material. So do groves of trees or maybe surrounding farmland. The kinds of amenities you have on the grounds should enter your thinking. If you have swimming pools, tennis courts, playgrounds, sailing, fishing, ice-skating—all of these point to activity as part of your theme.

In considering a theme, you should consult with the owner and architect who may have had a theme in mind when the place was built. You should certainly consider the market you are trying to reach. It would be a mistake to develop a refined French theme and expect to reach a market of active young people. It would likewise be inappropriate to come up with a relaxed informal theme for a luxury high-rise apartment in the most exclusive part of town.

Names and Symbols

Themes are evident in the name of the development and the symbolism chosen to represent it. Most garden-apartment complexes are identified by a distinctive name—Knollwood, Glenfield, Versailles—whereas in-city apartments are commonly identified by the street number—One City Center, 1000 Lake Shore Drive.

It's very important that the name and symbol be presented in a unified manner. Too often the property manager will find the name printed one way in the newspaper, appear in another style on the building sign, be used in still another way on the brochure, and continue to vary in every other use. All of this is self-defeating because a consistent image is not being built up in the mind of the prospect.

Consistency is a key element in merchandising. It conveys a sense of order that is very reassuring to the prospect. When he sees you following a clear plan of uniformity, he gains respect for your operation, something he doesn't have if he sees a slapdash approach. But consistency is also important for another reason, and that is to reinforce your impressions.

If the prospect sees many variations of the development's name—variations of color, style, placement—he may not recognize it as the same development. The name is the same but the impression is different. But if the name and symbol are always the same, the impressions are the same, and they build up in the prospect's mind so he is less likely to forget you and is more likely to carry away a favorable image.

It's important that you *develop a unified presentation of your name and symbol very early,* so you will be able to use them consistently throughout your presentation. To do this, you should work with a competent *graphics designer,* either an independent studio or someone on the staff of an advertising agency. Select someone good, because you'll have to live with the results of his or her work for years.

The importance of good graphics can't be overestimated. Corporations spend millions of dollars to develop trademarks and logotypes to help identify their products and promote them in the marketplace. Fortunately, with apartments the task and costs are much less and are incurred only once.

In developing the graphic treatment of the name and symbol, try to keep it simple. Bear in mind that it must be suitable for use in a variety of applications—on signs, on letterheads, on vehicles, on brochures. The simpler a design is, the more places it can be used.

A Unified Graphics System

A professionally designed treatment of your development's name and symbol is just the first step. You also need a *unified graphics system* that will spell out how the name and symbol are to be used, and how everything else that appears in print on or about your property is to be treated. Your graphic designer should prepare a graphics manual for you that shows exactly what is permitted and what is not. Among the elements you should include in this manual are the following:

- **Name and symbol**—typeface, style, type sizes, exact color number.
- **Stationery** (letterheads, envelopes, statements, labels, etc.)— exact placement of development name, symbol, address, tele-

phone number, specific color of paper and ink, type of paper.

- **Business cards**—placement of development name and symbol, person's name.
- **Signage**—sizes, type style to be used, placement of development name and symbol colors.
- **Brochures**—type style, placement of development name and symbol, color.
- **Advertisements**—format of ads, type sizes to be used, placement of development name and symbol, margins, use of abbreviations.
- **Vehicles** (company cars, trucks)—color, placement of development name and symbol.

These are starting points. Your graphics designer should examine everything you have or could have that will bear the development name or symbol and include these in the graphics manual. Then you should make sure that everyone in your organization who has anything to do with ordering signs, ads, printed materials, or similar items has the manual and follows it. You should also give copies to your sign painter, printer, newspaper account executive, and advertising agency and insist that they, too, follow the manual.

Signage

Once your theme has been selected, your name and symbol designed, and your graphics manual prepared, you're ready to tackle the all-important challenge of signage. As a general observation, signs are both badly designed and grossly overdone. The average American is exposed to some 43,000 signs every day; most are totally ignored. If your signs are going to have any effect at all, they must at least meet these standards:

1. They must look as *fresh and clean* as if they had just been put up that day. Otherwise they will convey a poor image of your development and people will automatically ignore them.
2. They must be at *right angles to traffic,* not parallel. Otherwise they will be hard to notice and read.
3. They should have *six and no more than eight words.* Too many words and people riding by in autos won't be able to read them.

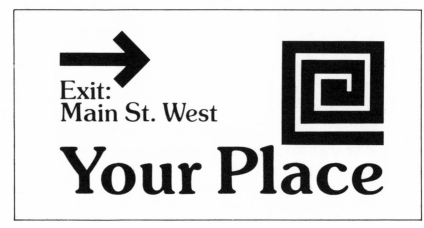

Directional Billboards

These signs are intended to direct, not sell. The sign illustrated at the top is an example of an off-site directional billboard which might be used on a limited-access highway. The directions are clear but brief. The lower illustration shows an example of an on-site billboard commonly used during the early rent-up period of a new development. An arrow or further directions are not always necessary if the way to proceed is obvious.

Signage falls into four broad categories: promotional, directional, identification, and informational.

Promotional signs are primarily offsite billboards and are discussed under Advertising (p. 245).

Directional signs can be located off- or on-site to direct prospects to both your complex and your rental information center.

Just how many directional signs you use and where you use them depends on how difficult it is to find your property. Generally if you are on a well-traveled road in the midst of competing developments, a good entry sign (as we'll describe later) is sufficient. But if you're in a remote location, such signs can be helpful. These signs have value only if they can be read by a motorist through the windshield of his car traveling at the posted speed limit. This requires that the sign be at the proper height, at right angles to traffic, of sufficient size, and have a short, clear message. The sign is to direct; don't try and do a selling job, too. Another form of off-site directional signage is a sign called the *reassurance sign*, or sometimes *trailblazers*. It reassures the prospect that he has indeed made the proper turn and is on the right track. When you go to a company or American Legion picnic at a rural grove, you will often see homemade signs on telephone poles to help lead the way. These are reassurance signs. Yours mustn't be homemade but they do need to be inexpensive because road crews remove them on a pretty regular basis.

Once the prospect makes the turn into your driveway, he should see a sign directing him to the rental information center. As he proceeds along this road, similar signs should be used wherever there is a turn or an intersection with another road so the driver knows exactly how to proceed. Once he reaches the parking lot, other signs should direct him to the visitor parking spaces. When he leaves his car, signs should point the way to the rental information center. If needed, continue the directional signs into the building so the prospect knows exactly where to go.

All of these signs should conform to the graphics manual so they reinforce the image you're trying to convey.

Identification signs perform some of the more important signage functions. The most important of these signs is what is called the *permanent identification* or *keystone* entry sign. This is a permanent sign which is both substantial in its construction and architectural in its design. This sign establishes the character of the

Directional Signs

The two signs at the top are examples of reassurance signs, sometimes called trailblazers. They are usually small, inexpensive, and placed on poles along the route. Note the use of reverse colors. This attracts greater attention and is easier to read. The model and information sign at the bottom is an on-site lead-in sign used to direct prospects. These signs should be used sparingly but often enough to avoid confusion.

development. It usually says little more than the name of the development. When done correctly, these signs are expensive. They should be lighted and made part of a landscaped setting designed for change of seasons or year-'round plantings. The majority of renters will come from drive-bys. This sign will be one of their first contacts and impressions of your property. If given $5,000 to spend on an entry sign and a brochure, the property manager would be better off spending $4,900 on the sign and the remainder on the brochure. He'll draw more traffic and make more of an impact that way.

Other identification signs include building address signs, and signs identifying recreational and supporting amenities such as swimming pools and laundry rooms. Signs identifying the Rental Information Center, Visitor Parking, and Recreation Center are also included in this category. These signs as well as all other forms of signage should be used sparingly so as not to clutter either the landscape or the residential appearance. They must also be consistent with your graphics program.

Informational signs have the least value and are the most offensive of all forms of signage. The most common of these are called command signs. They include signs put up by property managers who like to give commands. They say: "Keep off the grass," "Close the door," "Put garbage in dumpster," "Don't post messages on mailbox," "No galoshes in hallway," etc.

Usually the manager posts these signs to deal with a current problem and then forgets they are there. Often the signs are crudely made with plastic strips or with felt-tip markers. Tenants quickly learn to ignore these signs if they read them in the first place. Sometimes these signs can be confusing. One manager posted a "No hot water" sign when the plumbing in the laundry room was being repaired but forgot to take it down; imagine the confusion when the sign was seen by tenants who used the laundry room a few days later, after the plumbing was back in order.

You should forbid your managers to use such signs. Instead of posting a "Close the door" sign, get a door closer. Rather than tell your tenants via a sign not to put their galoshes in the hallway, send them a letter at the start of the snow season. If you see signs telling people to put their garbage in the dumpster or not to post notices on the mailboxes, remove the signs as quickly as you find them.

If you want to evaluate the impact of such signs, consider what your impression would be if you walked into the lobby of a fine

Permanent Identification Signs

Sometimes called a keystone entry sign, this type of sign is one of the most important. It falls under the classification of identification signs. Its purpose is to identify the development and to mark the main entranceway. This sign should be substantial in construction and its style consistent with the development's architecture.

continental-style hotel and saw signs reading: "Put cigarette butts in ash trays." That would alter the atmosphere considerably, wouldn't it? The same applies in your apartment development.

Some informational signs are necessary or required by law. OSHA posters and swimming pool signs are two common examples. Comply with the law but don't add any unnecessary signs or posters.

Finally, there is another type of informational signage which finds its way into apartment complexes. Contractors, suppliers, and others like to post signs on developments to advertise themselves. Furniture rental companies and apartment locator services are common examples. Calendars, scratch pads, ash trays, and the like with other firms' advertising have no place in your office or rental areas. Don't allow them and remove them if they appear.

Rental Information Center

The typical rental office looks the part; it's cold, harsh, commercial. The furnishings are typical of an office. They include a metal desk and some uninviting hard side chairs. The desk is covered with calendars, appointment books, application forms, and five-day notices. Everything shrieks out: "This is the place where the landlord does his business."

But the prospect hasn't come necessarily to do business. He or she has come for information. The appearance of most rental offices puts the prospect on the defensive. He is on his guard and antagonistic if he walks into an office situation that makes him think he's applying for a loan.

You want to avoid this atmosphere. Begin by calling the facility a *rental information center,* not a rental office or any other kind of office. Office means business, and that's what the prospect may want to avoid at this stage.

Furnishings

Next, furnish your rental information center with *residential scale furniture*—comfortable chairs and round tables for discussions. Create a warm, inviting environment that says, "Welcome!" Use bright colors to liven up the surroundings. Serve coffee in the winter, iced tea or lemonade in the summer, plus cookies. All of this puts the prospect at ease.

Identification Signs

These signs are used to identify important buildings and locations as well as to provide address identification of the individual apartment buildings. They can be installed either as plaques affixed to buildings or as free-standing signs on standards. Their design, use of logo, color, and type style should be consistent and should conform to your established graphics system.

The round tables we mentioned are important. When you and the prospect sit down to discuss the apartment and lease application, you want to avoid having him sit on one side of a desk and you on the other. That again creates the head-to-head selling situation. Instead, you want to be on his side. The round tables accomplish this very adroitly because there are no sides.

Exhibits

The *exhibits* in the rental information center are important. You need them not just to give information about the development but to allow visitors to occupy themselves in case you're involved with another prospect. No one wants to stand around gaping at plain walls; people welcome the opportunity to look at something informative. Exhibits serve another function; they give the prospect and his spouse a chance to step off into a corner to discuss a detail of the lease terms in the guise of checking the exhibit. They don't want to be embarrassed by asking for a moment to discuss things between them. Instead, the man or woman will suggest that "there's an interesting feature on that wall exhibit" and step over to look at it, using this opportunity to talk things over.

For exhibits you can use *scale models* of the development, *a site plan, photos* of the building, enlargements of *floor plans, photos or sketches of amenities,* and *lists of features.* One of the best exhibits is a *large aerial photograph* of the development showing its relation to the rest of the community. People enjoy locating themselves on the photo and seeing where other familiar features are.

Some apartment developments go so far as to have the brochures of competing developments on display. This enables the rental agent to compare the subject development with others and to counter prospects who say they want to see what the competition has to offer before making up their mind.

If your model apartments are in the same building as the rental information center, you may want to extend the graphics or exhibits into the connecting corridor so the prospect continues to get a favorable impression of the information center as he walks to the model apartments.

Model Apartments

A well-furnished model apartment is an essential part of the merchandising program for developments in their initial rent-up or

Pool Rules

Hours: 10:00 am to 10:00 pm Daily
Children under 12 years of age must
be accompanied by an adult.
No glass in pool area.

Office Hours

Weekdays
11:00 am to 6:30 pm

Weekends
11:00 am to 5:00 pm

STOP

Speed

20

Limit

Informational Signs

Shown here are examples of informational signage. Care should be taken
to minimize the use of such signs. Signs that fall into this classification
typically are command signs that are hand-lettered on-site. Frequently,
they are graphically inconsistent, are rarely obeyed, and are irritating to
tenants. Use them only when absolutely necessary.

those suffering with an undue number of vacancies. A good model establishes an atmosphere and life-style which cannot be verbalized but can only be felt.

You should observe these points in setting up a model:

- **Furnish two models,** one a one bedroom unit, the second a two bedroom unit. If you furnish just one, your model tour will be short. If you furnish more than two, you really are showing nothing more than additional bedrooms; don't furnish the three and four bedroom models unless you are having great trouble renting them.

  By furnishing two models, you can show two different life-styles, one that appeals to the younger renter, the other that caters to a more mature person. By taking the prospect from one to the other, you can convey an idea of how adaptable the apartments are without creating confusion.

- **For your model apartment, select one of the least desirable units,** not one of the best. This sounds odd, but it isn't. Prospects are quick to detect the advantages of an apartment with a good layout and location. The decorated model apartments can work as a great equalizer of your best and worst apartment layouts. The poorer layout will gain desirability when shown with creative decorating. The better layout can stand on its own without the help of the sample furnishings. Owners and developers often push to model the best layouts to gain ego satisfaction. This leads to an unbalanced rent-up, with the better layouts renting faster and the less desirable units moving slower at less than the greatest potential rent.

- **The model apartment should be a real apartment,** not a mock-up in a detached temporary building. Experience shows that renters react best to the real apartment. This may not always be possible, particularly with condominiums where pre-sales are very important.

  Many developers who put up new buildings are in a hurry to get leases signed before the building is finished. This feeling is understandable. But prospective renters are no longer in a hurry and would rather see the apartments in the finished building.

  Meanwhile, the developer has spent precious dollars to build and furnish the mock-up plus extra dollars to maintain it. When the building is ready, he now faces the added cost of decorating the actual apartment model and transferring the furnishings. He has gained little in the interim and would have been better off waiting to furnish the real apartment.

- **Make the decorating and furnishings of the model truly outstanding,** not mediocre, regardless of what market the building is designed for. The more dramatic the approach, the better.

A model apartment is intended to be *looked at, not lived in.* It shouldn't contain a triple dresser in the bedroom or a TV or hi-fi set. Its purpose is to establish an atmosphere and to suggest a life-style that has eluded the prospect.

In years past, property managers and developers used to get department stores and furniture stores to decorate the models, expecting that the store would do the job for little or no cost in return for the chance to promote the store name in the models and in advertising. The result of this approach was usually a very "homey" type of model that may have been very comfortable to live in but left no impact on the prospect. Too often this arrangement reflected the taste and inventory of the store rather than the goals of the rental program.

The same applies to the use of rented furniture for models. The style and quality are often cheap and mediocre, adding absolutely nothing to the appeal of the apartment.

A far better way is to *hire a competent interior designer* and give him or her free rein to decorate the apartment to its best advantages. You may get results that are "way out" and startling, but they will be memorable as well. People will come to see and talk about the apartments, helping you build traffic. You may not want to live in such a daring apartment, but your prospects will remember it. Your high-income prospects will expect to see something innovative in decorating and your moderate-income prospects will be flattered by this approach. Either way, you'll impress your prospects and give them something to remember.

Don't worry about recovering the cost. When the time comes to close the model, if you have used a trendy decor, chances are you can recover 60 percent or more of the original cost of furnishings. With mediocre furnishings, you'll be lucky to recover 30 percent. The difference is that people are willing to pay more for decorator merchandise, whereas they know they can get conventional furnishings anywhere.

- **Do a complete decorating job, down to the accessories.**
This includes flowers and place settings on the tables and books on the shelves, plus guest towels in the model bath and interesting utensils in the kitchen.

  But don't go too far. Some managers think it wise to put food in the refrigerator, towels in the closet, even a half-eaten cookie on a plate to give the idea that someone lives in the apartment. This is wrong. If prospects get this idea, they'll think they're intruding into someone's private domain. The minute they open a closet and find towels inside, they'll shut it quickly and feel embarrassed. Furnish the apartment like a model, not like a real-life home.

- **Maintain your model apartments so long as they are useful in your leasing program.**
Once you have your model set up, you should *maintain it* in first-class condition. Have your maintenance crew go over it daily to vacuum carpets, see that ash trays are cleaned, bathroom fixtures sparkling, and everything else is in good order. If you discover that some accessories have been pilfered, expect this and have them replaced. Don't let your model take on a run-down appearance.

  When you reach 90 percent occupancy, you're in a good position to sell off your model furnishings and rent the rest of the apartments by showing vacant units. At this point your models will probably begin to show wear and tear as well as their age. Despite their daring good looks when they were new, fashion soon catches up and they will begin to look dowdy. So this is a good time to close them out.

  If you are managing a phased development where new buildings are being opened in successive years, you should *relocate the models* to the newest building. You may be able to reuse some of the furniture by having it cleaned or recovered. The point is to emphasize the newness in the new buildings by having new models rather than trying to rent from the old ones. One risk you face is that some of your tenants living in the earlier phases will be attracted to the new models and some may want to transfer to one of the new buildings. This risk is worth taking in view of the appeal the new models will have in drawing entirely new prospects to the newly opened buildings.

Brochures and Collateral Material

Contrary to what many people think, a brochure has very little value in renting apartments. This is certainly not true of brochures for condominiums or new houses. In these cases, the brochure is an important selling tool because the sale is rarely made on the first visit.

But in the case of renting apartments, 75 to 80 percent of rentals are made on the prospect's first visit if all elements of the program are right. So for these people, the brochure is a post-selling tool, to help them reinforce the feeling they've made the right decision, and to answer any questions that may not have been answered during their visit. That leaves the other 20 to 25 percent to be convinced later on, and it is for these people the brochure is intended. They visit five or six developments in a day's time, are confused by what they see, can't remember one project from the next, and need to refer to facts to help them sort out one development from another. But keep in mind when planning your brochure, you're doing it for the benefit of a minority of prospects.

Your brochure should be *simple, direct, clear,* and *inexpensive.* The slicker and more filled with superlatives it becomes, the more damage it does. Remember we said that renters don't want to be sold; they want information. Give them the facts with a straightforward narrative message. Don't try to win them over with mood copy that they'll see right through.

For example, here's the kind of brochure copy to be avoided:

"Four hundred acres of natural beauty. The cool tranquility of a mile-long lake and winding streams. Oak trees, pine trees, and willows. Brooks, glens, and glades. Wildlife. Flowers. Heavenly Manor offers apartments set in the midst of one of the most beautiful settings in our area."

That's a lot of atmosphere copy that says nothing and turns off the reader. Instead, use copy like this:

"We're at Lake Drive and Lynn Lane, with easy access to shopping, business, churches, and schools. Lake Louise, just 5 minutes away, offers sailing, fishing, golf, park, and picnic areas. The airport and downtown are 20 minutes away. Choose from 4 large floor plans—1, 2, 3 bedrooms and 3 bedrooms with den. Each has lots of closet and linen space, washer and dryer in each unit, modern all-electric kitchens, and individual climate controls."

Just the facts.

When it comes to illustrating the brochure, use actual photographs where possible, stay away from renderings of buildings. People regard renderings as unbelievable.

One word of caution: *Don't illustrate anything in the brochure or write anything that won't be in your development.* The brochure will go into the prospect's drawer and it comes out later as an implied warranty. If you picture tennis courts for atmosphere, for example, but don't actually have them, the prospect will hold this against you and claim that you promised tennis courts. The same goes for any other feature or service referred to but not actually provided.

Finally, be sure your brochure includes the complete *name of your development;* complete *street address, city, state,* and *zip code;* and *telephone number* with area code. This is particularly important for prospects who visit a number of developments in different suburbs or cities. Without this information, the prospect may not remember who or where you are.

This same identifying information should be on *floor plans* and the *site plan* if these are inserts to the brochure. Floor plans should be as large as possible: more than six by eight inches is recommended. The larger the floor plan, the larger the apartment appears in the prospect's mind. People have problems relating to small floor plans, so make them big. Also remember to include dimensions on the floor plans for all rooms except the bath and closets, where dimensions aren't needed.

Site plans are good if yours is a multi-building development. The site plan identifies all the amenities and helps the prospect orient himself to a particular building and its relative location.

Besides the brochure, floor plans, and the site plan, there are other items that come under the general heading of collateral sales material. These include:

- **A form letter or card** sent to prospects after they leave to thank them for their visit and signed with the name of the rental agent who helped them.

- **Books of matches** bearing the name and symbol of the development to be passed out in the rental information center.
- **Postcards** with a picture of the development. These can be picked up by prospects in the rental information center. They can also be used by new tenants to notify friends of their change of address.
- **Lapel buttons** with the building name and symbol. If these are freely distributed in the rental center, you'd be surprised how many people will pick them up and take them home where they act as reminders of the prospect's visit.
- **Hard candy** wrapped in paper with the building's name and logo.

You'll discover other items of collateral for yourself. Just make sure they tie in with your development's theme and are designed to match the unified graphics system.

Advertising and Public Relations

In our chapter on preparing your product, we noted that 55 percent of the people who rent apartments do so because they liked what they saw when they drove by. That leaves 45 percent who visit the property for other reasons. As a matter of fact, experience shows that of the prospects who become renters, only 15 percent were attracted by paid advertising, usually newspaper advertising. So while advertising has a role to play, its value in renting apartments has been greatly overrated. You should keep this point in mind when you are attempting to step up a lagging rental program by increasing the advertising.

There are many types of advertising you can use for your property: daily newspapers, community newspapers, radio, television, billboards, direct mail, telephone directory, etc. We'll discuss the merits of these one by one. But first, let's consider the two major types of advertising you can use.

- The first is *institutional advertising*. Its purpose is to establish an image, theme, status appeal, life-style, character, and reputation for a development. It does not zero in on specific apartments for rent or call for an immediate response. Rather, it seeks to remind the public that you are there.

Institutional advertising is good if you are renting a large community that will take several years to complete, such as a planned unit development or a multi-phase garden complex. This kind of advertising helps to establish and keep the name of the community before the public. In some cases, it may stimulate a person who is in the market for a new apartment to come out and see what you have to offer. But the purpose of institutional advertising is not to prompt an immediate response but to establish a long-term image.

- The second kind of advertising is *promotional advertising.* Here the objective is to produce immediate buying action for a specific product or service. Promotional advertising focuses on one or two items, uses media with a great sense of immediacy (such as the newspaper), and calls for action now.

You can understand the difference between institutional advertising and promotional advertising this way:

Institutional advertising says: "Come live in Happy Acres, where we have 1, 2, and 3 bedroom apartments renting from $200 to $350 per month."

Promotional advertising says: "For rent: 2 bedroom apartment, utilities included, washer-dryer in apartment, recreation facilities, $280 per month. Happy Acres, 415 Lynn Road, Westbury, Conn."

In one case we're talking generalities, in the other case specifics. You'll discover that most of the time, promotional advertising will be more effective for you than institutional advertising in renting apartments.

Be aware that in our discussion, we are talking about *advertising of rental properties,* not condominiums or for-sale properties which require an entirely different kind of advertising philosophy and approach.

Newspaper Advertising

Many property managers believe that a continuing program of newspaper advertising, especially on weekends, is absolutely essential if they are to rent apartments. They believe that if they run an ad on Saturday or Sunday, prospects will come streaming out to rent apartments.

This isn't so. To find out for yourself, make this test: discontinue all your newspaper advertising for one or two weekends and notice the difference in traffic count. You'll discover there has been no change in rental traffic.

Why is this? There are several reasons. As we said, most of your rental prospects are drive-bys; they come in whether you advertise or not. A good portion are drawn by the advertising of your competitors and while they're in the neighborhood, they stop in to visit you. This works in the opposite way when you advertise; you help draw traffic that will visit your competitors. The property which looks the best will always come out ahead in this traffic trading. Finally, many prospects are already aware of you and are not influenced by any further ads or lack of advertising.

This doesn't imply that you can do without advertising. Before you can make the test of discontinuing your ads, you must have a newspaper advertising program to start with, to get your name established. The point we're making is that beyond a certain point, newspaper advertising seldom produces any additional traffic and in fact may be safely discontinued for short periods without affecting your rental traffic. You can't discontinue it altogether, of course, because then that 15 percent portion of the rental market that is drawn by advertising will have no way of knowing about you. The point is, don't rely on newspaper advertising to produce miracles.

Let's look at the limited impact of newspaper advertising from another angle. We said that you can't sell apartments to a prospect; instead, you give him the information he needs to make his decision. Actually, people make up their minds to change living quarters several months before they set out on their first outing to look at available housing. People can be expected to scan newspaper ads for a full six weeks before leaving their living rooms.

What does prompt a person to start looking for a new apartment is a whole series of incidents. The situation is much like that of a person whose car begins to give him trouble. It begins to burn oil, the tires need replacing, it won't start on cold mornings, and so on. The owner begins to ask himself: "What's my car worth? What would a new car cost?" He begins to casually notice new car ads and then looks at the classified pages to see what used cars are selling for. In his mind he calculates what difference he'll have to pay between what he'll get for his old car and the price of a new one. He is now paying close attention to different car styles and makes as he drives about. Then, after one or two more mishaps with his old car and one or two more whopping repair bills, he makes up his mind to buy a new or better one and starts his shopping in earnest. That's when he begins to pay serious attention to the ads.

The prospective renter does the same thing. He is vaguely discontented with his present apartment. The closets are too small and overstuffed. The landlord or property agent gave him a hard time when he asked to have a leaky faucet fixed. Maybe his children are having bad experiences at school. He is getting fed up with the heavy traffic on the long drive to work. All of this discontent is building up and reaches a peak in the two- to four-month period just before the renter decides that enough's enough.

During this time, he and his wife have been aware of institutional ads that tell about the wonders of this community and that one. These ads contribute to their feeling of dissatisfaction. But these institutional ads don't spur the prospect to come out. As a matter of fact, they often have the opposite effect. Because of their size and image-building character, they may convince the prospect that the development is out of his league and too expensive. But at least the institutional ad does keep him stirred up about moving in general.

Finally, in the few weeks before the actual shopping begins, the prospect starts studying the classified ads. Instinct tells him that if there are any real bargains, they will be in the smaller classified ads and not in the larger display/classified ads placed by major complexes or realty companies.

Then one weekend when the weather is nice but not too nice, or the present landlord has failed again, or a particular ad promises an unusual value, the prospect will actually take to his car and begin to shop. The people who respond to your ad have undoubtedly followed a similar pattern. Their need or desire for different housing accommodations began months before, followed by weeks of ad comparisons and searching, and ending with the actual physical inspections. Assuming your ad appears on the weekend the prospect decides to shop, he might well show up at your doorstep in response. This, however, requires a bit of coincidence, the right timing, and some skill in the art of writing an effective ad.

Coincidence is only luck; timing will come with experience; but the skills of preparing an ad can be learned. Consider these points in understanding newspaper advertising.

There are three types of newspaper advertising:

- **Classified,** so called because the advertising is classified by

Classified Ads

Classified ads are the most common form of promotional advertising for rental apartments. Every ad, regardless of size, must answer three basic questions prospective tenants ask themselves: What do I get? How much does it cost? and, Where do I find it? A series of different ads of varying sizes is recommended to attract maximum readership.

subject matter—jobs wanted, jobs available, goods for sale, homes for sale, apartments to rent. The ads are all ganged together in one section of the paper and generally run in one-column widths, using the uniform type style and format of the newspaper.

- **Display.** These are the ads that run throughout the newspaper, using illustrations and a variety of type styles.
- **Display/classified.** This is a hybrid type of ad that combines the artwork and variety of type styles of a display ad in the classified section of the newspaper.

In most cases you'll find that classified advertising will be the most productive for you. It is recommended for all promotional advertising. Display and display/classified are better suited for institutional advertising.

Regardless of what kind of newspaper ad you run, the ad should answer three questions:

1. **What do I get?** This means spelling out the features of the property, beginning with the apartment. Start with the number of bedrooms; that's the first thing prospects want to know. Then list the number of baths, kitchen equipment, carpeting and drapes if included, air-conditioning and individual climate controls, utilities, fireplace, vanities, washer and dryer connections, closets. Go on to list the recreational amenities: swimming pool, sauna, tennis courts, playground, sun deck, lake, putting green, etc.

   You can set down these features either in a *narrative* style, running the items together in a continuing sentence, or in a *bulletin or list* style, running them one under the other. In fact, it's a good idea to vary the form so your ad doesn't look the same each weekend.

   Don't abbreviate! BR, Kit., fpl., tn. ct., and A/C may be understandable to you, but the reader may not understand and in any event, abbreviations impede easy reading of the ad. Generally understood abbreviations—St., Ave., Blvd., Dr.—are permissible.

   As another technique for variety and to attract different markets, you can switch what you have to offer from week to week. For example, one week you can advertise one and two bedroom apartments to catch one segment of the market.

Display Ad

Display ads are used primarily to create a mood and awareness. They are generally used in conjunction with a grand opening campaign or on a sustaining basis for a large, multi-phase development. The sample ad shown here (which has been reduced in size) might be used as a full-page ad in a magazine or newspaper.

The next week you can advertise three and four bedroom units to catch the family market. The point is not to put everything you have to offer in a single ad, or else you'll confuse the prospect. Remember, each prospect is looking for one kind of apartment, and he is not really impressed by your ability to accommodate all family sizes. You are better off by running separate ads if you have many sizes of apartments to offer than by cramming them all into one ad.

2. **What does it cost?** Some property managers are not confident of their rental pricing so they don't list the rent in the ad. Their hope is that once the prospect sees the apartment, he'll accept the rent being asked. However, for every prospect who is drawn by such an ad without a price, the manager will lose 10 to 15 who won't come because the rent isn't listed. This is a terrible waste.

   If you don't want to list a specific price, it's perfectly all right to use a leader price: "From $185." Or you can give a rent range: "Apartments from $225 to $480." In fact, the high end of the range adds to the status appeal of the property, even though the prospect may be interested in only the low end.

3. **How do I find it?** It's hard to believe it, but the directions in the vast majority of ads for suburban garden complexes will lead the prospect somewhere else. The person who writes the ad knows how to get there and, because of this knowledge, omits a vital step in spelling out the directions.

   To prove this point, we have made it a practice when visiting apartment complexes in various cities never to be picked up at the airport or telephone for drive-out instructions. Instead, we attempt to locate the place from the instructions in the newspaper ad. In the course of visiting almost a thousand developments in five years, we have seldom found the place we are looking for by following the ad.
   Location instructions should be crystal clear. Start from a major expressway or major arterial street. Identify this street by its most commonly known name and route number. Sometimes a major expressway or street is known by different names as it passes through different communities or even in the same large community, which is why a route number is helpful.

Your Place

1 & 2 Bedroom Apartments

Your Place offers you all you would expect in apartment living and more, "a place to call home." Each Apartment is carefully designed to offer you the most in custom features including:

- Shag Carpeting
- Central Air Conditioning
- Self Cleaning Oven
- Dishwasher
- 2 Door No Frost Ref.
- Garbage Disposal
- Master TV Antenna

For your leisure time, Your Place offers a beautifully decorated Club House with a Large Pool and Lighted Tennis Courts.

From $220.00 to $310.00

Your Place is conveniently located only minutes from Schools, Shopping and Expressways.

Directions: Take I-101 to Main St. Exit—go West 1½ Blocks to Your Place. Only minutes to Schools and Shopping.

Furnished models open daily 11:00 am to 6:00 pm

Your Place
200 Place Drive
388-2000

Display/Classified Ad

This type of ad is a hybrid of both classified and display ads. It appears in the classified section of the newspaper. Normally, an ad of this type and size is too expensive for weekly use and should be reserved for grand openings or other institutional advertising programs. A smaller classified ad will generally bring out more prospects than the larger, more expensive display/classified ad. Use the latter sparingly.

Then identify the exit by name and number. Be sure this name and number are visible to the person on the expressway. You may know the exit as 22nd Street because you drive it every day, but all the prospect has to go by is Exit 14. Drive out to the exit sign yourself to make sure you have it right.

Also make sure the exit is identified from all directions. A prospect driving from the east may be able to turn off at Exit 14, but there may be a different number from the west or, worse yet, there may be no west exit. In that case, you'll have to direct him to another exit.

Tell the prospect which way to turn from the exit—right or left—and then continue to guide him along the various streets until he gets to your place. Spell out the instructions carefully. It helps if you have directional signs along the way. As we noted earlier, these signs may be knocked down, so don't count too heavily on them. Make sure your drive-out instructions are complete and clear so the prospect can find you without signs.

You may have a *choice of routes* to get to your development. The most direct route may lead the prospect past unattractive scenes or perhaps in front of your competitors. Real estate agents who sell homes are careful to take the prospect along the most scenic route, even though it's longer, so the prospect won't see the garbage dump two blocks away on the direct route. Consider which is best for you and write your instructions accordingly.

If prospects continue to have trouble finding you, your answer may be a display classified ad that includes a map. The map should be to scale, not distorted, and it should indicate mileage distances so the prospect can get some indication of how he's proceeding and where you are from major points.

What about a *telephone number* in the ad? While a telephone number is helpful as part of your signature to aid people who get lost, that's about all it is good for. A telephone number should not be a major element of your ad.

You are looking for people to come out to see you, not to call. The task of selling a prospect by telephone is next to impossible.

If you rely on the telephone, you'll be faced with mostly unfulfilled appointments. Aside from prospects who want drive-out instructions, people who telephone in response to your ad fall into one of three categories:

- They really aren't serious but are calling to get an unpleasant duty out of the way. Perhaps it's a man who is comfortably watching Sunday football on television and now makes the call to please his wife who sees the ad. He makes the call and then tells his wife the place isn't for them.

- They have unrealistic expectations. A young couple expecting to live in $500 luxury for $300 a month calls to ask about all the conveniences and amenities. When they find you don't have washer and dryer connections in the apartments, they hang up. If they saw your place with its modern laundry room and all the other conveniences, they might rent. But the telephone gives them an excuse to rule you out.

- They are fearful of being misled by the ad. These people don't believe what you say in print and they will discount what you say on the telephone. But if they visit your property, they can see your features for themselves. The telephone rules out this possibility.

In short, include the telephone number as a convenience, but don't feature it in your ad or rely on it to bring out prospects.

Advertising Details

Now that we've covered the three questions that every apartment ad should answer, let's consider a number of other details of newspaper advertising:

- **Headlines.** Catchy headlines don't catch. They may make the prospect think that some clever salesperson is out to get them. The serious classified ad reader doesn't want to be entertained. All he wants to know is how many rooms you have, the features and amenities, the price, and the location. For a headline, it's better to use either the name of your property or the number of bedrooms.

- **Size.** Prospects think that the true bargains are in the smaller ads. So the smaller your ad, the more likely you are to attract prospects. Just make sure that the ad answers the three questions, no matter how small it is. We have found that the most successful classified ads are those that are the smallest and that advertise the fewest number of units.

Large ads are self-defeating. The prospect who sees a large ad is apt to think that you have a correspondingly large number of apartments to rent. Apartments in plentiful supply or that appear to be slow moving attract little response. Prospects are looking for the rare find. The small ad helps convey that image.

Newspapers traditionally arrange classified ads on the page by size, the larger ads on top, the smaller ones toward the bottom. It's a good idea to vary the size of your ad from week to week so the newspaper will move it around on the page. That way you have a better chance of catching the roving eye of the prospect and you won't get stuck in one position.

- **Type size.** The newspaper ad salesman will tell you that large type is easier to read. Naturally he wants to sell you large type because that makes the ad larger and the newspaper gets more money for it. But don't be afraid of using the standard newspaper type size for classified ads. When people read the classified pages, their eyes adjust to the small type on the page and they'll have little trouble reading your ad.

- **White space.** Again to sell you a larger ad, the newspaper ad salesman will advise you to use plenty of white space in your ad. But this can be overdone. Don't use white space simply for the sake of using it. You can run an effective ad that is crowded from corner to corner.

- **Choice of paper.** In most metropolitan areas with more than one daily newspaper, one paper is the recognized leader in apartment ads. That's the paper to be in. You're wasting your money in the others.

Community newspapers offer another opportunity. These papers are usually published weekly and they cover a smaller geographic area than the large dailies. A prospect who is looking for an apartment in a particular area may very well look in that local paper.

If you use both the leading daily and a community paper, *alternate your placements* so you are not in both of them the same week. This will stretch your advertising dollar and give you a better evaluation of the response.

- **Frequency.** Sunday advertising is essential; that's the day most prospects are looking. Beyond Sunday, one other day is all that is ever recommended. Don't advertise more than twice a week in any one newspaper.

Weekday advertising once a week can be effective. Your weekday ad can be smaller than your Sunday ad because there are generally fewer weekday ads competing against you. Also the person who looks for apartments during the week is a more serious shopper than a Sunday prospect. Many transferees, who must locate housing quickly, shop during the week and may be attracted by your weekday ad.

In scheduling your ads, take into account holidays, season of the year, and weather. Don't blame your advertising if the weekend turns out to be the first balmy days after a dreary winter when people would rather stroll in the park than visit apartments. Don't expect advertising to draw people in July and the first two weeks of August when many people are on vacation. The last two weeks of August and the first part of September, on the other hand, are good periods for attracting prospects.

Finally, while these are not, strictly speaking, details of advertising, they are points you should consider in your advertising strategy:

- **Grand-opening ads.** The exception to the rule of the smaller the apartment ad the better is the grand-opening ad. Here you may want to use a large display or display/classified ad for a series of weekends to establish your presence. People expect a large ad in connection with a grand opening, but if the large ad continues to appear long after the grand opening is over, prospects become suspicious and they'll avoid you.

- **Pre-leasing ads.** These ads aim to draw prospects for apartments that are not yet available. We advise against them. If you draw prospects, you need an apartment to show them; without an apartment, you are wasting advertising money. Rely on drive-by traffic for any pre-leasing business you hope to do.

- **The best ad.** An unusual but effective ad might contain the following message: "Thank you for your tremendous response. We're all filled up. If you want to get on our waiting list, stop by and leave your name." Such an ad will pull tremendous traffic. People want what they can't have, and they'll come out to see what makes you so successful.

Radio Advertising

Radio has a lot of things in its favor. Rates are low, much lower than most people think. For FM radio, the rates are even cheaper than for AM. Radio is also one of the most effective traffic builders there is. We have seen cases where rental traffic has built up tremendously within minutes after a message is on the air during a weekend. Why? Because many radio listeners are in their cars driving around and when they hear something interesting, they turn around to respond to it. This is certainly true of prospects who are out driving on a weekend. The stations that generate the most traffic are those that cater to young people and teenagers. AM radio reaches a larger audience than FM radio does, principally because AM radio has a greater range and there are fewer FM radios in use, especially in cars. But the number of FM radios is increasing year by year.

Unfortunately, while radio generates a lot of traffic, this *traffic seldom rents.* It consists mainly of curiosity-seekers who want to know what's going on and who come out for any premiums you may be offering. Certainly the teenagers who are drawn by your radio messages aren't prime rental prospects.

This doesn't mean that radio has no value in renting apartments. Radio can be especially effective in connection with *grand openings.* The heavy traffic built up by radio can help convey a feeling of success that may convince the serious prospects that they ought to rent before all the apartments are taken.

If you use radio, it's a good idea to schedule your advertising to build up from Thursday through Saturday, and then slack off by midafternoon on Sunday. Pay particular attention when buying time. Many stations have *restrictions* on what's available and when you can buy time. Some popular programs are filled up, with no time available. You may have to buy a package of undesirable time periods in order to get the time you want. Sometimes the station will schedule your commercials at its convenience. You have to be aware of these possibilities and take them into account when planning your campaign.

Television Advertising

Television is a great but expensive selling medium. Spot commercials for apartment developments are almost always used as a form of institutional advertising. They are only rarely intended to promote the leasing of individual apartments.

In smaller cities and towns, television time is somewhat cheaper; in most metropolitan areas, the cost is prohibitive except for the top luxury apartments with large promotion budgets. Besides the cost of time, there is also the cost of production. A good television commercial costs a lot of money to make and it must be done with great care or else the product will suffer. One way to cut cost is to make commercials using videotape rather than film. In fact, most TV stations will offer to do this for you.

Another way to cut costs is to advertise on UHF stations which have lower rates and smaller audiences than VHF stations.

Be wary of certain television traps. One is the low rate for late night shows and for Friday and Saturday nights. The reason the rates are low is because the audience is smaller, and chances are your prospect market isn't watching.

Another trap is the station that strings a series of real estate commercials together on the same show. You want a show on which you're the only real estate advertiser. At least you don't want to be seen in the same hour with two or three other developments.

A third trap is your desire to advertise on stations and shows that you prefer, without regard for what your market is watching. Don't let your personal viewing or listening preference dictate your television or radio advertising strategy.

Local TV stations may offer opportunities to participate that don't require paid advertising. One such opportunity is the auction for charity benefit. Local merchants are asked to contribute goods and services which are then auctioned off to viewers. The station will generally prepare a commercial showing your complex. This commercial will be run several times each day during the telecast auction in return for your donation of, say a year's free rent on a one bedroom apartment. This can be an opportunity for an apartment development to gain tremendous television exposure and perhaps the free production of a taped commercial, all while benefiting a worthwhile charity.

But in any case, be sure to get competent advice from your advertising agency or other communication professional when dealing with TV.

Magazine and Program Advertising

Included here are regional and city editions of national publications such as *Time* and *Newsweek*; magazines put out for specific cities by local publishers; and programs for concerts, operas, and plays.

In most cases these media are restricted to major cities and in all cases are good only for institutional advertising. You are borrowing the prestige of the publication and associating it with your development. The effect is one of image-building over the long term, but expect little immediate response. For this kind of advertising to do you any good, you have to do it on a sustained basis for a long period. Such advertising is probably most beneficial to luxury apartments.

Direct Mail

This is one of the most effective and most expensive forms of advertising. Many people think this is surprising, especially when they think of the amount of "junk mail" they receive. But postage, whether it's first class or third class, is expensive. Add to this the cost of paper, envelopes, printing, addressing, handling, and the cost per person reached is far higher than any other kind of advertising.

The major advantage of direct mail is its extreme selectivity: it enables you to *reach exactly the prospects you want to reach.* With newspapers, magazines, radio, television, and billboards you are presenting your message before thousands of people who have no possible interest in your development; all of this is waste. But with direct mail you can control your audience.

A direct mail campaign for an apartment complex should consist of a mailing to 300 to 500 names per week. This is a manageable number to handle using your own manpower, and it also is a good number on which to base an evaluation. If you mail to fewer than 300, your evaluation base is small and you also run the risk of reaching too few prospects with a successful mailing. More than 500, and you run up the costs if the mailing is unsuccessful and may get too much of a response if the mailing hits home. The 300-to-500 range is a safe middle ground.

The content of your mailing should be a simple letter inviting the reader to inspect your development. If your brochure is designed to be mailed, this can be included. Don't ask the prospect to phone for an appointment; telephone transactions are a waste of time.

Try to avoid gimmicks or incentives in your letter, such as a free house plant or free transistor radio. Incentives will increase the response, but they will also lead the reader to think you are desperate. Incentives also tend to weaken your status appeal.

You can pre-stuff your letter and brochure into plain white envelopes, then write the name and address of the recipient by hand; don't type or use labels. Please note that you don't need a printed envelope with your return name and address. The plain white envelope with the hand-written name and address will get the most attention. Of course, the mailing should go first-class. A third-class mailing signals a sales pitch or something unimportant.

Don't bother to personalize the letter itself. The reader will recognize the letter for what it is, and personalizing won't add enough to justify the additional cost.

Time your mailing to go out on a Tuesday for arrival Thursday, no later than Friday. This gives the prospect plenty of time to plan for a visit on the weekend. There's nothing more wasted than a direct mail letter for an apartment development that arrives on a Monday. By the weekend it's forgotten.

A good direct mail campaign will draw a 4 percent response; that is, if you mail to 500 names, you should get 20 prospects to visit you. If you score 4 percent or better, mail the same letter to the same list the following week. You'll most likely get the same response on the second weekend. That's because the second group originally intended to come out the first weekend but for one reason or another postponed it.

If your response is less than 4 percent, consider other approaches. You may want to switch to another list of names or change the appeal in your letter. Remember the effect of weather—bad or good—on weekend traffic and take this into account when evaluating a poor response.

There's no magic formula for successful direct mail. You'll have to work out your own. If you'll stick to the 300-to-500 sample, keep your letter simple, and experiment with different approaches, you will find the formula that works for you.

Yellow Page (classified telephone directory) Advertising

People don't normally look in the Yellow Pages for unfurnished apartments, unlike people who shop for furnished apartments. The higher the caliber of the tenant, the less likely he is to consult the Yellow Pages.

Add to this the high cost of an eighth-page or quarter-page ad and the waste circulation, and the value of a Yellow Page advertisement becomes even more questionable.

A simple listing of your apartment development name in boldface type is adequate. If you like, you can include the hours your rental information center is open and an emergency telephone number for the benefit of tenants who may use the Yellow Pages instead of the regular telephone directory.

Apartment Guides

Many communities have these booklets which are usually pages of display ads of different apartment developments. These guides are distributed free at high-traffic points: shopping centers, airports, train depots, drug stores, etc. In some communities these guides are very effective; in others they are not. The people who pick them up and read them are nearly always in the market. You will have to learn from experience whether the apartment guide in your area is a useful tool. If it is, you should be in it. The cost is usually a fraction of what a newspaper ad costs and the usefulness of the guide is usually over a period of months, maybe as much as a year.

Handbills and Flyers

These pieces of throwaway literature are not recommended except for grand openings and special promotion. They tend to cheapen your product when used on a sustaining basis.

Newsletters

As far as tenants are concerned, newsletters produced by the management have little value. Tenants regard them as propaganda pieces, even if they contain information that is useful. A newsletter can backfire and spark a tenants' newsletter to answer management's claims and to air grievances of unsatisfied tenants.

Prospects tend to look at the newsletter as sales literature, more institutional and less commercial than the brochure. The newsletter does tend to create the impression of a viable community, which may be an important point to make. Also, the newsletter can be updated periodically so it reflects the current status of the

Promotional Billboards

Not intended to direct, promotional billboards are designed to establish an awareness and an identity. They must be large, properly placed, and contain few enough words to be read and understood quickly. The use of the "reverse" color combination as shown on the lower sign will attract more attention from a greater distance so long as the message is short.

development. If the rental program for the development extends long enough, several editions of the newsletter can be produced to report on construction progress, tenants moving in, opening of amenities, the relationship of the development to the surrounding community, and so on. Such a newsletter can be useful in repeat mailings to prospects as part of a direct mail campaign.

If you're going to do a newsletter, do it well and make sure it meets the requirements of your unified graphics approach.

Billboards

These can be used to convey an institutional message as part of an overall campaign. More commonly they are used for directional signage near highly traveled roads as explained earlier. The primary value of the billboard is to direct people who are already heading your way.

Be aware of the *limitations of billboard advertising.* If the salesman claims that 10,000 people see the sign every day, figure it's largely the same 10,000 seeing it going to and from work. A billboard loses its impact almost as soon as it is put up because people get used to it. The sign needs to be lighted at night if you are to get full value from it. You may have to take a series of billboard placements on a rotating basis which includes poor locations as well as good ones. Finally, the number of billboards is decreasing because of environmental pressures which are driving up the rates for remaining billboards.

All of this means that billboards have limited value so far as apartment renting is concerned. Billboards may be powerful for soft drinks, but apartments are something else.

Transit Advertising

Like billboards, transit ads are usually exposed to the same people all the time. Many of the people who use public transit are not in the market for your apartments, especially if yours is a suburban garden complex. Transit ads on the outside of vehicles get dirty quickly and reflect poorly on your image. The man stuck in a traffic jam behind a bus spewing diesel fumes is not likely to react favorably to your ad staring him in the face from the rear end of the bus. Also, you may not be able to get the routes you want for the exposure of your ad. For all of these reasons, transit advertising is not recommended for apartment renting.

Airport Displays

These displays reach one of the most active and most affluent segments of the housing market, including executives being transferred. But in large metropolitan airports, the cost of these displays is prohibitive and many times the airport has control over how your display looks. In smaller cities, airport displays, including kiosks in airport lobbies, can be reasonable in cost and make sense as part of a major advertising program.

Benches

Advertising on benches at bus stops and elsewhere is usually for reminder purposes. An apartment ad on a bench at a key corner close to your development might be acceptable. If you can afford to erect your own bench and bus-stop shelter, with architecture and landscaping that matches the character of your development, so much the better. Otherwise, bench advertising is wasteful and also reduces the status of your development.

Miscellaneous Advertising

Included here are skywriting, sponsorship of baseball and bowling teams, participation in a parade float, etc. If these have value, the value is strictly institutional. Don't expect prospects to come running out to rent an apartment because they saw your apartment development name on a parade float.

Traffic Builders

There are other strategies and techniques that can be used to draw traffic and prospects, either as part of an advertising program or on their own.

- **Premiums.** You may consider offering a premium in newspaper advertising or direct mail to get people to visit your development. Premiums are frequently used successfully by savings and loan associations, banks, gasoline stations, and appliance dealers to attract customers. But no one will change his place of residence for the sake of a premium. All they'll do is come out to help build up traffic. If that's your goal, fine.

Don't use premiums as an inducement for people to sign a lease application. Nothing will induce them if the apartment doesn't fit their needs. And if they do sign, they would have signed without the premium inducement.

- **Giveaways.** Included here are buttons, balloons, matches, tee-shirts. These are harmless attention-getters. People accept them as token gestures. But if done to excess, they can damage your image and smack of commercialism.

- **Celebrity appearances.** These are good traffic builders for grand openings. They may also be good if the celebrity lives in the building and is willing to appear for the benefit of other tenants. Otherwise, a constant stream of celebrity appearances gives your building a Las Vegas atmosphere which many prospects and tenants won't like.

- **Charitable and public service activities.** Your development may be so conveniently located that you'll be approached to make it the center of various public service activities. The local public health service may ask if it can set up a TB x-ray trailer on your premises. Or the Red Cross chapter may want to hold a blood donor drive in your development, drawing outsiders as well. Perhaps your development might be considered as a good drop-off point for bottles and cans to be recycled, or as the starting point for a charity bike-a-thon.

All of these are good legitimate activities to stimulate public awareness of your development and to increase the number of visitors to it. It may be difficult to trace rentals to such activities, but if it doesn't cost you anything and does not downgrade your image, go ahead and do it.

One thing to be cautious of is any activity that draws large crowds of young people, such as rock concerts, which will drive away prospects, irritate tenants, and probably do great physical damage to your property.

Other Prospect Sources

Besides drive-by traffic and advertisement, there are other sources you can use to produce prospects.

- **Apartment locator services.** These are commercial services that will direct prospects to your property; if the prospect becomes a tenant, you pay the service a fee which is typically a half-month's rent.

  These services have cropped up in many areas with high vacancies. In major metropolitan areas with low vacancies, they play less of a role. They offer the prospect the advantage of centralized searching. The prospect doesn't have to spend time traveling around. Instead, after determining what the prospect is looking for, the locator service will point him in the right direction. What the prospect doesn't realize is that the locator service will refer him only to those apartments for which the service will be paid a fee.

  The trouble with locator services is that the property manager becomes dependent on them, rather than exerting his own efforts to attract prospects. If the manager has his own rental staff and say a 50 percent turnover ratio, he has added significantly to his overhead by using the locator service. The more he uses them, the less he rents on his own.

  If the property manager takes care to set up his own merchandising program correctly, chances are he won't need a locator service at all.

- **Tenant referrals.** Probably no one is a better prospect than the person who walks in to your rental information center saying that he's been referred by a tenant who already lives there. This prospect is probably of the same caliber as the tenant you've already rented to. Moreover, chances are the prospect has seen the tenant's apartment, likes the development, and is ready to rent. The tenant has already done the job of informing and exciting the prospect. Such a prospect is worth much more to you than one referred by a locator service.

  To let tenants know that you'll welcome and reward referrals, periodically send the tenants a letter announcing this. To qualify, the tenant must personally bring in and introduce the prospect, so there's no question later on that a proper referral has been made. You don't want the situation in which a prospect comes in by himself, rents an apartment, and then later on a tenant claims he referred the prospect. The personal introduction eliminates this possibility. When the prospect signs the lease, the tenant who referred him then gets a referral bonus; a suggested bonus is a rent credit of $50 to $100, depending on the rental range.

- **Housing directors.** These include housing directors and personnel managers of nearby corporations, hospitals, and colleges who are seeking housing for people transferring into the area. Contacts with these people are fairly well dominated by full-service real estate firms which can offer a variety of services including home sales and mortgage financing as well as apartments to rent. Few property managers can afford the constant contact with housing directors to cultivate them properly.

  The best you can hope for is that the day you call on the housing director, or the day your mailing reaches his desk, he'll be looking for an apartment for one of his people and you'll be there to capitalize on it. If you can afford the time to make these contacts, you may be lucky.

- **Waiting list.** Unless an apartment becomes available within a day or two after a prospect puts himself on a waiting list, fewer than one percent of the names on such a list ever remain good prospects. Very few will go home and wait for one of your apartments to become available. They'll look elsewhere. The primary advantage in maintaining a waiting list is to add to status appeal. People want what is in demand and hard to get. Word of this will get around which will increase further interest and traffic.

- **Follow-up list.** This is a list of people who say they'll be back but never show. The chances of converting these people to renters is not very good. Once they've left your rental information center, they've lost interest. If you couldn't reach an agreement with them when you had them on the premises, it will be difficult to rekindle their interest over the telephone. A good many will resent your call. Out of 100 prospects you follow up, 20 may agree to come back, 12 may actually show, and three or four may sign. During periods of slow traffic, however, it may be worthwhile to spend the time to follow up and gain this additional traffic and the resulting rentals.

Public Relations

As applied as part of your merchandising campaign, public relations refers to publicity used to gain attention for your development, establish its image and theme, and keep it in the news. Public relations, of course, is much more than merchandising. It includes policy making, product design, personal relations with prospects and tenants, complaint handling, community relations, etc. But since we are dealing with merchandising the product and attracting prospects, we'll look at only the merchandising role of PR.

The power of public relations is in its believability. People regard what they read in the news column of the newspaper as truth; what they read in an ad, although it may say the same thing, is regarded with some suspicion. However, for public relations to have this believability, it must be totally divorced from advertising. If people know that a newspaper regularly trades off editorial space in exchange for advertising, they regard the publicity as advertising and discount it accordingly.

To a great extent, the success of a PR program for an apartment development depends on the ability to come up with stories and photos that will be published in local newspapers and picked up by local radio and TV. This is no job for an amateur. Just as the property manager shouldn't be the designer of the development's symbol and graphics (unless he is a professional designer), he shouldn't be the development's PR expert, either (unless he is a professional PR person). He should go out and hire the best talent available.

Contrary to what many people think, public relations or publicity aren't free. True, the newspapers run it free, but you have to pay someone to create the publicity. Try to conserve on what you pay for good talent and you'll wind up getting few or no results.

Once you have the PR talent on hand, make it clear that what you're after is publicity to build traffic, not publicity to tickle someone's ego. Publicity that builds traffic focuses on the building and its features and appears in newspapers where the public can see it. Ego-building publicity focuses on the developer and manager and is restricted to real estate news corners or trade publications where the general public isn't even aware of it.

Beyond local publicity, your PR counselor may be able to generate interest on the part of *national magazines* to do a story about your development. While these magazines cover far more than your market, their prestige will boost the image of your apartment development. In addition, *reprints* of national magazine stories can be used as information pieces in the rental information center and as direct mail material.

Dealing with Prospects

The performance of your rental staff is of crucial importance. You may have done everything perfectly up to this point and expect large prospect turnouts. But if your rental staff doesn't follow through with its part of the merchandising program, you won't get the signed applications you anticipate.

As we said in the chapter dealing with personnel policies, the people part of property management is often the weakest link. That's because the staff is very seldom trained or motivated to do the right job. Rental agents must understand that their job is to help the prospect select the right place to live. When this is done sincerely, we provide the prospect with a needed service and as a result we have one less apartment to rent. Take a minute and think about the merchants you have dealt with who have taken the extra time and interest to see that you choose the right product, style, or size. This has become such a rare event in our high-speed world that you find yourself amazed and flattered with the extra interest and concern. A man, for example, often feels like a lost sheep when making his annual trip for new business suits. He is tired of his old patterns and styles but lacks the know-how and confidence to experiment with the latest fashions. A skilled haberdasher quickly spots these hidden desires as well as the customer's uncertainties. The man needs more than a suit, he needs help in coordinating his wardrobe. This often includes shirts, ties, contrasting slacks, etc. The customer will certainly spend more than intended but will be happier for it. For a change, he will feel in style and will stand taller and walk brisker in his new coordinated wardrobe. The haberdasher has provided a valuable service. Some novice observers may term this high-pressure selling but the customer in our example doesn't, so how can it be? A true merchandiser who involves himself in helping the customer satisfy a need or desire will always do better, more easily, than the person who simply trys to sell a product or service.

A common greeting by unskilled rental agents typically includes the question: "Would you like a one bedroom or two bedroom apartment?" Many agents do this without rising out of their seat or moving from behind a cluttered desk. We are convinced that the agents do this almost in hope that the prospect will ask to see an apartment size that isn't available so that the agent can quickly dismiss the prospect and resume what he was doing. Even when a tour is given, it lacks interest and enthusiasm, which are essential if the prospect is to be properly served.

Getting Prospect Information

Without substantial involvement that must originate with the rental agent, there is little chance of serving the prospect. You must know something about the prospect; the exchange of names is certainly one of the first items. Offer your name and you'll generally learn his name in return. Americans, when doing business, almost play a game of Ping-Pong. A cordial welcome begets a cordial response. A sharp comment brings a sharper reply. An offer brings a counter offer. If the prospect doesn't offer his name—ask for it. Then remember it and use it. You'll want to know something about where the prospect lives now, why he is considering moving, family size, rent budget, etc. If you ever hope to be of service in finding proper housing accommodations for this prospect, you will need this information.

It takes a great deal of time and patience for a rental agent to learn how to win the prospect's confidence and gradually obtain the needed information without the prospect being aware of it.

Some developers make up a guest card or prospect questionnaire in an attempt to gain this information. This is a brutal method which is almost guaranteed to put the prospect on the defensive.

Consider what would happen if you walked into a cocktail party, were introduced to someone, and then took out a card and pencil and began recording the person's name, occupation, number of children, and so on. Then you repeated this with the next person you met. Before long, you'd be all alone in one corner of the room and everyone else in another. That's what happens when the prospect walks into your warm, inviting, rental information center and suddenly finds himself being badgered with a series of personal questions and sees his answers being recorded on a guest card or questionnaire form. You need the information if you are to be involved and effective, but you must obtain it in a conversational manner, the same way you meet and get to know people at a cocktail party or other gathering.

Your dress will have something to do with how easily you develop rapport with the prospect. You need to dress close to the manner of dress of your prospects; which is probably casual or sporty. There was a time when the rental staff was expected to dress in business attire: suits, shirt, and tie for the men; dresses and high heels for the women. Then came the era of the uniform, usually in the form of a blazer worn by men and women.

In today's more relaxed and casual atmosphere, it's perfectly proper for the rental staff to dress in more casual wear. Suits and ties for men are too stiff and formal for most rental information centers; they remind the prospect of a business setting and put him on his guard. Just how casual you can be depends on your area of the country. The West, Southwest, and South are more casual in dress than the East, with the Midwest being somewhere in between in dress as well as in location.

Learning by Observation

Getting back to the prospect, there are many things that can be learned simply by observation. For example, if the woman is well dressed, she'll probably be interested in boutiques and department stores near the development. If the man looks athletic, he may like the tennis courts and swimming pool. If the person is overweight, perhaps he'd like to know about the restaurants in the vicinity. If the prospect is a young couple dressed in the latest mod fashions, the discotheque nearby might intrigue them. If a man and woman come in with young children, they may like information about the recreation programs and the Cub Scouts. Combining the information gathered in conversation and through observation, you will begin to know how best to serve the prospect.

Knowing Your Product

A thorough knowledge not only of the apartment community but also of the neighborhood and beyond is essential. This information can't be gained through hearsay. The rental agent must know about all of the community facilities, first-hand. Go to the schools, shops, and churches, and speak with the principals, merchants, and ministers. Walk through the YMCA, parks, and community centers. Understand the bus routes and expressway systems. When you actually experience these things you will be not only more natural in your presentation, but you will also be far more helpful and thus more effective. This first-hand knowledge extends to the competition also. With actual knowledge of what the competition has to offer and at what rent levels, you will be more confident and helpful. The information must be current. A tour two years ago is of little value. You will learn far more about the competition by introducing yourself rather than pretending to be a prospect searching for an apartment. The world of property managers is small and normally quite friendly, even though we find ourselves competitors.

Showing the Product

The prospect should be given a complete tour of the apartment community. Often this begins with the recreation facilities and the decorated models if you have them. Show both models (this assumes they are reasonably close to one another). Prospects enjoy visiting models to garner decorating ideas. If the recreation facilities and models are done properly, they will be a great help in establishing a mood and atmosphere. They can demonstrate life-style far better than you can verbalize it. If you wait until the end to show the recreation package, you may not get a chance to show it at all. Prospects might leave before seeing the recreation facilities, but they won't leave before seeing the apartments. Hold the apartments until last and your tours won't be cut short. Supporting amenities are less important and can be held until the very last or even skipped if the prospect shows little interest.

After seeing the models, the prospect will be interested in inspecting the actual unit that is available for rent. Deciding what to show requires a feel that comes from your information gathering. It also demands skill and some finesse. No matter how many vacant units you have, a prospect should only be shown two, never more than three. People want things that are in demand. There is much less desire or urgency for things that appear to be in abundant supply. When it appears that every other apartment is available for rent, the prospect gets wary and interest dulls. As stated earlier, housing is an important status symbol. It's a primary means of demonstrating a person's success. It's hard to feel satisfaction in your housing choice if no one else seems to want to live there.

Showing the first apartment gives the agent a chance to see if he has made the right conclusions about the prospect. For example, to the athletic-looking man who might be a tennis enthusiast, the agent shows an apartment near the tennis courts. To the mother with two children, the agent shows an apartment on the first floor with the shortest distance between the parking lot and the apartment. To the young girl with a deep suntan, the agent shows an apartment near the swimming pool. At this point the agent must have rapport with the prospect. The agent must interpret the prospect's reaction accurately because if the apartment being shown isn't right, the next one has to be.

A complete knowledge of the inventory of available apartments is also essential. This is no time to go back to the information center to look through the available apartment list. If neither of the first two units fills the needs of the prospect you may try showing a third apartment but only if you have gained further information which tells you that the third showing *will* fit the needs of the prospect.

Questions and Objections

When the prospect begins asking questions and raising objections, that's a sign he's warming up. Questions and objections are used by the prospect to escape the necessity to make a decision. They are signals that he wants to say "yes" but can't make the decision to do so. This is very true of most people, particularly when faced with major decisions such as with housing, automobiles, and expensive clothing. Most rental agents misinterpret these objections as a negative reaction on the part of the prospect. This is far from correct. If there was little interest, the prospect would simply say, "No, thank you," and leave. That's easy. When the prospect takes the time to spell out objections, he is interested but needs help.

Almost all rental agents can quickly recite all of the plus features about the competition and all of the negative ones about the complex which employs them. This results from absorbing prospect objections. Rental agents must learn the most fundamental principle of merchandising: *People need help in making decisions.* When the objections and questions begin, the prospect is ready. Now is when your knowledge of the prospect, the neighborhood, and the competition will come into full use. Your ability to overcome objections and to answer questions depends upon it. The better you have prepared yourself, the easier the task. No one method can be taught. Each case will be somewhat different. You will have to experiment. In time, experience will help point the way. All objections do not have to be overcome. A good many of these are raised only as a means of defense so that the prospect can avoid a decision.

Getting Action

It is not uncommon that you will have to actually make the decision for the prospect. Another method is to hurdle the decision and to go on to something that's easier for the prospect. For example, a salesman can help a person who is resisting a decision to purchase a new refrigerator by jumping over the decision to buy and asking if the refrigerator should be delivered on Tuesday or Wednesday. The choice between delivery dates is far easier to make and brings with it automatically the commitment to purchase the particular refrigerator. The same delivery or move-in alternatives can frequently be used in closing a deal for an apartment rental. Knowing the prospect's situation will provide you with a number of approaches. Of course, if you haven't obtained this information, there is little that you can do now to assist in closing the deal.

Decisions almost always become final with the transfer of money. Without money, there is a high risk of the prospect changing his mind. A couple can be totally "sold" on a particular apartment and leave without placing a deposit. On their way home they might look at other places and find a better deal. Once they put money down, they go home because a decision has been made. At that point they are removed from the market as a prospect. Their minds begin to focus on the better living style or larger quarters or whatever expectations the change in housing accommodations seems to offer. A deposit, even an amount as small as $25, or for that matter even a postdated check, will signal a decision and trigger a stream of expectations for a better life-style. If the prospect leaves without making a deposit, he leaves without making a decision.

Only the most basic principles of merchandising techniques can be learned through books. Most of these skills must be acquired through actual trial and error and constant self-evaluation.

Evaluating Your Progress

If you have developed a merchandising program based on everything we've said so far, you can expect a good amount of traffic and a corresponding amount of lease applications. But how good is good?

There's no general answer to what you can expect in the way of traffic. That depends on your location, your area of the country, and competition. You have to get the feel of the market over a period of weeks before you can arrive at your own measure of what constitutes good traffic.

A far better gauge of your success is your *conversion rate.* If yours is a new development, you should convert one out of every 10 to 12 prospects. In an existing building, you should convert one out of every 6 to 8 prospects. The reason for the difference is that a new building attracts more curiosity-seekers and "tire-kickers" than an older building, hence more people who are not true prospects.

If you are converting one out of every 8 prospects in a new building or one of out 4 in an old one, you're doing very well; so well, in fact, that your rent levels are probably too low. Raise them to get back to the proper ratio.

But if you are converting fewer than the recommended ratio, then something is wrong with your product or your merchandising technique. You will need to analyze your particular situation to determine where the breakdown has occurred. A thorough inspection will tell the story about maintenance levels. The use of shoppers can tell a lot about sales techniques or the lack of them.

Using Shoppers

Most rental agents detest shoppers. To them, the shopper is no better than a spy. But you should let your rental agents know that you are going to use shoppers to spot mistakes and learn how to correct them, not to punish anyone.

As a matter of fact, it's a good idea to use shoppers even though your rental agents are converting prospects at a ratio of six- or eight-to-one. The shopper might discover if the agents were doing everything they are supposed to, they would be converting at an even lower ratio. In that case, your rents may be too low and you can safely raise them. Have your development shopped two or three times a year just to make sure you aren't letting down.

The shoppers you hire should be young couples who look like prospects. If they have a baby or small child with them, that makes it even better. Have them dress casually and act like prospects. You should have *two or three teams of shoppers* who can each visit the development on the same day but at different times. The reason for this is that you want to be able to support any report by more than one person, thus helping to counteract the denials which can be expected when the rental agent is confronted with a negative report.

If the same report is made by two shoppers, the agent has little argument.

The shopper should note the *date* and *time* of the visit, plus the *name* of the rental agent. The shopper's report should be strictly factual, in narrative form, with no subjective comments. You'll be amazed at what the shopper's report can show. In one case, the rental agent never introduced himself. In another, the shopper asked for but wasn't given a model tour. In still another, the rental agent wouldn't give the shopper a brochure. In a fourth, the rental agent walked around in her bare feet. And in a fifth, the rental information center wasn't open when the shopper visited, even though the time was clearly within the hours stated.

You should review the written report individually and privately with each rental agent so that he or she understands what is being done incorrectly. Don't let the agent be defensive or negative. Let him understand what was wrong and point out the correct techniques.

Setting Goals

When you are satisfied that your rental staff is doing a good job, have the staff set their own performance goals. Ask them how many apartments they would *like to rent* this month. Chances are the staff will set a high goal, much higher than you'd set for them. Then ask them to tell you how many they actually *expect to rent.* The new figure will be somewhat lower than what they would like to rent, because you have now asked for their commitments. Once those are given, the staff will generally meet their own goals. If they fall below that figure, help them analyze their performance to see why.

To improve the productivity of your rental staff, consider *incentives* other than money. As we said in our section on personnel policies, money is one of the least powerful motivators. Contests that involve the spirit of competition are much better to spur better performance. By publishing results and awarding prizes, you can do wonders with your rental staff. Remember, all people want one thing more than to be first; they never want to be last.

A Final Check

If after doing all of the above you're still not happy with your traffic and conversion rate, go back and check every link in the rental chain step by step: policies, rents, product preparation, merchandising, or even the product itself. If you find something that can be improved, change that without changing anything else. Then change other elements one at a time until you get the proper results. But remember that the weakest link is usually the rental staff, with product preparation the next weakest. Concentrate on these two and you'll solve most problems.

Chapter Six

Records and Record-Keeping

Too many property managers overemphasize the importance of record-keeping. Ask them what they do all day, and they're likely to tell you about the forms they filled out, the notices they filed, the letters they wrote, and the filing to be done. Rarely will they talk about the business of renting apartments, dealing with tenants, and keeping up the brick and mortar.

While record-keeping is important to keep track of your position and to meet legal requirements, it's of minor importance in the overall business of property management. Given a choice between doing the best job of record-keeping and the best job of management, you'd be better off choosing the latter.

Don't equate record-keeping, which is keeping score, with property management, which is the game. The less time you spend on record-keeping, the more time you have to devote to the property. Therefore, simplify your record-keeping as much as possible. Use the minimum amount of forms and the minimum amount of time. Do only what's necessary.

With this much said to put record-keeping in its place, let's go into the matter of what record-keeping you need to do.

Management Agreement

Throughout this book we have addressed ourselves to the person who has management responsibilities over a property or group of properties. That person can be an executive property manager, a supervising property manager, or the site manager. When any of these manager types are directly employed by the owner, their duties and responsibilities are usually spelled out in a job description. When these managers are either proprietors or employees of a management company which acts as a managing agent for a particular owner, the duties and responsibilities are then spelled out in what is referred to as a *Management Agreement.* This document does several things:

- It serves as an *employment contract* between the owner and the managing agent.
- It establishes an *agency relationship,* giving the managing agent the right to act in the owner's stead and to assume obligations in the name of the owner.
- It spells out the *rights, responsibilities,* and *limitations* of the managing agent.
- Finally, it spells out the managing agent's *compensation.*

To undertake the management of real estate without a management agreement is foolish. The main reason for having an agreement is that it sets out everything in writing, thereby reducing the chance of misunderstandings. The agreement is more for the managing agent's protection than for the owner's.

Powers

As the managing agent, you are more than the owner's representative; you are in effect acting as the owner and have the powers that the owner would have if he were acting for himself.

As the owner's agent, you have the power to *set rents* and to execute, extend, and cancel *leases,* as well as *make settlements* with tenants. You also have the power to *collect money* and *spend it* on behalf of the property. In this respect you have a fiduciary responsibility to the owner to act honestly and in good faith, which requires you to render a precise accounting of collections and expenditures.

The management agreement also gives you the power to *execute contracts* for building services, to keep the property in good condition, and to *make repairs.* What you spend on maintenance and repairs may be limited by a dollar amount beyond which you need the owner's further approval, except in emergencies when life or property are threatened.

You also have the power to *hire, fire, and supervise personnel.*

The staff employees are generally employees of the building, not direct employees of the managing agent. However, even when this is the case you still can be considered an *alternate employer* because of your powers to hire, fire, and supervise. That is, you may be held responsible for observing all requirements of the federal Wage and Hour Law, for instance. You can't escape this responsibility even though the personnel are employees of the owner. With your authority to hire, fire, and supervise, you have the corresponding responsibilities to see that all employment conditions required by the law are fulfilled. The owner in turn holds you responsible to see that you professionally fulfill the obligations you have undertaken for him.

You have the *power of attorney* to act in the owner's behalf. This power of attorney should be clearly set forth in the management agreement in three areas specifically:

*   First, to establish that you have the right to *execute a lease.* A tenant may challenge your right to do so. By referring to the power of attorney in the agreement, you can support this right.
*   Second, to meet Internal Revenue Service requirements that you are empowered to *file employee tax payments* in the owner's name.
*   Third, to *distribute net proceeds* to the owners. This can be tricky. You must get the power of attorney from all of the owners for any percentage distribution of net proceeds. It's not uncommon for a managing agent to receive a contract from two owners, and then discover later on there are other owners who demand their share of the proceeds. Your only protection is to identify all of the owners and see that they all sign any distribution instructions.

Obligations

Your overall obligation is to act in a professional manner with the owner's interest as your prime concern. Most management contracts place obligations on the agent to:

*   See that the property achieves maximum occupancy with the most efficient outlay of operating expenses.
*   Collect rents.
*   Pay bills incurred for the property.
*   Submit a report to the owner of collections and disbursements.
*   See that the insurance is maintained.

- Pay taxes from building funds.
- File employee payroll tax returns.
- Maintain the property using building funds.
- Notify the owner of property shortcomings and defects as well as citations.
- Maintain records such as leases, tax payments, mortgage payments, original paid invoices, and insurance policies, all of which are the owner's property. (Correspondence files and books of account which the managing agent generates in the course of managing the property remain the property of the agent, not the owner.)

Associated Risks

The managing agent is exposed to certain risks. The "hold harmless" provisions of the management agreement are designed to minimize these risks by placing many responsibilities on the owner and to provide for the payment of legal defense in certain matters unless the agent has been negligent. These matters generally include:

- Actions which stem from the owner's refusal to advance needed funds.
- Building code violations.
- Civil rights suits.
- Wage and Hour claims.
- Occupational Safety and Health Act (OSHA) claims.
- Lawsuits in general.
- Harmful or improper acts of employees.

Compensation

The most common method of compensation is the *flat percentage* of total collections for the property. One example is an amount equal to 6 per cent on all monies collected. This method is the easiest to get owners to accept because it is *traditional* and because it gives the managing agent an *incentive* to collect the maximum rents.

In addition to covering the managing agent's fee, the agreement should also spell out *who pays for on-site administrative help.* Usually this is the responsibility of the owner, not the managing agent.

Finally, the agreement should also contain any specifics on *commissions for renting apartments and renewal bonuses.*

Termination or Cancellation

The management agreement can be ended in one of four ways:

- When the term of the agreement expires.
- By notice from either the owner or the managing agent according to contract provisions.
- By mutual agreement. If the cancellation is negotiated, one party may ask for payment from the other in return for early termination.
- When the purpose is ended. A common reason is sale of the building. The owner has retained the agent to manage his property; if the property is no longer his, the purpose is gone and the contract is normally ended. The managing agent may seek protection against this by having the agreement state that a sale of the property does not affect the contract, or that if the building is sold, the agent will receive a specified sum as liquidated damages.

As you can see, the management agreement is an important document, one that should be kept in a safe place. But the agreement won't guarantee continuing employment; only effective performance will do that.

Collections and Disbursements

In Chapter 4, All About Rents, we discussed the types of rent, forms of payment, and where rents are paid. Our last discussion of rent deals with properly recording those rent payments. Historically, apartment rents have been posted to tenant ledger cards which are usually maintained at the point of collection. The problem with most tenant ledger card systems, and for that matter many other systems as well, is that they are designed to control the activities and payments of the tenant and do very little to control the status of the individual rental units within the property.

When you control the tenant you are controlling the *variable*. You should establish a system which is designed to control the *fixed* asset, namely the apartment units. The airlines, for instance, don't keep track of passengers; they keep track of seats. They want to know what their total seating capacity is. How many are sold? At what price? Only incidentally is the airline concerned with who filled the seats. In our case, the rental unit, not the tenant, is the factor to be controlled.

It is not our purpose to propose or lay out a system to track collections and to develop accounting procedures. That requires a complete study unto itself. Our point here is that when these systems are being studied or evaluated, bear in mind just what it is you wish to control.

Unscheduled Collections

While regularly scheduled rents can pose a problem in collection and recording, the matter of unscheduled collections can be far worse. More money is misappropriated, "lost," or stolen in this category than anywhere else. This money comes from several sources: from tenants to cover damages, from concessionaires, from charges for use of the hospitality or recreation room, from lease settlements or cancellation fees, from back-rent payments on accounts that have been written off, and from building-owned laundry equipment. Much of this money comes in the form of cash. It can amount to many thousands of dollars over a year's period. Because of this and the fact that collection cannot always be anticipated, the opportunity for loss through theft or misuse is great. Be alert that the situation exists and that the temptation is there also. There is no known system that is foolproof, but you should take the time to develop a system which will at least minimize the exposure.

Security Deposit Accounts

You need to know your local laws governing the use or escrow of security deposit monies. You may be required to maintain a separate escrow account and to compute and pay interest on the money being held. You may be called upon by the owner to place this money in interest-bearing bonds or treasury bills or in a bank or thrift institution. Whatever the situation, it will involve substantial record-keeping and attention.

Owner's Custodial Account

All monies collected for the owner should be put in a custodial account separate from the funds of the managing agent; there should be no commingling of the owner's and management company's funds. Separate owner's custodial accounts are required by most state laws and ethics codes and by the Federal Housing Administration for all FHA-insured or -assisted apartment properties.

It's not necessary that every building have its own bank account, although this may be done and may be required in some areas and by some management agreements. It's more desirable to put all funds from properties under your management in a single bank account. That greatly simplifies check writing and record-keeping. Each owner still gets a statement showing his own cash position. The single bank account for all owners' funds is a matter of convenience for the managing agent.

One word of caution: with several different owners' funds in a single account, it's possible to inadvertently overdraw one owner's funds using the surplus funds of another. Unless you have approval for this you are making an unauthorized loan of an owner's money.

Purchasing

As the managing agent, you are responsible for the maintenance and operation of the building, you'll have to purchase supplies, materials, and services using funds belonging to the owner. Your obligation to the owner is to generate the greatest possible net income. This means you must seek ways to get the most for his purchasing dollar. The best way you can do this is to establish *specifications* for the supplies, materials, and services you need and then shop around or take bids to get the best value. Besides giving you a basis for comparison, specifications also help settle disputes if there is any question later on of what was to be delivered or supplied.

It's always best to get a *firm price.* If this is impossible because of the nature of the job, place a limitation on what can be spent without further approval. Never give out an open-ended purchase order. Remember, too, that the time to negotiate a price is before you place an order, not after you get the bill.

Establish a *payment program* for major items before you place the order. Vendors generally will cooperate if they know when they can expect their money. Let's say you order a $9,000 compressor. The vendor expects you'll pay the $9,000 in one lump sum in the normal time, say 30 days after billing. He'll be irritated and uncooperative if after getting the bill you tell him you'll have to spread out the payments. But if you tell him in advance you'll make three payments of $3,000 each, he'll more readily accept this. Why? Because he knows that without this concession he may not get the order.

Most important of all, make all purchases with a *written purchase order.* This is essential if you are to keep track of what you ordered, what orders are outstanding, and whether the invoices agree with the quoted price. If you have a file of such orders and the building is sold, you can quickly contact vendors whose work has not been delivered or started and cancel. Otherwise, they may fill the order and then bill you or the former owner, a situation which can lead to disputes. The new owner may refuse to pay the bill, saying he never authorized the order. The supplier may put a lien on the building, further complicating things. All of this can be avoided if you cancel unfilled orders. Without a purchase-order file, you'll have trouble remembering what orders are open. The remedy: put it in writing.

Every purchase order placed by a managing agent should contain a notice to the effect that *your company is acting as an agent, not as the principal, and that you will disclose the identity of the principal if requested.* This signals to the supplier that your company is an agent and that the principal, not the managing agent, is responsible for the payment of the invoice. (This notice is not necessary if you are a direct employee of the owner.) Without this notice, the supplier can assume that the managing agent is acting on its own behalf and will look to the agent for collection if the building or the owner can't pay. It's very rare that a supplier will ask you to identify your principal but if you are asked, you should be allowed to disclose this information. Just make sure you include this notice to protect your company.

Bill Payments

As managing agent you need policies and procedures for paying bills. These are the major points you should consider:

1. **Choose a period** to pay bills when money is available and you have the time to do the paper work. Don't have suppliers submit bills by the tenth of the month for payment on the

first of the following month. While it's true that bank balances are highest in the opening days of the month, this is also the property manager's busiest time because he's handling move-outs and move-ins, collecting rents, taking complaints, and doing extra paper work. It would be better to select a time that's less hectic, say around the middle of the month, for bill payments.

In the same regard, it is unfortunate that most mortgage payments end up being due on the first of the month. Invariably there isn't enough money collected and in the bank to make the first-of-the-month payment date. At the time the mortgage was originally made, it would have been an easy matter to arrange for payments to be due later in the month. Even if the mortgage is established, it's worth the try to have the payment date set back into the month. By setting the date at the fifteenth, chances are you'll have more money on hand and more time to handle the payment.

2. **Let your vendors know what your bill-paying procedure is.** This will discourage calls from vendors who want to know when they'll be paid.

3. **Be alert to discounts and gross/net billings.** You should take these discounts as a prudent businessman. If you can't take discounts because of a short turn-around period or because of a lack of funds, put the owner on notice of this. Otherwise, if he finds that you're not taking discounts, he may claim that you owe him the money because you were negligent in missing the discount period.

In taking discounts, you may have to violate your own bill-paying schedule. For example, many discounts must be taken in the first 10 days. If you pay in 15 days, you'll miss the discount. Some vendors will honor a discount even if taken 30 days later, feeling that money is money. Others will police the discount strictly.

Utilities commonly bill on a gross/net basis: you pay the lower net amount in 10 days, the higher gross amount after 10 days. If you're a big enough utility customer, you may be able to get the utility to extend your net period to 15 or 30 days.

Another point about utility bills: you may be billed for a

vacant apartment even though it's leased to a new tenant. The same thing may happen if the tenant moves in early. To avoid this, have the tenant sign the utility application and turn-on card when he signs the lease so the utility billing will commence with the lease date or move-in date, whichever is earlier.

4. **Avoid paying bills C.O.D.** Some vendors insist on this, especially if they've had bad experiences with apartment owners and managers. Once a vendor gets you in the habit of paying C.O.D., he'll insist on it because it's the fastest way he can get cash; there's no incentive for him to change. But paying C.O.D. will complicate your record-keeping and bill-paying procedures.

   If necessary, to avoid C.O.D. billings, change vendors. With the new vendor, allow time to have your credit checked and become an approved account. This is recommended for purchases of all supplies, materials, and services. The only exceptions are payments for one-time things, such as emergency noncontract snowplowing or a special load of dirt for which the driver demands cash on delivery.

5. **Don't use petty cash funds to pay vendors.** If you do, you will need a large cash fund on hand to handle all the vendors who will now demand cash. These funds are subject to theft and misuse. It also leads to poor record-keeping. Petty cash is for incidental purchases such as postage stamps and postage due, small shipping charges, gas for lawn mowers, minor office expenses, etc. A revolving fund of $50 is adequate for most properties.

6. **Have bills approved by the on-site manager** who ordered the work, before they are processed for payment. Don't send the check back to the site manager for review or forwarding to the vendor. Some firms do this, saying that it enables the site manager to know who is being paid and to hold the check back if there's a last-minute question about performance. This should have been determined before the bill was approved for payment.

   The danger in letting the site manager approve the check or forward it to the vendor is that it gives him a chance to possibly extract a kickback from the vendor, even if it's nothing more than a free lunch. Simply by calling the vendor and saying, "I've got your check here," the site manager exerts some pressure on the vendor. This leads to bad vendor relations which will in turn cost the owner money.

Payroll Periods and Taxes

As we stated earlier, because of the workweek requirement included in the Wage and Hour Law, it is advisable to establish weekly or biweekly pay periods to avoid confusion and overlap. Monthly or semimonthly pay periods are acceptable; they just complicate your record-keeping chores.

It's a good idea on payroll checks to itemize deductions and show cumulative earnings to date, so the employee is aware of what's happening to his earnings. Otherwise, he may question what you're deducting money for.

The managing agent is generally responsible for deducting and depositing FICA and payroll withholding taxes. Filing the appropriate returns is also a normal function of the managing agent.

Reserves

In today's world of limited or nonexistent profits, it's difficult to think about establishing proper reserve accounts. It's foolhardy, however, to suggest that residential rental housing can go for extended periods without the need for substantial sums to cover major repairs and replacements. Prudent owners and managers will set aside funds in a reserve account to pay for the repair or replacement of major building components. The reserve account should be separate and distinct from the operating account. This money may even be invested for short periods in order to gain interest.

The Federal Housing Administration requires an exact amount be set aside each month for reserves in addition to the mortgage payment. Any monies which can be earned as interest on the investment of these funds accrues to the owner. A word of caution to the manager who is inexperienced in operating FHA-insured or -assisted properties: Don't forget to make periodic claims on the reserve account to reimburse the operating account for monies expended on replacements. Too many managers suffer with a cash-poor operating account because they make replacement expenditures, and forget entirely about the reserve account which has money for just that purpose. If you have such a reserve account, you may be better off to *replace* parts such as motors than to *rebuild* them. Reserve accounts often only cover replacements, not repairs or rebuilding.

A reserve account can also be established for short periods to build up money to cover large expenditures such as taxes, a new roof, or a big remodeling program. This type of reserve account may be discontinued after the particular project is completed and the bills satisfied.

Monthly Statement

As stated in the section on the management agreement, one of the major duties of a managing agent is to submit a monthly statement of receipts and disbursements. This is different from a profit-and-loss statement and a balance sheet which are prepared by an accountant or bookkeeper. It is very rare that a managing agent is required to generate this kind of accounting work. The monthly report of receipts and disbursements produced by the managing agent is simply a running history of the cash transactions.

Monthly management statements produced by managing agents take many forms. Some are simple, almost primitive reports while others are elaborate computer-prepared reports detailing endless information. The best system of reporting is probably in the middle of these extremes.

Most owners prefer receiving a monthly statement that can be read quickly and that can be readily understood. The statement must contain detail and perhaps some statistics but these items shouldn't be overwhelming. A comprehensive monthly management statement should include certain basic parts.

- **A listing of the rent roll.** Each apartment and all other rental spaces should be listed in their numerical sequence regardless if the unit is leased or not. Once this order has been adopted, it should not vary from month to month. Listed along side of each apartment should be all other *fixed* information such as unit size, floor, address, etc. Following on the same line is the *variable* information including the tenant's name, security deposit amount, term of lease, rent, and rent status. If a particular unit is vacant, this portion would be blank. It is possible that under a single unit, information will be detailed about more than one tenant in the same month (e.g., tenants moving during the month, collection from a delinquent past tenant).

The information concerning the tenant is a running history. It should show the status listed at the end of the previous month, all transactions during the current month, and the ending status. Without this detail, an owner cannot properly monitor the activities in his property nor evaluate the performance of the managing agent.

Some agents do not list the entire rent roll but instead report by *exception*. This type of reporting is quicker for an agent to prepare and quicker for an owner to read, but it lacks the unit-by-unit detail necessary to really understand what is going on.

- **A listing of disbursements and miscellaneous receipts.** This is a chronological listing of all checks written and all monies received from other-than-rental units (such as collections from laundry equipment, vending machines, and recreation room charges and collection of security deposits). This listing details the name of the vendor paid, the amount paid, and often the check number. It also lists the source of each miscellaneous receipt and its amount.

Most managing agents establish a *chart of accounts* to classify items of expense. By doing this, purchases can be easily categorized for budgetary and accounting purposes. These account numbers are completely arbitrary.

Be aware that this statement will include items other than building operating expenses. Common examples of these include debt-service payments, payments for capital expenditures, and distributions to owners.

Another point is that such a statement is on a cash basis and does not reflect any unpaid bills. This omission may give the owner the impression that his property owes no money. The way to avoid this is to include a total of unpaid bills at the bottom of this statement so the owner will be aware of them.

- **A listing of reserve account transactions.** These can include the monthly payment into the owner's real estate tax fund, with an indication of the balance; deposits for future capital expenditures; or a regular monthly accounting of an established reserve for replacement account. All of these show the owner what money is being accumulated for major expenditures. When these expenditures are made, the reserved money is generally transferred into the operating account where it will be used to pay the particular bill.

• **A running summary of all financial transactions.** This generally contains a beginning balance for the month, total of collections, total of disbursements, an update of the escrow or reserve account, remittances to owners, and the ending balance.

Copies of the monthly statement together with the original copies of the paid invoices and any distribution check are usually submitted to the owner a short time after the close of the particular month's business. The relationship between the owner and manager is often affected by the timeliness and accuracy of the monthly management statement.

Employee Records

The federal Wage and Hour Law, OSHA, equal employment opportunity legislation, and numerous state and local laws are specific on employee records, and these laws are becoming more involved and complicated every day. Good business practice demands that you keep adequate employee records.

You should have a file for each employee, including casual labor, that includes the following:

1. Employee application form.
2. Job description.
3. Current W-4 form for withholding tax.
4. Benefit application.
5. Time records.
6. Pay records, including regular pay, overtime, bonuses, commissions, and raises.
7. Vacation and sick-day records.
8. Social security payments.
9. Union benefits.
10. Accident reports.

11. Review and evaluation report.
12. Commendations and complaints.
13. Record of disciplinary action.

Application Form

Antidiscrimination laws prohibit you from asking anything about the person's age, sex, color, religion, creed, or national origin prior to being hired. However, for purposes of insurance and other benefits, you are permitted to get this information after the person is employed. Some application forms are divided into two parts, the first dealing with prehiring information, the second asking for more detailed information after the employee has been hired. Just be sure that none of the forbidden items appears in the prehiring section.

Time Record

As explained in the Personnel Policy section (p. 102), building employees including most managerial help are entitled to the minimum hourly wage for a 40-hour workweek and time-and-a-half for overtime after that. In effect, this makes all building personnel hourly employees whether they are paid a salary or an hourly wage. It's important that you keep records of the time they work and pay overtime if needed.

You can do this by giving each employee a time card each week. Have him fill in the hours worked each day. Then collect the card at the end of the workweek. These cards should be kept on file. You should also inspect them and monitor the time. If a person spends more than 40 hours in a workweek, see that he is paid overtime.

These time records are essential in any investigative hearings. The vast majority of Wage and Hour settlements are made on "proof of the record"—that is, what the time cards show. Without a card, it's your word against the employee's.

Taxes and Insurance

Real estate and personal property taxes are commonly called ad valorem taxes. An ad valorem tax means "(according) *to value*" or "*to worth* (of the property)" as opposed to income tax which is "according to income."

Tax File

Real estate taxes are probably the largest single item of expense in the buildings you manage. Good record-keeping requires that you maintain a separate tax file for each property. This file should contain:

1. The legal description of the property.
2. The permanent tax identification number.
3. Information concerning the valuation of the land and the building.
4. Timetables and procedures for handling reassessment.
5. History of the tax rate to the current date.
6. Name, address, and telephone number of the owner's tax attorney assigned to the property.
7. Copies of paid tax bills.
8. Special assessments and other taxes.
9. Correspondence regarding protests, appeals, and complaints.

In addition to the permanent tax file, you need a *tickler file* to remind you of approaching payment and protest dates. As managing agent, it's your obligation to see that real estate taxes are paid whether or not you receive a bill. If you don't get a bill, it's your obligation to see what's wrong. When you get the tax bill, check it carefully to see that it applies to your property.

If *personal property* taxes are collected in your area, you will need to maintain the same kind of file.

Some localities also collect *sales taxes* on rents; if this is true in your area, you must set up and maintain a record of payments made and returns filed.

Insurance

The managing agent usually assumes the responsibility to be aware of the insurance carried by the property, to pay premiums from the owner's funds, and to advise the owner of expiration and renewal dates. He has no responsibility for buying or renewing insurance or for paying premiums out of his own funds.

The owner will look to the managing agent to attend to the

details of insurance and to advise or tell him what should be done. So you must know what coverage is in effect, the amount, and the parties insured. We'll begin by discussing the *kinds of coverage* your building can or may have:

1. Fire and extended coverage (Fire and EC) insurance. Fire is self-explanatory. Extended coverage can include wind, hail, lightning, collapse, explosion, riot, smoke, and flood.
2. Vandalism and malicious mischief (VMM) insurance. This covers damage done to the property.
3. Liability insurance. This protects the owner and managing agent against claims, most commonly for accidents occurring on the property.
4. Rent loss insurance. This provides continuing rental income when the apartments are rendered uninhabitable by a fire or other loss.

All of the above can be included in a *multi-peril package policy* that offers significant savings over the same protection bought separately. Specialized insurance protection is also available. This may be part of the package policy or purchased separately, depending on the insurance company. This protection includes:

1. Contents insurance, for damage to building property such as lobby furniture.
2. Fine arts insurance, covering paintings and statuary the building may own.
3. Boiler insurance, covering explosion, ruptures, and related losses.
4. Dram shop or host insurance, to cover liquor-related incidents.
5. Auto insurance, including nonowner auto insurance to protect the owner against claims made against building employees driving their own cars on company business.
6. Fidelity insurance, to protect against losses caused by dishonest employees.
7. Plate glass insurance.
8. Sprinkler leakage insurance.

In addition, *workmen's compensation insurance* is required in most states. This coverage is never included in a package policy. It is always separate.

In the study of insurance it is important to know about a special clause being commonly used in the vast majority of fire and extended coverage policies being written; it is the *co-insurance clause*. Eighty percent co-insurance is the most common type, but 60, 70, and 90 percent co-insurance clauses are also available. Policies with these provisions came about as a way to encourage owners to carry proper amounts of fire and extended coverage insurance on their property. Because most fires are small and only damage a portion of the building, many owners began carrying insurance amounts which were substantially below what would be required to restore their property if hit by a major fire. They were, in effect, self-insuring themselves for the amount they were under-insured by. To entice owners to carry proper insurance coverage, the insurance companies began offering lower rates to owners who would take coverage with limits of at least 80 percent of the Actual Cash Value (ACV) or sound value of the building (at least 60 percent if 60 percent co-insurance; 90 percent if 90 percent co-insurance, etc.). The higher the co-insurance percentage, the lower the insurance rates are.

In the case of an 80 percent co-insurance clause, contrary to common belief, an owner, if he carries the proper amount of insurance, is not responsible for 20 percent of any damage loss. The theory behind co-insurance is that approximately 20 percent of the value of the structure is not subject to destruction, such as the foundations, water and sewer lines, heavy boilers, etc. Therefore, if the insurance is maintained at proper levels, the owner should not be exposed to sharing in part of the restoration costs.

The key is that proper insurance levels must be maintained. As construction costs increase, so do costs to rebuild a fire-damaged structure. If the cost to rebuild your building, less certain depreciation factors, goes up, and it does every day, you will soon be under-insured, assuming you don't increase your insurance in a corresponding fashion. When your coverage goes below the 80 percent that you committed to maintain—you become a co-insurer and will suffer part of the loss. Look at an example of this:

Assume your building has an Actual Cash Value (this is not market value; it is replacement value less certain depreciation factors) of $300,000 and you agree to the 80 percent co-insurance provision. You must maintain at least 80 percent of $300,000 or $240,000 worth of coverage. If you do, you will be covered on losses up to the limits of the policy ($240,000) by the insurance company. The formula is:

$$\frac{\text{Amount of insurance carried}}{\text{Amount of insurance which should be carried}} = \begin{array}{c}\text{Percentage of loss to be paid}\\ \text{by the insurance company}\\ \text{(up to the limits of the policy)}\end{array}$$

or using our numbers

$$\frac{\text{Amount carried \$240,000}}{\text{Should be carried \$240,000}} = \begin{array}{c}100\% \text{ of loss to be paid by}\\ \text{the insurance company}\end{array}$$

Now let's assume that the cost to restore buildings has increased and that our building now has an Actual Cash Value of $400,000 but our insurance coverage has remained at $240,000. We committed to maintain coverage of at least 80 percent of the current Actual Cash Value or $320,000. Now apply the formula again:

$$\frac{\text{Amount carried} \quad \$240,000}{\text{Should be carried \$320,000}} = \begin{array}{c}75\% \text{ of loss to be paid by}\\ \text{the insurance company}\\ \text{(up to the limits of the policy}\\ \text{or in this case \$240,000)}\end{array}$$

If the loss amounted to only $20,000, the insurance company will pay 75 percent or $15,000. You must make up the difference. If the loss was $200,000 your share would be $50,000.

The co-insurance clause saves many premium dollars because of its lower rates but it is essential that the coverage be checked and adjusted periodically to avoid being under-insured. Establishing the proper levels of insurance protection is the responsibility of the owner and the owner's insurance agent, but you should understand how it works and alert the owner if you see a problem developing.

Finally, you need to be aware of *who is insured.* The managing agent should be named as an *additional insured* on policies covering workmen's compensation, liability, nonowner auto, and dram shop or host insurance. In this way, you are protected in actions arising from problems in these areas. Lending institutions will be listed as an additional insured to the extent of the mortgage on policies covering fire, extended coverage, vandalism and malicious mischief, rent loss, or anything else that may affect their collateral, the mortgaged property.

In buying insurance, you should understand the savings possible in a prepaid three-year policy. Even if the owner has to borrow to pay for the policy, the savings often outweigh the costs of the financing and you are then assured of an established premium for three years.

Reminding the owner of renewals and expiration dates is just one part of the managing agent's insurance record-keeping job. Your greatest involvement comes when a loss occurs.

Your first duty when this happens is to *immediately report the incident* to the proper insurance company. If the loss, an accident, injury, or death, involves an employee, you must also report it to OSHA. Be sure you have all the necessary forms on hand in your office, and make certain you keep copies on file.

If there has been a physical loss to the property, you have the obligation to protect the property or what's left of it, including boarding up the building and arranging for emergency lighting and heating.

In the case of a fire or similar loss, the owner may also ask you to help with the *insurance adjustment.* Be careful. Unless you are particularly skilled and knowledgeable in loss adjustment and have an excellent relationship with the insurance company, stay out of it. Advise the owner to retain a professional adjuster to represent him. The owner might not receive the maximum loss settlement if the loss adjustment is not professionally handled.

You may also be asked by the owner to repair the damage in the case of a small loss. In effect, this is a request for you to act as a general contractor in hiring tradesmen to do the work. Normally your management agreement does not obligate you to do this. Managing agents who undertake this work are usually compensated with a fee ranging between 10 and 15 percent of the cost of the work.

Budgets

To some managers, budgets are an excellent textbook exercise, but not practical in the everyday business of managing an apartment complex. But budgeting is more than an academic concern; it is a highly practical necessity that establishes a spending plan and lets the manager know how he's doing. As a professional, you need to budget.

Types of Budgets

There are several types of budgeting methods. One is the *annual net operating income projection*. It's prepared by estimating annual collections and subtracting itemized operating expenses. At the end of the year you know how well you did. The trouble with this method is that it's of little use as a working tool. By the time the year is over, the damage is done. If you've miscalculated, there's no way to adjust.

A refinement of this method is the *monthly net operating income projection*. Because it's by month, you have the opportunity to make adjustments for the following month. This type of budget can also include data letting you know how you've done for the year to date and how you stand in comparison to last year at the same time.

The *annual cash flow budget* is another method that many property managers use. Cash flow is arrived at by subtracting debt service (mortgage payments) from the net operating income. Because the manager frequently makes the debt-service payments, he will have this information. But again it covers a year, which doesn't lend itself to periodic adjustments.

A more useful budget is the *monthly cash flow budget.* This lets the property manager know how much money he'll have each month and therefore lets him plan for peak spending needs, such as large fuel or other seasonal bills, real estate taxes, and capital expenses. These are seldom uniform but fluctuate from month to month. This budget type usually reflects expenditures in the month payment is made and not in the month the charge was incurred. Knowing what cash will be available, and when, you can plan more accurately.

Budgeting is particularly useful in giving you better control of certain variables, such as advertising and promotion, supplies, payroll, repairs, and maintenance. Over these you have *direct control.* Noncontrollable expenditures, which include debt service, taxes, utilities, and insurance, are either out of your control or difficult to change.

You'll also find monthly cash flow budgeting useful in planning for capital expenditures, such as remodeling and major improvements.

In marketing a brand-new building, *weekly marketing budgets* can help you measure the value of expenditures in comparison to rentals during the campaign.

Budget Tips

In setting up budgets, keep these points in mind:

1. The **fewer categories** there are in the owner's budget, the less chance there is for minor fluctuations to trip you up. For instance, supposing you list gas, electricity, and water as separate categories. In one month gas is up, and in another month it is down. The opposite happens to electricity. But total expenditures for all utilities remain constant. The owner will notice the variances in electricity and gas. If you combine all three under a utility category, without a specific breakdown, there won't be a variance between your budget and your performance. For your own purposes, however, the more categories you have, the easier it is to spot problems.

   The minimum categories you need are these:

   > Utilities
   > Services (rubbish collection, exterminator, window washer, etc.)
   > Supplies
   >
   > Payroll and related costs
   > Advertising and promotion
   > Management and administration
   > Legal and audit
   > Insurance
   > Real estate taxes
   > Repairs and maintenance
   > Miscellaneous

2. **Use rounded box-car numbers,** not exact dollar amounts. The box-car numbers allow for reasonable variations. When you set out budget amounts you are also establishing the parameter of acceptable variance. For example, a budget amount of $2,110 suggests a normal variance would be anywhere between $2,100 and $2,120. A budget amount of $2,100 allows for a variance anywhere between $2,000 and $2,200. A low budget number such as $2,000 would not allow an acceptable variance of $1,000 to $3,000. With larger numbers, say, of more than $8,000 or $9,000, it would be an acceptable variance. Remember this when inserting budget amounts. After all, budgets are only estimates and you must allow for some variance.

There's only one exception to using box-car numbers and that's with real estate taxes. Use last year's bill less the pennies, and identify the tax year.

3. **Use today's figures** for your budget estimates. If you depart to allow for inflation or known cost increases, state your assumptions.

4. **Propose a realistic budget** that leans toward the high side. Most property managers are afraid to do this. So they come in with an unrealistically low budget initially. This makes them look good at first, but when the budget is exceeded every month, the managers look bad.

5. **Prepare your budgets early, before the month or year begins.** Yearly budgets should be ready at least 30 days before the year begins, monthly budgets 15 days ahead of time.

Like any other tool, a budget has to be used if it's to do you any good. You need to review your budgets regularly and make adjustments if you're drifting. That way you can stay on target and prove your value to the owner.

Analyzing Budgets

Besides giving you a map to follow, your budget can also be used to tell you how well the property is doing in comparison with other properties in your portfolio and perhaps with certain competitive properties. Seldom will you be able to make a direct budget-to-budget comparison unless the properties are almost identical. But you will be able to compare certain common elements.

The most frequently used method of comparison and analysis, and the least valuable, is on the basis of *percentage of gross possible income.* Percentage of collections should not be used. The reason is that many major expenses such as taxes and insurance are the same whether the building is 100 percent full or 50 percent full; yet the percentages of expenses when compared to the two different collection levels will be dramatically different.

The percentage of gross possible income can yield some misleading figures because it's based on the rent which does not affect some factors. Take a family of two living in an $80 apartment; the water bill is $4, or 5 percent. Now take another family of two living in a $300 apartment with the same water bill of $4; the figure here is 1 per cent. Unless the properties are close in rent levels, these comparisons aren't valid.

Another method of comparison is *dollars per room per year.* For this method, you use the room count as explained in our chapter on The World of Apartment Management (p. 23).

Take the total number of rooms and divide this into the various individual income and expense categories. Example: you have 400 rooms and an annual water bill of $2,000. Your water cost per room per year is $5 ($2,000 ÷ 400). While this is a better indicator than percentage of gross possible income, it doesn't allow for significantly different room sizes which affect the costs of heat, light, insurance, taxes, etc.

Appraisers commonly use the method of *cents per gross square foot per year.* Property managers generally modify this to *cents per net rentable square foot per year,* excluding halls, stairways, elevators, lobbies, etc. To find the gross square footage, multiply the length by the width of the building by the number of living floors. To get the net rentable square footage, multiply the length by the width of each apartment unit, with no discount for partitions, plumbing chases, and other small niches. Then combine the totals for each apartment. Don't include balconies, patios, or unheated sun porches.

Either of these methods will provide a more accurate comparison and analysis than the dollars-per-room or percentage methods.

Regardless of the method used for comparison, make allowances for certain items unaffected by apartment rent, number of rooms or apartment size. For example, a 70 unit building and a 280 unit building may each have 24-hour doorman service or may each have the same-size swimming pool. Using any of these methods of comparison with dramatically different-size buildings, with expensive common facilities or services, will produce distortions which require adjustments.

Other Requirements

OSHA

The Occupational Safety and Health Act of 1970 has definite record-keeping requirements of employers, including managing agents. Since laws are constantly changing, you should contact your nearest U.S. Department of Labor office for details. Stiff fines are imposed for violations.

Antidiscrimination Laws

Federal law makes it illegal to discriminate in hiring employees or renting to tenants for reasons of age, sex, race, religion, creed, or national origin.

We have already discussed the inadvisability of calling for this information on employment application blanks. Also avoid asking for this information when dealing with prospects. Don't keep records on this data unless legally required to do so.

Building Code Violations

If you receive a citation for a code violation, immediately send a copy to the owner. On certain low-cost items, you may proceed without getting the owner's approval so long as it is within the spending limits set out in the management agreement. Otherwise you need the owner's additional approval. When the defect is corrected, notify the owner that the building is in compliance. Keep files of all correspondence pertaining to violations.

Posting of Notices and Licenses

You're required to obey the laws concerning the posting of

notices and licenses, including the following:

- Local business license
- Real estate salesmen's and broker's licenses
- Unemployment insurance notice
- Workmen's compensation notice
- Occupational Safety and Health Act (OSHA) notice.
- Equal employment opportunity notice
- Fair housing notice

In addition, you may also be required to distribute certain materials to your employees, such as first-aid pamphlets required by OSHA.

Contracts and Guarantees

Guarantees and contracts for services are the property of the owner. Set them up in permanent files. Have a tickler or reminder file to alert you to expiration or renewal dates.

Correspondence

Correspondence that you generate in the course of managing the property belongs to the managing agent, not the owner, although the latter may wish to see the files from time to time. For mutual protection, you should send carbon copies of all correspondence to the owner on matters that have a major impact on his ownership interests, such as real estate tax settlements, insurance adjustments, and transactions with the owner's accountant.

These are your major record-keeping requirements. In each particular instance, there will be more. Learn of them and keep them. But keep them as simple as you can so that you can devote the bulk of your time not to score-keeping but to profitable management.

Glossary

Abandonment A relinquishment or surrender of property or rights. Abandonment of leased premises refers to the relinquishing of the premises by the tenant without consent of the owner before the lease expires.

Abatement In real estate, a reduction of rent, interest, or an amount due.

Abjudicate To give away or transfer by judgment.

Abstract of title A summary of all the deeds, wills, and legal proceedings which show the nature of a person's right to a given estate, together with the mortgages, judgments, etc., which constitute liens or encumbrances thereon.

Acceptance The act of taking or receiving something that is offered.

Account A detailed statement of receipts and payments of money or of trade transactions which have taken place between two or more persons.

Accounting The theory and system of setting up and maintaining the book of a business organization; analyzing the operation of a business from a study of income and expenses.

Accounts payable Monies due to others for services rendered or goods ordered and received.

Accounts receivable Monies due for services rendered or goods ordered and delivered.

Accredited Management Organization (AMO) A designation conferred by the Institute of Real Estate Management of

286

the National Association of Realtors® to real estate management firms which are under the direction of a Certified Property Manager and which comply with stipulated requirements as to accounting procedure, performance, and protection of funds entrusted to them.

Acknowledgment The act of going before a competent officer or court and declaring the execution of a deed or other instrument. The acknowledgment is certified by the officer and his certificate is sometimes called an acknowledgment.

Acre A measure of land area, 43,560 square feet.

Actual authority The authority expressly or impliedly conferred by a principal on his agent to act in his behalf.

Ad valorem tax A tax levied according to the value of the object taxed; a tax in proportion to the value. Most often refers to tax levies by municipalities and counties against real property and personal property.

Adjustment In the law of insurance is the settlement of the amount to be received by the insured.

Adverse possession The actual, visible, hostile, notorious, exclusive, and continuous possession of another's land under a claim of title; possession for a statutory period may be a means of acquiring title.

Agency management Management by an agency, authorized to do so, of property owned by another.

Agent One authorized by another (the **Principal**), to do an act or transact business for him, and to bind his principal within the limits of that authority.

Aggregate rent The total or gross rent amount for a lease term.

Agreement An expression of assent by two or more parties to the same object.

Amenities Features of a property that render it more useful and/or attractive. Satisfactions of possession and use arising from architectural excellence, scenic beauty, and social environment.

Amortized mortgage A mortgage loan in which the principal as well as the interest is payable in monthly or periodic installments during the term of the loan.

Ancillary income   A common term to describe additional, unscheduled income such as laundry room receipts and commissions.

Annual statement   In real estate—a fully detailed and annotated statement of all income and expense items involving cash and covering a twelve-consecutive-month period of operation of an individual property; and including the disposition and application of net funds for the period concerned and accumulated funds from prior periods. Variations in form and content are effected to conform with owner directives.

Apartment   A residential unit found in a variety of properties such as walk-ups, garden-type projects, elevator buildings, condominiums, and the like.

Apartment building   A building designed for the separate housing of two or more families and where mutual services are supplied for comfortable and convenient occupancy.

Appraisal   An estimate of quantity, quality, or value. The process through which conclusions of property value are obtained; also refers to the report setting forth the estimate and conclusion of value.

Approaches to value   An appraiser employs three approaches to estimate the value of real estate: cost approach, income approach, and market data approach.

Arbitration   The submitting of a matter in dispute to the judgment of one, two, or more disinterested persons called arbitrators, whose decision, called an award, is binding upon the parties.

Assessed value   The value placed on land and building by a government unit (assessor) for use in levying annual real estate taxes.

Assessment   The imposition of a tax, charge, or levy, usually according to established rates. (see **Special assessment**)

Assignee   One to whom some right or interest is given, either for his own enjoyment or in trust. The person receiving the assignment.

Assignment   The transfer of an interest in a bond, mortgage, lease, or other instrument, by writing.

Assignor   One giving some right or interest; the person making the assignment.

Attorney in fact   One who holds a power of attorney from another allowing him to execute legal documents such as deeds and leases on behalf of the grantor of the power.

Authority   Power or right conferred on a person; usually by another to act on his behalf, so that the person authorized may do such act without incurring liability. (see **Agent**)

Balloon payment   The final payment of a mortgage loan that is considerably larger than the required periodic payments; results from the fact that the loan amount was not fully amortized.

Balustrade   A railing on a staircase held up by balusters.

Base line   A reference survey line of the government or rectangular survey, extending east and west and crossing a principal meridian at a definite point.

Base rent   The minimum amount of rent payable under the terms of a percentage lease.

Bench mark   A permanent or semi-permanent identifiable reference point for the determination of elevations; customarily used by surveyors.

Beneficial interest   Profit, benefit, or advantage resulting from a contract or estate, as distinct from legal ownership or control.

Beneficiary   A person designated to receive funds or other property under a trust, insurance policy, mortgage loan, etc.

Best use   In real estate—economically the most productive in net income over a foreseeable period of time without prejudice to the total capital investment or fair market value of a property.

Betterment   Substantial improvements upon real property other than mere repairs.

Bill   An account of money owed for goods or for services rendered or for the use of property (such as rent).

Binder   Temporary insurance contract, in effect pending execution of the final policy.

Blanket mortgage A mortgage covering several pieces of property.

Blanket policy A policy covering all of a specified quantity or class of property, or a variety of risks, or both.

British thermal unit (BTU) A measure of heat, being the quantity needed to raise the temperature of one pound of water one degree Fahrenheit.

Brochure A pamphlet or booklet designed to give by illustration and narrative complete information on a specific subject.

Broker An agent who buys or sells for a principal on a commission without having title to the property.

Budget An itemized estimate of income and expenses for a given period of time in the future.

Building codes Ordinances specifying minimum standards of construction of buildings for the protection of public safety and health.

Business cycle The periodic change from a maximum to a minimum of general business activity.

Calculated risk A foreseeable remote disadvantage in a business transaction that the participants discount because of other certain valuable advantages.

Cancellation Act of cancelling. Termination before the time of expiration. To render nonoperative.

Cancellation agreement Agreement between two or more contracting parties to a cancellation of an existing contract between them.

Cannibalization To strip equipment or housing units of parts for use in other units to help keep them in service.

Capital Any form of wealth capable of being used to create more wealth.

Capital gain A profit from the sale of assets.

Capital improvement A structural addition or betterment to real property other than a repair or replacement. The use of capital for a betterment that did not exist before.

Capitalization The process employed in estimating the value of a property by the use of a proper investment rate of return and the annual net income expected to be produced by the property, the formula being expressed:

$$\frac{\text{Income}}{\text{Rate}} = \text{Value}$$

Carport A roofed sideless shed for the storage of a motor vehicle.

Cash flow The amount of cash available after all payments have been made for operating expenses and mortgage principal and interest.

Cautionary judgment Where an action in tort is pending and the plaintiff fears the defendant would dispose of his real property before judgment, a cautionary judgment is entered with a lien on the property.

Caveat emptor (Let the buyer beware) A principal of law which imposes on the purchaser of property the risk of defects in title or quality of the thing purchased, unless there is an express or implied warranty, or some fraud or mispresentation on the part of the seller.

Cede To assign or transfer.

Cedent An assignor.

Census A numbering of the population, now taken every ten years in the United States.

Census tract A standard area in certain large cities used by the U.S. Bureau of Census for population.

Certified check One that has been presented to the bank on which it is drawn and marked good by the proper officer. Such certification is a warranty that the signature is genuine, and that the drawer has funds in the bank to meet it and obligates the bank to pay it on presentation.

Certified copy One signed and certified as true by the official in whose custody the original is.

Certified Property Manager (CPM®) The professional designation conferred by the Institute of Real Estate Management of the National Association of Realtors® on individuals who fully comply with the professional standards as specified by the Institute.

Chain   A surveyor's unit of measurement equal to 66 feet, consisting of 100 links of 7.92 inches each.

Chart of accounts   An arbitrary classification or arrangement of account items according to grade or class.

Chattel   A movable article of property other than land, buildings, or things legally and physically annexed or attached to real property.

Chattel mortgage   A mortgage on movable personal property.

Client   One who hires another person as his representative or agent and agrees to pay his fee.

Code   A collection of laws, rules, or regulations.

Co-insurance clause   A form of fire insurance coverage in which an insured is obliged to carry at least a fixed insurance amount as a percentage of the total Actual Cash Value (ACV) in consideration of a reduced premium charge; and where there is failure to do so, the insured becomes a co-insurer in proportion to the amount carried in relation to the amount required.

Collateral   Security given as a pledge for the fulfillment of an obligation.

Collateral materials   As applied to advertising and promotion, includes printing and devices such as brochures, leaflets, floor plans, posters, photographs, lapel pins, book matches, etc.

Collection   A sum of money collected. In real estate usually refers to rentals paid or collected.

Collusion   Agreement for fradulent purposes; a conspiracy to do an illegal or fradulent act.

Comaker   One who, with another, signs a negotiable instrument on the face thereof and thereby becomes primarily liable for its payment.

Commercial property   Real property used for the conduct of retail or service businesses and inviting public patronage by display of signs, merchandise, advertising, and other stimulants for public participation.

Commingling of funds   The illegal act of a real estate broker or managing agent in mixing the money of other people with his own.

Common wall A shared wall; where one wall is a part of more than one dwelling unit.

Community property A system of property rights of Spanish origin affecting property of married persons, whereby it is considered as separate property of one spouse if acquired before marriage or by gift or inheritance; or community property owned one half by each, if acquired during marriage with joint funds.

Company An association of individuals for the purpose of carrying on some joint business or enterprise, whether incorporated or not.

Complex A group of buildings that together form a single comprehensive group.

Compound interest Interest upon interest, i.e., when the simple interest on a sum of money is added as it becomes due to the principal, then bears interest, becoming a sort of secondary principal.

Concessions Things conceded or granted. In real estate, to induce the making of a lease or sale.

Conclusion A deduction or final decision resulting from interpretation of all available information on the specific subject.

Condemnation The taking of private property for public use; also the official act to terminate the use of real property for nonconformance with governmental regulations or because of the existance of hazards to public health and safety.

Condemnation clause A provision in a lease stating the agreed rights, privileges, and limitations of the owner and tenant respectively in the event of the taking of the subject property for public use.

Conditional sales contract A contract for the sale of goods, the goods to be delivered to the buyer but the seller to retain title to the goods until the conditions of the contract have been fulfilled.

Condominium The absolute ownership of an apartment or a unit, generally in a multi-unit building, by a legal description of the air space which the unit actually occupies, plus an undivided interest in the ownership of the common elements, which are owned jointly with the other condominium unit owners.

parcel (sometimes referred to as **development parcel**) The entire tract of real estate included in a condominium development.

unit One apartment or space in a condominium building or a part of a property intended for independent use and having lawful access to a public way. Ownership of one unit also includes a definite undivided interest in the common elements.

common elements All portions of the land, property, and space comprising a condominium property including land, all improvements, and structure; and all easements, rights, and appurtenances, excepting therefrom all space comprising all the units. Each unit owner owns a definite percentage of undivided interest in the common elements.

Consideration Something that suffices to make an agreement legally binding; something given in exchange for a promise.

Constant A percentage derived by dividing the annual principal and interest payment by the original amount of the loan.

Constructive eviction Inability of a tenant to obtain or maintain possession by reason of a condition making occupancy hazardous or unfit for its intended use.

Constructive notice Notice given to the world by recorded documents. All persons are charged with knowledge of such documents and their contents whether or not they have actually examined them. Possession of property is also considered notice that the person in possession has an interest in the property.

Consumer price index A ratio of the cost of goods at the present time in relation to a base period said to be 100. This index is published monthly by the United States Department of Labor, Bureau of Labor Statistics.

Contiguous In actual close contact; touching, adjacent.

Contingent Dependent upon something not yet certain; conditional.

Contingent liability A liability that can fall to one as an implied participant or contributor.

Contour Surface outline or shape.

Contract An agreement entered into by two or more legally competent parties by the terms of which one or more of the parties, for a consideration, undertakes to do or refrain from doing some legal act or acts.

Conventional mortgage A mortgage loan which is not insured or guaranteed by governmental agencies: FHA or VA.

Convey To transfer: pass title to.

Conveyance The instrument or document by which a transfer is made or title passed from one person to another.

Cooperative A residential multi-unit building with title in a trust or a corporation which is owned by and operated for the benefit of persons living within, who are the beneficial owners of the trust or the stockholders of the corporation, each possessing a proprietary lease.

Coping The top layer of a masonry wall, usually sloped to carry off water.

Corporation An artificial person or body of persons, established under a corporate name, for preserving in succession certain rights differing from those of the individuals or corporators who constitute the corporation from time to time.

Correction lines A system of compensating for inaccuracies in the Rectangular Survey System due to the curvature of the earth. Every fourth township line (24-mile intervals) is used as a correction line on which the intervals between the north and south range lines are remeasured and corrected to a full six miles.

Cost The price paid to acquire, produce, maintain, or accomplish anything.

Cost approach The process of estimating the value of a property by adding to the estimated land value the appraiser's estimate of the replacement cost of the building less depreciation.

Cost plus Usually an agreement for compensating a contractor to the extent of a percentage of the actual cost of labor and materials used to complete a specified job. The percentage most often includes the contractor's overhead and his profit.

Covenant An agreement written into deeds and other instruments promising performance or nonperformance of certain acts, or stipulating certain uses or nonuses of the property.

Creative Having the power to originate, bring into existence, or to be productive.

Credit The allowance of time for payment of goods delivered or services rendered; reputation for the ability and willingness to meet an obligation. The balance in one's favor in an account.

Credit rating Reputation for meeting financial obligations.

Cumulative Increasing or growing by successive additions.

Cycles Period of time within which a round of regularly recurring events is completed, as in business cycles.

Data Known available information including facts and figures.

Date of commencement In a lease on real property—the date upon which the lease term starts and rental begins to accrue; the day upon which the tenant comes into possession subject to the provisions of the lease.

Date of lease The date that the lease instrument is signed by the contracting parties.

Date of termination In a lease on real property—the date upon which the lease term ends, rentals cease to accrue, and the tenant gives up possession to the owner or agent.

Datum In surveying—a horizontal plane from which are measured heights and depths.

Death clause A special clause in a lease which provides for termination of the lease before its expiration date in the event of the death of the tenant.

Debt That which a person is bound to pay or perform for another.

Debt service A real estate term meaning principal and

interest payments made on a mortgage. To service the debt.

Decorate To improve appearance by ornamentation or embellishment.

Decree A judicial decision or order.

Dedication The voluntary giving of private property by the owner of a development for some public use (streets, parks, etc.).

Deed A written document executed under seal and delivered to effect a conveyance of title to real estate.

Deed restrictions Clauses in a deed limiting the future users of the property. Deed restrictions may take many forms; they may limit the density of buildings, dictate the types of structures that can be erected, or prevent buildings from being used for specific purposes or used at all. Deed restrictions may impose a myriad of limitations and conditions.

Deed of reconveyance An instrument delivered to reconvey a trustee's interest in real property where the trustee held the property under a deed to secure the payment of a debt due to a third party or beneficiary.

Deed of trust A written document by which title to land is conveyed as security for the repayment of a loan.

Default The nonperformance of a duty, whether arising under a contract, or otherwise; failure to meet an obligation when due.

Defect of title A claim, restricted use provision, or other imperfection that adversely affects the customary use and marketability of a property.

Deferred charge A charge or debit where payment is postponed to a future date.

Deferred maintenance Ordinary maintenance of a building that has not been effected, and which noticeably affects the use, occupancy, welfare, and value of the property.

Deficiency discount A reduction in rent to induce a tenant to accept a substandard apartment.

Deficiency judgment A personal judgment levied against the mortgagor when the foreclosure sale does not produce sufficient funds to pay the mortgage debt in full.

Deflation An abnormal decline in the level of commodity prices.

Delete To strike out, erase, or remove anything written or printed.

Delinquency An overdue debt, as rent not paid on the due date.

Demised premises Property conveyed by a lease.

Demolition To pull down a building completely; to destroy.

Department of Housing and Urban Development (HUD) A federal department created in 1968 charged with the supervision of the Federal Housing Authority (FHA) and a number of other government agencies charged with administering various housing programs.

Depletion A reduction of or the removal from a presumed fixed inventory of goods or benefits. A diminishing.

Depreciation Loss of value due to all causes; usually considered to include: (1) physical deterioration (ordinary wear and tear), (2) functional depreciation (see **Obsolescence**), and (3) economic obsolescence.

Description A narrative giving a detailed account of a thing so that it may be easily identified and completely understood or evaluated.

Devalue To deprive of or reduce in value; to fix a lower legal value; to devaluate.

Developer A person who develops real estate on a speculative basis.

Development In real estate—the physical improvement of land for higher and better use such as the subdivision of land for residential, commercial, or industrial purposes; the erection of buildings, etc.

Devise To assign or transmit real property by will.

Disability clause A special lease covenant that provides for the alteration of the lease terms or the termination of the lease before expiration, in the event that the tenant is physically disabled and unable to continue his use of the leased premises. Most often included in leases for residential property.

Disbursement The expending of money. In real estate—the payment of charges for the operation and maintenance of property usually recorded in detail as to the distribution of payments; also payments as directed by an owner.

Disbursement ledgers Ledgers showing the expenditure of funds for operating and capital expenses.

Discount A reduction in price usually as a reward or allowance for the payment of a charge prior to the date of delinquency.

Dividend A pro rata share of an amount to be distributed in the form of money or goods.

Down payment An agreed initial increment payment to secure the delivery of property or goods upon payment of the total agreed price in accord with a specific agreement.

Due process of law Conformance with all of the legal rights, privileges, and obligations granted and required by law.

Duly authorized Properly authorized to act for another in accordance with legal requirements and in conformance with a written series of conditions and covenants. A power of attorney. An agency.

Dumpster A container for accumulating waste, generally over two cubic yards in size, which must be emptied by hydraulically lifting the container and dumping the contents into a truck.

Duplex One building with two separate living units.

Dwelling unit A place to live in, residence, abode.

Earnest money Money given to bind a contract.

Easement A right or interest in land of another which entitles the holder thereof to some use, privilege, or benefit out of or over said land.

Economic alternatives The determination of highest economic and most productive use after a study of alternative uses.

Economic life The number of years during which a building will continue to produce a higher net percentage yield.

Economic obsolescence Impairment of desirability or useful life or loss in the use and value of property arising from economic forces outside of the building or property, such as changes in optimum land use, legislative enactments which restrict or impair property rights, and changes in supply-demand relationships. (see **Obsolescence**)

Economics   The science that deals with the production, distribution, and consumption of wealth and with the various related problems of labor, finance, taxation, etc.

Economy   The existing system for the management of national resources in their relation to money, community, or national welfare and the management of production and distribution of goods and services of a material value or nature.

Efficiency   The ratio of work done to the energy expended. Performance or competency.

Efficiency apartment   A small, bedroomless apartment usually with less than a standard-size kitchen.

Egress   The right to leave a tract of land. Often used with ingress.

Ejectment   A suit brought by a property owner to regain possession of real estate and payment of damages from the party who has occupied it illegally.

Elevation   A drawing or design representing a vertical side or portion of a building. A place above the level of the surrounding ground.

Elevator   A moving platform and cab for transporting goods or persons in a vertical direction from one level to another.

Elevator cab   The housing or enclosure on an elevator platform.

Emancipation   Release of a minor from parental control and supervision often allowing the minor to contract as an adult.

Emergency   A sudden, generally unexpected occurrence or set of circumstances demanding immediate action.

Eminent domain   The right of a government or municipal quasi-public body to acquire private property for public use, through a court action called condemnation, in which the court determines that the use is a public use and determines the price or compensation to be paid to the owner.

Empty-nesters Persons whose children have left home permanently.

Encroachment A building or some portion of it, or a wall or fence which extends beyond the land of the owner and illegally upon some land of an adjoining owner or a street or alley.

Encumbrance Any lien, such as a mortgage, tax lien, or judgment lien. Also, an easement, a restriction on the use of the land or an outstanding dower right which may diminish the value of the property.

Endorse To sustain; to approve, guarantee payment. To alter a document by adding a covenant.

Enhance To improve; to give greater value or benefit; to raise to a higher degree, intensify, magnify.

Entity Something that has a real existence.

Equalization The raising or lowering of assessed values for tax purposes in a particular county or taxing district to make them equal to assessments in other counties or districts.

Equity The interest or value that an owner has in real estate over and above the mortgage against it.

Escalator clause A clause in a contract, lease, or mortgage providing for increases in wages, rent, or interest based upon fluctuations in certain economic indexes, costs, or taxes.

Estimate To form an approximate opinion as to value, amount, etc. To give an opinion; to calculate approximately.

Ethics The rules of conduct recognized in respect to a particular class of human actions. A code of the principles of morality.

Eviction A legal process to oust a person from possession of real estate.

Evidence That which tends to prove or disprove something.

Examine To inspect; investigate; to interrogate a person to determine his knowledge, experience, etc.

Exclusive agent An agent with exclusive rights to sell property owned by another for a fixed period of time.

Exclusive right In leases, reserves the right for one tenant exclusively to conduct a certain business in the leased property during the term of the lease.

Exculpate   To free from blame.

Execution   The signing and delivery of an instrument. Also, a legal order directing an official to enforce a judgment against the property of a debtor.

Expense   Money paid to discharge a charge or cost.

Experience   Observing, encountering, and performing things that occur in the normal process and course of time.

Expert   A person who has special skill or knowledge in some particular field.

Extended coverage (EC)   An endorsement to a standard form of fire insurance policy adding to the coverage insurance against financial loss from certain other specified hazards.

Facility   A building, special room, etc., that facilitates or makes possible some activity, e.g., a recreation facility.

Fair market value   At a specific time—the price paid or that might be anticipated as necessarily payable by a willing and informed buyer to a willing and informed seller, neither of whom is under any compulsion to act and where the object sold has been reasonably exposed to the market.

Feasibility study   A study made to discover the practicality, possibility, and reasonableness of an undertaking that is proposed.

Fee simple   The largest possible estate or rights of ownership of real property continuing without time limitation. Sometimes called fee or fee simple absolute.

Federal Housing Administration (FHA)   Insures loans made by approved lenders in accordance with its regulations.

Fenestration   The arrangement of windows and doors in a building.

Fidelity bond   A form of casualty insurance guaranteeing one individual against financial loss that might result from dishonest acts of another specific individual.

Fiduciary   One charged with a relationship of trust and confidence, as between a trustee and beneficiary, attorney and client, or principal and agent.

Financial analysis Projection of income and expense, financing considerations, tax implementations, and value charged, used in a management survey.

Financing The availability, quantity, and terms under which money may be borrowed to assist in the purchase of real property and using the property itself as the sole security for such borrowings.

Fire and extended coverage insurance (Fire & EC) Insurance for property which covers loss by fire, as well as the perils of windstorm, hail, explosion, riot attending a strike, civil commotion, aircraft, vehicles, and smoke.

Fire insurance Insurance on property against all direct loss or damage by fire.

First mortgage A mortgage which has priority as a lien over all other mortgages.

Fixed assets Properties, goods, or other things of value that cannot be readily sold or otherwise converted on short notice, at their true or fair value. Things possessed mainly of value in use as is, and of little value if removed, such as trade fixtures and machinery.

Fixture An article of personal property attached permanently to a building or to land so that it becomes part of the real estate.

Flashing Sheets of metal or other material used to weatherproof joints and edges, especially on roofs.

Flat building Two or more separate suites of living quarters, one above the other or contiguous to each other, each having independent means of ingress and egress and otherwise independent of each other.

Floor plan A scale drawing of the layout of rooms, halls, etc., on one floor of a building or in one unit of a building.

Foreclosure A court action initiated by the mortgagee, or a lienor, for the purpose of having the court order the debtor's real estate sold to pay the mortgage or other lien (mechanic's lien or judgment).

Four-plex A flat building of four separate living units.

Fraud Intentional deception to cause a person to give up property or a lawful right.

Fringe benefits Extra compensation to employees such as housing, pension plans, hospitalization and sickness provisions, and vacations.

Functional obsolescence Defects in a building or structure that detract from its value or marketability.

Fund A stock of money; money in hand; financial resources.

Furnishings Fittings, appliances, and other chattels used in a house or a room.

Furniture Movable articles such as tables, chairs, desks, and bedsteads, usually for personal use or comfort.

Garnish To attach a debtor's property, wages, or other assets, by the authority of a court, so that these can be used to pay the debt.

Garnishment A proceeding whereby property, money, or credits of a debtor in possession of another (the garnishee) are applied to the payment of debts by means of process against the debtor and the garnishee.

General partnership The business activity of two or more persons who agree to pool capital, talents, and other assets according to some agreed-to formula, and similarly to divide profits and losses, and to commit the partnership to certain obligations.

Graduated rent Rent which has two or more levels in the same lease term.

Grant To transfer or convey by deed or writing.

Grant deed A conveyance of fee title.

Grantee A person to whom an interest in land is conveyed by deed, grant, or other written instrument.

Grantor A person who, by a written instrument, transfers to another his interest in land.

Gross income The total monthly or annual revenue from all sources as rents and other receipts before any deductions, allowances, or charges.

Gross lease A lease of property under the terms of which the landlord pays all property charges regularly incurred through ownership (repairs, taxes, insurance, and operating expenses).

Gross receipts The total cash income from all sources during a specific period of time as monthly or annually.

Gross rent multiplier A figure which, when used as a multiplier of the gross income of a property, produces an estimate of value of that property.

Gross national product (GNP) The total value of a nation's annual output of goods and services.

Gross possible income The total monthly or annual possible income before uncollected income is deducted.

Ground lease A lease for land only on which the tenant usually owns the building or is required to build his own building as specified by the lease. Such leases are usually long-term net leases; tenants' rights and obligations continue until the lease expires or is terminated for default.

Guarantee A warrant; a pledge; a formal assurance.

Half-bath A term used in real estate to describe a bathroom with a basin and water closet but no bathing facilities such as a tub or shower.

Head rent Rent charged to a person or persons occupying premises independently of each other.

Heterogeneous Unlike; variable; a nonuniform or haphazard mixture of objects or people.

High-rise A building with ten or more stories.

Highest and best use The most productive use to which real property may be put for the most desirable period of time considering all economic quantities.

Hold harmless Declaring that one is not liable for things beyond his control.

Holdover tenancy A tenancy whereby the tenant retains possession of leased premises after his lease has expired, and the landlord by continuing to accept rent from the tenant thereby agrees to tenant's continued occupancy as defined by state law.

Home A house, apartment, or other shelter that is the fixed residence of an individual, a family, or a household.

Homestead A dwelling with its land and buildings, occupied by the owner as a home and exempted by law from seizure or sale for debt.

Homogeneous   Essentially alike, generally uniform.

Hotel   A public house offering lodging, food, etc., for travelers.

Hotel apartment   An apartment building offering hotel services to residential tenants, usually on a permanent basis.

House   A building for human habitation: a place of residence.

Housing act   An act by the Congress of the United States creating programs and procedures for federal assistance in the creation and improvement of residential facilities for residents of the United States and its territories.

Improvement   Something done or added to real property in order to increase its value.

Income   The returns that come in periodically from all sources as salaries, rents, dividends, and interest.

Income approach   The process of estimating the value of an income-producing property by capitalization of the annual net income expected to be produced by the property during its remaining useful life.

Income property   Property that produces an income.

Increment   Something added or gained; a profit; amount of insurance.

Indemnify   To promise to make good or secure against a foreseeable loss or damage.

Independent contractor   A person who contracts to do a piece of work for another by using his own methods and without being under the control of the other person regarding how the work should be done. Unlike an employee, an independent contractor pays for all his expenses, personally pays his own income and social security taxes, and receives no employee benefits.

Industrial district or park   A controlled parklike development designed to accommodate specific types of industry and providing public utilities, streets, railroad sidings, water, sewage facilities, etc.

Infant   A minor in the eyes of the law. (see **Minor** and **Majority**)

Inflation   Undue expansion or increase of the currency of the country with resultant decrease in worth of the unit of that currency.

In-house management   Management originating from within an organization or company, i.e., by the staff of the corporation owning the property, rather than brought in from outside.

Installment contract   A contract for the sale of real estate wherein the purchase price is paid in installments over an extended period of time by the purchaser who is in possession. Title is retained by the seller until final payment.

Institute of Real Estate Management (IREM)   A professional association of men and women, affiliated with the National Association of Realtors®, who meet professional standards of experience, education, and ethics with the objective of continually improving their respective managerial skills by mutual education and exchange of ideas and experiences.

Insurable value   A commonly used term to describe the Actual Cash Value (ACV) of a property which is the cost to replace the building or structure less certain depreciation factors.

Insurance   An agreement to assume a foreseeable financial loss in consideration of a premium payment by the one insured (the insured) to the one insuring (the insurer, carrier, insurance company, etc.) as fire, casualty, liability, or property damage.

Interest   A share in the ownership of property. A payment for the use of money borrowed.

Interest rate   The percentage of the principal sum charged by a lender for its use, usually for a yearly period.

Invest   To put money to use by purchase or expenditure for something that will foreseeably yield a profit or income.

Investment   A means for putting money to work as buying real estate, lending money, or buying stocks or bonds.

Investment trust   A trust created for the joint ownership of real property or other securities where the participants or investors share in the profits or income in proportion to their trust shares or cash invested, and where title to the investment is held in trust for the shareholders. A joint venture under a trusteeship.

Invoice An itemized bill for goods delivered to a buyer.

Joint tenants Two or more owners of a parcel of land who have been specifically named in one conveyance as joint tenants. Upon the death of a joint tenant, his interest passes to the surviving joint tenant or joint tenants by the right of survivorship which is the important element of joint tenancy.

Joint venture As association of persons to carry out a single business enterprise for profit, for which purpose they combine their property, money, and skills.

Judgment clause A provision in notes, leases, and contracts by which the debtor, tenant, etc., authorizes any attorney to go into court and confess a judgment against him for a default in payment. Sometimes called a cognovit. The use of this clause is prohibited in many jurisdictions.

Jurisdiction The district over which the power of the court extends.

Landlord One who owns property and leases it to a tenant.

Latent defects (Hidden defects) Physical deficiencies or construction defects not readily ascertainable from a reasonable inspection of the property, such as a defective septic tank or underground sewage system, or improper plumbing or electrical wiring.

Lease A contract, written or oral, for the possession of a landlord's lands for a stipulated period of time in consideration of the payment of rent or other income by the tenant. Leases for more than one year generally must be in writing to be enforceable.

Lease conditions The provisions or covenants setting forth the agreed privileges, obligations, and restrictions under which a lease is made. Lease terms.

Lease extension agreement A covenant or other written and executed instrument extending or agreeing to extend the lease term beyond the expiration date as provided in the body of the original lease.

Leasehold   Land held under a lease.

Legal   Permitted by law; authorized by law; not in conflict with the law.

Legal description   A description of real property setting its dimensions, metes and bounds, or other definite identification in accordance with the description recorded in official governmental records and given in a manner that marketable title of the fee is unimpaired by such description. The description used to identify the property in legal instruments as deeds or mortgages.

Lenders loss payable   An endorsement on a policy of hazard insurance which provides that any compensation for losses sustained shall be made to the order of a lender to whom the property has been pledged as security for a loan.

Lessee   The tenant in a lease.

Lessor   The landlord in a lease.

Let   To lease; to grant the use of a thing for compensation.

Levy   To impose or assess a tax on a person or property. The amount of taxes to be imposed in a given district.

Libel   Defamation by written or printed words, pictures, etc. Anything defamatory or that maliciously or damagingly misrepresents.

License   Official authorization to engage in a business, profession, or other activity with or for the public or affecting the public interest. Freedom to act or express oneself. Also, the revocable permission for a temporary use; a personal right which cannot be sold.

Lien   A right given by law to certain classes of creditors to have their debt paid out of the property of the debtor, usually by means of a court sale.

Life estate   An interest in property that continues for the life of an individual and terminates in favor of others in the event of his death.

Limited partner   A partner in a business, who by agreement and notice shares in the profits of that business, but is not liable for any portion of any net losses or other obligations of the business beyond his original investment. An individual who invests money in a business to share only in the profits of that business and does not actively engage in the conduct of the business.

Limited partnership   A partnership arrangement which limits certain of the partners' liability to the amount invested and also limits the profit he can make; a limited partner is not permitted to have a voice in the management.

Limited power of attorney   A legal authorization to act in behalf of another for a specified purpose.

Limiting conditions   Restrictive consideration in the determination of a conclusion.

Loan   The giving of money or goods with a promise of repayment, usually with interest or other benefits added to the whole.

Loan commitment   An agreement to lend an amount of money, usually of stated terms and conditions.

Loan correspondent   An agent employed by a lender for the securing and servicing of loans in accord with established policies and requirements of the lender.

Loan cost   The cost in money for securing a loan, as loan fees, legal charges, title or abstract costs, recording charges or notary fees. The total charges for effecting a loan, customarily paid by the borrower.

Loan payment   The payment of an installment on the principal balance plus accrued interest on the entire unpaid balance that accrued since the immediately preceding interest payment.

Loan value   An estimate of value of profits which is a basis for determining the amount of money to be loaned when the property is pledged or otherwise conveyed as security for repayment of a loan.

Lockout   The refusal by an employer to allow his employees to come to work until they agree to certain terms.

Loft building   A building of two or more stories, designed for industrial use; originally developed to accommodate the needs of small manufacturing enterprises.

Low-rise   An apartment building containing five stories or less.

Maintenance Care, preservation; keeping in good physical and operating condition and appearance.

Maintenance cost The periodic cost, usually on an annual basis, for completing all of the required maintenance work in a building.

Majority The age at which an individual has the legal right to manage his own affairs and is responsible for his actions. The age of majority varies from state to state. (see **Infant** and **Minor**)

Management The skill and executive ability for the direction and control of physical, financial, and accounting matters related to the successful and rewarding operation of real property.

Management agreement A contract or letter of understanding between the owner(s) of a property and the designated managing agent, describing duties and establishing powers, responsibilities, rights, and obligations of the parties thereto.

Management fee The monetary consideration paid monthly or otherwise for the performance of management duties.

Management organization A real estate organization that specializes in the professional management of real properties for others, as a gainful occupation.

Management procedures The regular and programmed processes followed in the day-to-day management of real estate.

Management records The important and necessary accumulation of segregated and easily identifiable historical and accounting records, useful to both manager and client in the interpretation and understanding of the physical and financial welfare of a managed property. The recorded facts concerning the productivity and physical aspects of a property.

Management survey A detailed expert analysis of the physical condition, income, expense, operating procedures, trends, and other factors that affect the highest and most productive use of a parcel of real property.

Managing agent An agent duly appointed to direct and control all matters pertaining to a property that is owned or controlled by another.

Man-day 8 work hours.

Man-week   40 work hours.

Man-year   2,080 work hours.

Ma-pa management   The management of real property by a husband and wife team where typically the wife assumes the duties of renting and record-keeping and the husband performs the maintenance chores.

Market analysis   A determination of the characteristics, purchasing power, and habits of the population segment who are expected to be tenants of a property, used in a management survey.

Market data approach   The process of estimating the value of property through the examination and comparison of actual sales of comparable properties.

Marketing   All business activity involved in the moving of goods from the producer to the consumer, including selling, advertising, packaging, etc.

Market value   The highest price which a buyer, ready, willing, and able but not compelled to buy, would pay, and the lowest a seller, ready, willing, and able but not compelled to sell, would accept.

Mechanic's lien   A lien created by statute which exists in favor of contractors, laborers, or material-men who have performed work or furnished materials in the erection or repair of a building.

Merchandising   To advertise, promote, and organize the sale of a particular product.

Metes and bounds description   A legal description of a parcel of land by beginning at a point and reciting the boundaries of the land, using directions and distances, around the tract and back to the place of beginning.

Mid-rise   An apartment building containing at least six stories but not more than nine stories.

Mile   A measurement of distance: 1,760 yards or 5,280 feet.

Minor   One who has not reached the age set by state law to be legally recognized as an adult, therefore one not legally responsible for contracting debts or signing contracts. (see **Infant** and **Majority**)

Modernize   To give modern character or appearance (of buildings). To improve; to meet modern standards in appearance and use.

Module   A sectional unit of a building measured between column centers in a rectangular set of directions in which utilities and other facilities are directly available.

Monetary consideration   A cash payment to secure a promise to act or not to act.

Month-to-month tenancy   An agreement to rent or lease for consecutive and continuing monthly periods until terminated by proper prior notice by either the landlord or the tenant. Notice of termination must precede the commencement date of the final month of occupancy. The time period of prior notice is usually established by state law.

Monument   An object set in the ground to mark boundaries of real property.

Moratorium   An authorization to delay payment of money due.

Mortgage   A conditional transfer or pledge of real property as security for the payment of a debt. Also, the document used to create a mortgage lien.

Mortgagee   The lender in a mortgage loan transaction.

Mortgage lien   The claim on his real estate given to the mortgagee when the mortgagor executes a mortgage or trust deed to secure his note.

Mortgagor   The borrower, the owner of the real estate who conveys his property as security for the loan.

Narrative   A detailed account in prose, concerning events, facts, experiences, knowledge, etc., about a subject.

National Association of Realtors®   The national nonprofit corporation whose membership is principally composed of local members in subscribing local real estate boards throughout the United States and its possessions, and dedicated to the highest principles and performance by real estate licensee members.

Neighborhood   A district or locality often with reference to its character or inhabitants; a limited area as to size and used for residential, commercial, or other purposes or a combination of such uses integrated into an accepted pattern.

Neighborhood pattern The direction of development and the observable trends, qualities, and characteristics.

Neighborhood stores Usually small stores of individual proprietorship and dealing principally in services and food products. Service stores, as shoemakers, cleaning and laundry, hardware, markets, and drugs.

Net cost Cost after all incidental charges are added and all allowable credits are deducted.

Net lease A lease requiring the tenant to pay rent and all the costs of maintaining the building including taxes, insurance, repairs, and other expenses of ownership.

Net operating income Total collections less operating expenses.

Net prior to debt service (NPDS) The cash available from collected rental income after all operating expenses have been deducted, before capital expenses and debt service have been deducted; the net operating income.

Net worth The remainder expressed in dollars after deducting all known liabilities from all known assets.

Notary public An officer licensed by the state to take the acknowledgment of persons executing documents and to sign the certificate and affix his seal.

Note An instrument of credit given to attest a debt.

Notice to vacate A legal notice requiring a tenant to remove himself and his removable possessions from the premises within a stated period of time or upon a specified day and date, and to deliver up the premises to the owner or his agent or to a designated successor.

Nuisance An obnoxious or annoying thing or person. Something offensive to individuals or a community and to the prejudice of their legal rights.

Nullify To render or declare legally void and inoperative.

Obsolescence Lessening of value due to being out-of-date (obsolete) as a result of changes in design and use; an element of depreciation. (see **Economic obsolescence** and **Functional obsolescence**)

Occupancy Characteristics of tenants as to their use, care, permanence, etc., relating to real property let for rent or other valuable consideration. Actual possession.

Occupancy agreement A simple agreement which spells out the conditions of occupancy of a property for a specified length of time for a specified amount. A simple or modified lease.

Occupational Safety and Health Act of 1970 (OSHA) A law requiring employers to comply with job safety and health standards issued by the U.S. Department of Labor.

Office building A single- or multi-story building generally offering space for rent or lease. Usual tenancies are for the conduct of service businesses or professions such as real estate, insurance, lawyers, doctors, or architects.

Off-site management Management of a property by persons not residing or keeping office hours at the subject property.

Omission Something left out. Failure to do something required, expected, or necessary.

Opinion A belief or conclusion based upon reasoning, observation, experience, information, etc., which creates a firm belief but not a certainty.

Optimum The best or highest attainable. The most favorable.

Option A right given for a valuable consideration to purchase or lease property at a future date for a specified price and terms; the right may or may not be exercised at the option holder's (optionee's) discretion.

Overage The excess rental, above a specified minimum or base rent, that is chargeable as a result of a lease provision based upon a percentage of gross business enjoyed by a tenant.

Owner, landlord, and tenant liability (OLT) Insurance protecting claims against a property owner, a landlord, or a tenant arising from personal injury to a person or persons in or about a subject property and including the improvements on the land and any other contiguous areas for which the insured is legally responsible, such as sidewalks.

Ownership Legal right of possession; proprietorship.

Owner's improvements Additions, alterations, and other

capital improvements to a building completed at the cost and expense of the owner and becoming a part of the fee estate.

Parcel A separable, separate, or distinct part or portion or section of land often identified as a numbered lot with designated boundaries.

Parking Space for in-and-out parking and storage of motor vehicles. The number of vehicles that can be parked at one time with adequate provision for ingress and egress of vehicles.

Partition suit A legal action to dissolve a tenancy in common by requiring one of the common owners to purchase the interest of another owner or to sell an interest to another common owner or to liquidate or sell the entire fee estate, all based upon a stipulated and established fair market price; prorating the proceeds in event of a sale of the fee to others in proportion to the respective legal interests of the common owners and after deducting all legal costs as determined by the court.

Party at interest A person having a legal interest in real property.

Party wall A wall for the common benefit and use of two owners, their respective property being separated by the wall.

Passageway A hall, corridor, or similar facility for ingress, egress, and movement of persons into and within the public areas of a building or between or around barriers. A means of access on foot or by small vehicles and not for general public use.

Patio A paved area or court, open to the sky and adjoining a living space or spaces.

Pay-off penalty An extra stipulated charge for prepayment of all or a part of a loan on real property. A cash penalty for paying off a mortgage loan before its date of maturity.

Peaceful enjoyment The use of real property without illegal or unreasonable interference or annoyance within the control of the party granting the use.

Penalty A loss or forfeiture imposed on one for his failure to fulfill his obligation to another.

Penthouse A separate apartment, dwelling, or enclosure on the top floor of a building.

Per capita By the individual. Allocation on an individual basis.

Percentage lease A lease commonly used for commercial property that provides for a rental based on the tenant's gross sales at the premises; it generally stipulates a base monthly rental plus a percentage of any gross sales exceeding a certain amount.

Personal property Movable property belonging to an individual family, business, etc., that is not permanently affixed to real property, such as clothing, furniture, furnishings, and appliances.

Planned unit development (PUD) A group of buildings sometimes with varying uses (e.g., apartments, offices, shops, schools) which are completely planned before groundbreaking. Generally they are large in scale and built in several phases over a number of years.

Plat A map representing a piece of land subdivided into lots with streets and other details shown thereon.

Pledge A solemn promise of something to do or refrain from doing something.

Plot A scale drawing of a parcel of land or several parcels of land, oriented as to directions, and important facilities, and showing the location of buildings, rights-of-way, easements, etc., thereon. Also, a piece of land.

Plumbing chase A duct space or enclosure inside partition walls to house plumbing lines and vent stacks.

Points A unit of measurement used for various loan charges; one point equals one percent of the amount of the loan. Discount points represent the percentage by which the face amount of an FHA mortgage is reduced in order to bring its fixed interest rate yield into competition with the conventional money market.

Police power The right of the government to impose laws, statutes, and ordinances to protect the public health, safety, and welfare; this includes zoning ordinances and building codes specifying safe, sanitary construction.

Population The total of all individuals in a fixed or stipulated geographical area or in a building or a group of buildings. The body of inhabitants in a place.

Population density The average number of inhabitants per square mile of a geographic entity, most often a corporate city or other delineated community area.

Population movement The shifting of a large number of people from one place to another over a period of time, as the movement westward or southeastward, in the United States. In-and-out movements of people from place to place geographically, usually evidenced as a trend.

Power of attorney A written instrument authorizing another to act in one's behalf as his agent or attorney.

Pre-fab (prefabricated structures) Standardized parts or sections of a structure manufactured for rapid assembly and erection.

Price The amount of dollars spent or paid for an item at a particular time (may not be the same as value).

Prima facie On its face; presumptively, as prima facie evidence.

Prime interest rate The lowest interest rate currently being charged to the most financially responsible persons or with the security of highly rated and easily converted securities, on loans repayable on demand by the lender.

Principal (1) A sum of money lent or employed as a fund or investment—as distinguished from its income or profits, (2) the original amount, or remaining balance of a loan, or (3) a party to a transaction—as distinguished from an agent.

Principal meridian One of the 35 north and south survey lines established and defined as part of the rectangular survey system.

Process server One who serves an official notice or summons on another.

Progress payment Periodic payments on account to a contractor as various portions of a construction project are completed.

Property analysis Study referring to items such as deferred maintenance, functional and economic obsolescence, land location and zoning, exterior construction and condition, plant and equipment, unit mix, facilities, and expected income and expenses.

Property damage insurance   Insurance against liability for damage to property of others that may result from occurrences in or about a specified property and for which the insured is legally liable.

Property lines   The legal lines that bound a piece of real property.

Property manager   The chief operating officer or administrator of a particular property or group of properties.

Public area   A space in a property for general public use and not restricted for use by any lease or other agreements, as a lobby, corridor, or court.

Public improvements   All improvements to real property belonging to government, as schools, court houses, libraries, streets, sewers, and utility supply systems.

Publicity   Advertisements, press reports, letters, etc., used to secure public notice, attention, respect, acceptance, and prestige for a business, an individual, or a cause.

Pullman kitchen   A small non-walk-in kitchen, often in a closet-size space, with appliances and equipment that are smaller than standard.

Purchase money mortgage   A note secured by a mortgage or trust deed given by buyer (**as mortgagor**) to seller (**as mortgagee**) as part of the purchase price of the real estate.

Quick assets   Assets that are readily converted to cash without prejudice to the principal value or the stated value; cash itself; accounts receivable; demand or matured notes, etc.

Quit   To depart from, leave, relinquish, or give up.

Quit claim deed   A conveyance by which grantor transfers whatever interest he has in the land, without warranties or obligation.

Range   A part of the rectangular survey system, being a strip of land six miles in width extending north and south and numbered east or west of the principal meridian.

Raw land Large areas of ungraded land not possessing the necessary facilities, utilities, or other improvements required for development and improvement for residential, commercial, or industrial uses. Land that has not been subdivided into parcels for sale and use.

Real estate Land; a portion of the earth's surface extending downward to the center of the earth and upward into space including all things permanently attached thereto by nature or by man; freehold estates in land.

Real estate broker Any person, partnership, association, or corporation who for a compensation or valuable consideration sells or offers for sale, buys or offers to buy, or negotiates the purchase, sale, or exchange of real estate, or who leases or offers to lease or rents or offers for rent any real estate or the improvements thereon for others. Such a broker must secure a state license. For a license to be issued to a firm, it is usually required that all active partners or officers must be licensed real estate brokers.

Real estate investment trust (REIT) An unincorporated trust set up to invest in real estate. Management and control rest in the trustees who hold title to the property. One hundred or more investors are required to own the beneficial interests, no five of whom may own over 50 percent of the trust shares. No corporation taxes need be paid provided a series of complex IRS qualifications are met. Sale of beneficial shares are controlled by state and federal regulations governing securities.

Real estate salesman Any person who for a compensation or valuable consideration is employed either directly or indirectly by a real estate broker to sell or offer to sell, or to buy or offer to buy, or negotiate the purchase, sale, or exchange of real estate, or to lease, rent, or offer for rent any real estate, or to negotiate leases thereof or improvements thereon.

Realtor® A registered trademark term reserved for the sole use of active members of local boards of **Realtors**® affiliated with the **National Association of Realtors**®.

Rebate A return of a part of an original amount paid or charged for goods or services.

Recapitulation statement ("recap" statement) An annual balanced cash statement customarily prepared by real estate managers showing all receipts, disbursements, and reserves accumulated for an established twelve-month period.

Reclamation The conversion to use of otherwise nonusable land by means of draining, filling, drying, clearing, etc.

Rectangular survey system A system established in 1785 by the federal government and providing for surveying and describing land by reference to principal meridians and base lines.

Recurring expenses Regular operating expenses that recur monthly or periodically, such as those for utilities, supplies, salaries, scavengers, insurance, and taxes.

Redemption period A period established by state laws during which the property owner has the right to redeem his real estate from a foreclosure or a tax sale by paying the sale price, interest, and costs. (Many states do not have mortgage redemption laws.)

Redevelopment The complete removal or restoration of unsightly, unsafe, uneconomic, or otherwise blighted improvements from land for re-improvement. Often by governmental action or legal authority.

Redress Relief or compensation for wrong or injury.

Regional analysis A detailed study of a region, usually surrounding and including one or more neighboring cities, to determine the force of various factors affecting the economic welfare of a section of the region, such as topography, population growth and movement, transportation facilities, employment, industrial and business activity, tax structures, improvements, and trends.

Release deed (release of mortgage) An instrument executed by the mortgagee or the trustee reconveying to the mortgagor the real estate which secured the mortgage loan, after the debt has been paid in full. When recorded it cancels the mortgage lien created when the mortgage or trust deed was recorded. Partial releases may be issued to clear title of a lot from the blanket mortgage on a group of lots, upon receipt of a prescribed part payment of the mortgage debt.

Re-lease or re-let   To rent again. Usually involving a cancellation of the previous lease.

Remodel   To convert a building to other or better uses by effecting structural changes or additions.

Renewal   The renovation, rehabilitation, or modernization of an existing building or buildings.

Rent   A periodic payment (usually made in money, but which may be in kind or in service), due by a tenant of land, or other man-made improvement, to his landlord.

Rentable area   The total interior area in a building, usually expressed in square feet, that can foreseeably be leased to tenants.

Rent ledger   Record of rent received, date, period covered, and other related information.

Rent loss   The deficiency increment resulting from vacancies, bad debts, etc., between total projected rental (for a given period) and the actual rents collected or collectible.

Replacement cost   The estimate of cost to replace or restore a building to its exact pre-existing condition and appearance.

Rescind   Invalidate, annul, cancel, repeal, etc.

Research   A diligent and systematic inquiry into a subject in order to study and record the basic principles and facts affecting the subject.

Reserve account   An account of records in which accumulated funds are set aside for foreseeable expenses or charges.

Resident caretaker   An employee residing in a building for the purpose of overseeing and administering the day-to-day building affairs in accordance with directions from the manager or owner.

Resolution   A formal determination by an assembly or a body to do or not to do something.

Restitution   Compensation for a wrong done; reparation for a loss, damage, or injury. Giving back something that has been wrongfully or improperly taken away.

Restrictive covenant   A covenant in a deed restricting the use to which a property may be put.

Revocable trust   A trust estate that may be terminated at will.

Right of re-entry The act of resuming possession of lands, or tenements, in pursuance of a right reserved by the owner on parting with the possession. Leases usually contain a clause providing that the owner may terminate the lease, and re-enter for nonpayment of rent or breach of any of the covenants by the tenant.

Right-of-way A right of passage over land belonging to another.

Riparian rights Rights of an owner of land which borders on or which includes a stream, river, lake, or sea. These rights include definition of (and limitations on) access to and use of the water, ownership of stream bed, navigable water, and uninterrupted flow and drainage.

Rod A measure of length, 16½ feet.

Room count A count of rooms based on a generally accepted formula of what constitutes a room.

Row house A term given to housing units which are built in a row and are separated by common walls, sometimes called party walls.

Second mortgage A mortgage loan secured by real estate which has previously been made security for a prior mortgage loan. Also called a junior mortgage or junior lien.

Section A portion of a township under the rectangular survey system. A township is divided into 36 sections, numbered 1 to 36. A section is a square with sides one mile long and an area of one square mile or 640 acres.

Securities and Exchange Commission (SEC) A regulatory body created by the federal government to control the sale of securities.

Security deposit A preset amount of money advanced by a tenant and held by an owner or manager for a specified period to cover damages and to ensure the faithful performance of the lease terms by the tenant.

Sentimental value The value attributable to a property or other article resulting solely from emotional reactions. Sometimes called "heart" value.

Setback Usually a deed or zoning restriction requiring that the front face of a building be erected not less than a certain distance from various property lines.

Site plan A plan, prepared to scale, showing locations of buildings, roadways, parking areas, and other improvements.

Special assessment A charge against real estate made by a unit of government to cover the proportionate cost of an improvement such as a street or sewer.

Specific performance A suit brought against a party to a contract who has failed to fulfill his promise. This suit is brought in the case of unique goods or property (including real estate), when damages will not be adequate compensation for the breach of the agreement.

Square foot cost The cost per square foot of area to build, buy, rent, etc.

Standby charge An extra charge made for keeping a thing or a service available for a fixed period of time, as the charge made by a lender for money that will be made available as a specified loan on a future date.

Statute of frauds That part of a state law which requires that, in order to be enforceable, certain instruments must be in writing, such as deeds, contracts for the sale of land, and certain leases. Patterned after a seventeenth-century English law.

Storage space Usually unfinished space in a building for the storage of equipment and supplies or for chattels, etc., not being regularly needed or used.

Store A ground-floor section of a building used for the conduct of business.

Store front The front face of a store including the bulkhead, show window, entranceway, and ornamentation.

Strip stores An adjacent horizontal group of small stores along a roadway serving an outlying neighborhood or passing traffic.

Studio apartment Commonly used term to describe an efficiency or bedroomless apartment. In certain areas, the term refers to a small apartment with two levels.

Subdivision A tract of land divided by the owner into blocks, building lots, and streets by a recorded subdivision plat; compliance with local regulations is required.

Subletting The leasing of premises by a tenant to a third party for part of the tenant's remaining term.

Subordination clause A lease covenant in which the tenant agrees to take any action required to subordinate his claims against the property to the rights of the lender under a first mortgage or deed of trust, so long as it does not affect his right to possession.

Subrogation The substitution of one creditor for another. The substituted person succeeds to the legal rights and claims of the original claimant. Subrogation is used by insurers to acquire rights to sue from the insured party to recover any claims they have paid.

Survey A plot or map showing the exact legal boundaries and location of a parcel of real property identifiable on the ground by certain designated markings, together with the location of any easements, rights-of-way, overlaps, or encroachments; often including ground elevations at various designated locations, and the boundary lines of any improvements.

Syndication A combining of persons or firms to accomplish a joint venture which is of mutual interest.

Tax A governmental levy or charge for ownership or a benefit based in principle upon the relative value of the object being levied.

Tax lien A lien against property for taxes due but not necessarily delinquent.

Tax participation clause A covenant in a lease wherein a tenant agrees to pay a proportion or all of any ad valorem tax increases on the leased premises during the term of the lease in addition to any rents otherwise provided for.

Tenancy agreement Any agreement, usually in writing, between a landlord and another permitting the use of property by the other under specific terms, such as use, term of occupancy, or rent.

Tenancy at sufferance The tenancy of a tenant who lawfully comes into possession of the landlord's real estate, but continues to occupy the premises improperly after his lease rights have expired.

Tenancy at will An estate which gives the tenant the right to possession until terminated by notice or death of the landlord. The term of this holding is indefinite.

Tenancy in common A form of co-ownership by which each owner holds his undivided interest as though he were sole owner of it; each owner has the right to partition.

Tenant One who pays rent to occupy or gain possession of real estate. The estate or interest held is called a tenancy.

Tenant at will One who holds land at the will of the owner.

Tenant improvements Additions or alterations to a leased premises for the use of the tenant, at the cost and expense of the tenant and becoming a part of the realty unless otherwise agreed in writing.

Tenant in possession One having a possessory interest in real property.

Tenant profile A study and listing of the similar and dissimilar characteristics of the present tenants in a property.

Tenant selectivity An established set of standards used in the selection of tenants for a particular property.

Tenant union An organization of tenants formed to use their collective powers against an owner to achieve certain goals such as improved conditions, expanded facilities, and lower rent.

Tier Apartments in a vertical line in a building.

Time is of the essence A phrase in a contract which requires that the performance of a certain act by one party be within a stated period of time before the other party can be required to fulfill his part of the contract.

Title The evidence of right which a person has to the ownership and possession of land.

Title insurance policy A policy insuring an owner or mortgagee against loss by reason of defects in the title to a parcel of real estate, other than those encumbrances, defects, and matters which are specifically excluded by the policy.

Topography Surface features of land; elevation, ridges, slope, contour.

Tort A person's private or civil act that wrongs or injures another party. A tort is a violation of general law and is not based upon any contract or agreement.

Townhouse A one, two, or three story dwelling with a separate, outside entryway sharing common or party walls.

Township The principal unit of the rectangular survey system. A township has sides 6 miles long, and contains an area of 36 square miles.

Trade fixtures Articles installed by a tenant under terms of a lease; removable by the tenant before the lease expires. These remain personal property; they are not true fixtures.

Trading area The area from which a business draws its customers.

Trespass The illegal act of entry onto another person's real estate.

Turnover The number of units which are vacated during a specific period of time, usually one year. Turnover is usually expressed as a ratio between the number of units vacated and the total number of units in a particular property.

Unit A single, distinct part of the whole, e.g., a single apartment.

Unit area The square footage contained in a unit, such as an apartment.

Unit mix A number or percentage total of each unit size or type contained in a particular property.

Unit size A listing of the number of bedrooms and baths an apartment contains.

Urban Relating to or characteristic of a city.

Usable area The total interior area of a particular unit or space, including partitions, which is used exclusively by a tenant.

Utilities The service of electric power, gas, water, telephone, etc.

Vacancy An area in a building that is unoccupied and available for rent.

Value The power of a thing to command other goods in exchange; the present worth of future rights to income and benefits arising from ownership.

Value in use The value of a certain piece of real estate to an owner using the property for a specific and often unusual use.

Vendee One who purchases; the person to whom a thing is sold.

Vendor One who sells something to another.

Void Null, having no legal force or binding effect.

Voidable A valid act which may be avoided or declared void.

Walk-up An apartment building of two or more floors where the only access to the upper floors is by means of stairways.

Warranty deed A deed which contains a covenant or assurance by the grantor of real property for himself and his heirs, to the effect that he is the owner and will defend and protect the grantee against claims.

Wear and tear The using up or deterioration that results from normal use, age, and necessary exposure to the elements.

Work order A written form, letter, or other instrument used for authorizing work to be performed. A means for controlling and recording work ordered.

Workmen's compensation acts Laws passed in most states which provide for fixed awards to employees or their dependents in case of industrial accidents. Similar provisions cover occupational diseases contracted gradually in the ordinary course of employment due to conditions characteristic of the employer's business.

Zoning ordinance Exercise of power by a municipality in regulating and controlling the character and use of property.

INDEX